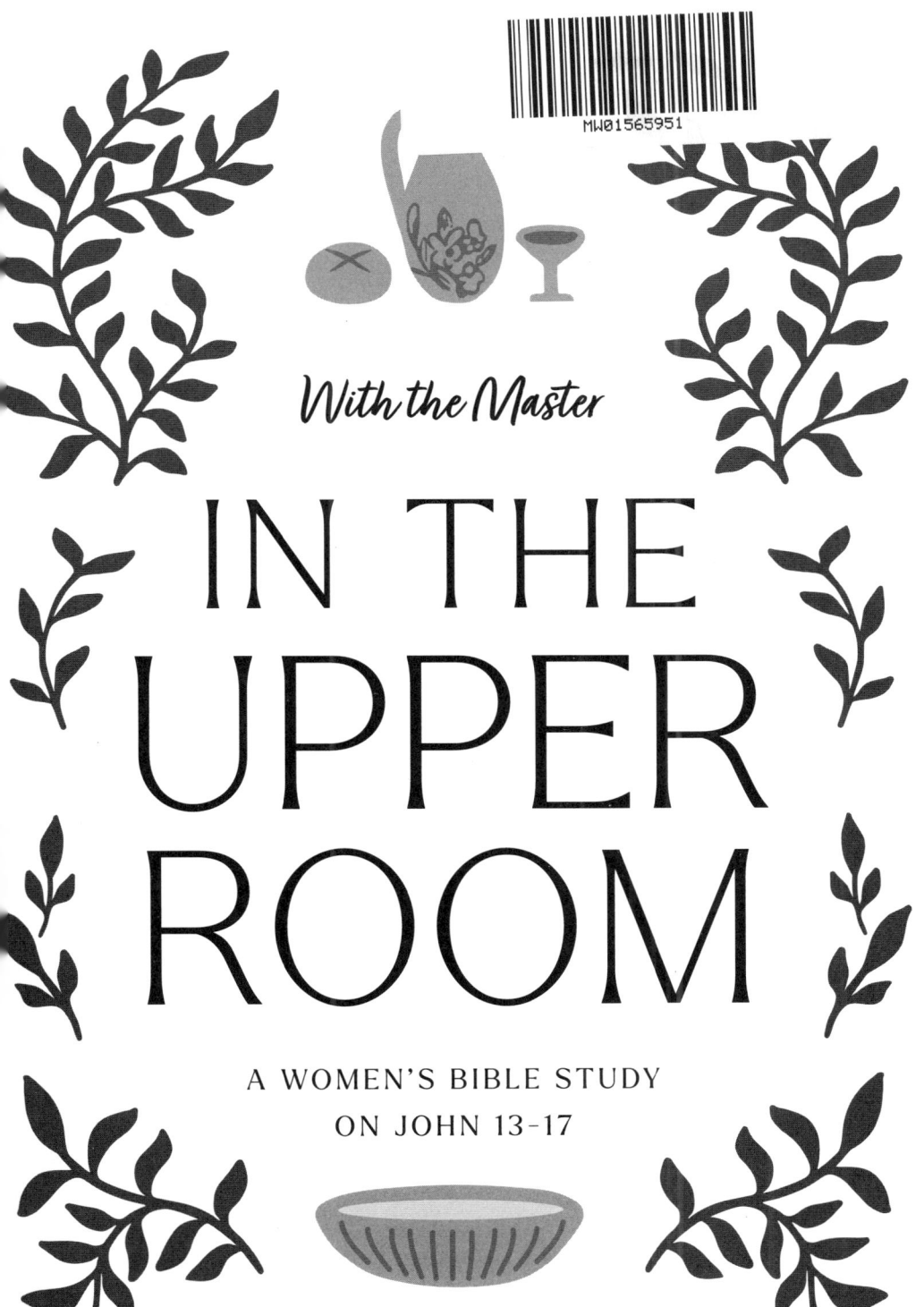

Unless otherwise indicated, Scripture taken from the New King James Version®. Copyright © 1982 by Thomas Nelson. Used by permission. All rights reserved.

Scripture quotations marked LSB are taken from the Legacy Standard Bible, Copyright © 2021 The Lockman Foundation. Managed in partnership with Three Sixteen Publishing Inc. LSBible.org

Copyright © 2023 by Three Sixteen Publishing Inc. All rights reserved. No part of this book may be reproduced or stored in an electronic retrieval system in any form. This includes photocopying, recording, or any other mechanical device without prior written permission of the publisher. This work is protected under United States copyright law. 316publishing.com

Printed in Korea
27 26 25 24 23 / 1 2 3 4 5

ISBN: 978-1-63664-318-2

To Pam Sheehan who has dedicated endless hours of sacrificial labor for the Kingdom of God and With the Master Ministries. She has "washed the feet" of many saints.

If you are like me and have become weary of women teaching the Word because of their compromise with worldly ideologies like feminism, legalism, new age, emotionalism, and CRT then you need to study Scripture with Susan Heck from "With the Master." Susan is not only a teacher of God's Word, she is a student. If you want Christ-exalting, verse-by-verse no-fluff teaching, coupled with heart-penetrating application, then there's no better place to be discipled in the Titus 2 ministry than by Susan.

Susan has enriched my own walk with Christ through her studies, books, and Scripture memory method and her friendship is a constant encouragement to me in my pursuit of holiness. My prayer is that every woman who professes the name of Christ would be familiar with Susan's ministry. I recommend her to everyone I know. I have no doubt that if you are in need of female discipleship in your own church, Susan's resources will help you to more fully glorify Christ in this pursuit of godliness.

For Christ's glory alone,

Erin Coates, Pastor's Wife
Women's Ministry Director, Gracelife Church of Edmonton

Susan Heck is one of my "must read" authors because of her faithfulness to handle God's Word carefully, accurately, and in a God-honoring way! Her newest offering, *With the Master In the Upper Room*, explores the Lord Jesus' last days on earth before His death. In this study of John chapters 13-17, she teaches us verse by verse *through* the text, helps us understand the passage better, and then like the true friend she is, asks the searching questions we must consider so we can bridge the gap from head knowledge to life application. This insightful look at Jesus' last days will make an indelible impression upon your heart and life!

Lisa Hughes, Pastor's Wife
Author of *Unmet Expectations* and *God's Priorities for Today's Woman*

TABLE OF CONTENTS

1. Having Loved, He Loves Again!
   John 13:1-5 .... *1*

2. Are You Washing the Saints' Feet?
   John 13:6-17 .... *17*

3. Judas, the Betrayer
   John 13:18-30 .... *31*

4. The Glory of God as Seen in His Son and in His Children
   John 13:31-35 .... *47*

5. A Shocking Prophecy
   John 13:36-38 .... *61*

6. Five Cures for a Troubled Heart
   John 14:1-6 .... *73*

7. Jesus and the Father Are One
   John 14:7-12 .... *87*

8. The Method, the Motive, and the Miracle of Prayer
   John 14:13-14 .... *99*

9. The Promise of the Spirit
   John 14:15-18 .... *113*

10. Christ's Comforting Promises to Those He's Leaving
    John 14:19-26 .... *125*

11. Five Peace-Stealers
    John 14:27-31 .... *139*

12. The Vine and the Branches (Are You Producing Fruit?)
    John 15:1-6 .... *153*

13. The Blessings of Abiding in Christ
    John 15:7-11 .... **169**

14. What a Friend We Have in Jesus!
    John 15:12-17 ....**183**

15. The World's Twofold Response to Christians: Hatred and Persecution
    John 15:17-21 .... **199**

16. The Three Witnesses
    John 15:22-27..*213*

17. Warning: Persecution Is Coming!
    John 16:1-4 .... *225*

18. The Threefold Work of the Spirit in the World
    John 16:5-11 ....*239*

19. The Spirit's Ministry to the Eleven
    John 16:12-15 ....*253*

20. Sorrow Turned to Joy!
    John 16:16-24 ....*265*

21. Christ's Final Words to the Eleven
    John 16:25-33 ....*279*

22. The High Priestly Prayer, Part 1: Christ Prays for Himself
    John 17:1-5...*293*

23. The High Priestly Prayer, Part 2: Christ Prays for the Eleven Disciples
    John 17:6-19 .... *309*

24. The High Priestly Prayer, Part 3: Christ Prays for Future Believers
    John 17:20-26 ....*327*

    God's Plan of Salvation *340*

Having Loved, He Loves Again!
John 13:1-5

THERE is a wonderful collection of Puritan prayers in a book entitled *The Valley of Vision*. It is a book I have grown to love and use often in my personal time with the Lord. There's a specific prayer in it that has become one of my favorites; it's called "Morning Dedication." The ending of this prayer is something I meditate upon often. It reads like this: "May I speak each word as if my last word, and walk each step as my final one. If my life should end today, let this be my best day."[1]

I've often pondered to myself, "When will be my last day on this earth? What will I have said and what will I have done in the moments before I leave this life to enter into the next life?" As we study John 13-17, *With the Master In the Upper Room*, we'll have the wonderful privilege of peering into our Lord's last day on earth before His crucifixion. We will listen to His last words, and we will read about His final actions. What did He say? What did He do?

For certain, Jesus said some comforting things, like: "Let not your heart be troubled; you believe in God, believe also in Me," "I will not leave you orphans; I will come to you," "Peace I leave with you," and "Holy Father, keep through Your name those whom You have given Me, that they may be one as We are" (John 14:1, 18, 27a; 17:11b).

But He also said some difficult things, like: "one of you will betray Me," "love one another as I have loved you," "You are My friends if you do whatever I command you," "If the world hates you, you know that it hated Me before it hated you," "the time is coming that whoever kills you will think that he offers God service," and "Indeed the hour is coming, yes, has now come, that you will be scattered, each to his own, and will leave

---

[1] Arthur Bennett, ed., *The Valley of Vision: A Collection of Puritan Prayers & Devotions* (Edinburgh: Banner of Truth Trust, 1975), 221.

Me alone. And yet I am not alone, because the Father is with Me" (John 13:21b; 15:12b, 14, 18; 16:2b, 32).

He even said some mysterious things, like: "If I then, your Lord and Teacher, have washed your feet, you also ought to wash one another's feet," "when He, the Spirit of Truth has come, He will guide you into all truth," and "Father, the hour has come. Glorify Your Son, that Your Son also may glorify You" (John 13:14; 16:13a; 17:1b).

In addition to all the things Jesus said, He also did some pretty amazing things, considering that it was his final day on earth—things like washing 24 dirty feet, giving numerous instructions to His disciples, loving the one who would betray Him, praying for His disciples, and praying for us! People often say that a person's last words are important, and our Savior's last words and actions are indeed of utmost importance.

Jesus' words in John 13-17 have become one of the most beloved portions of the Word of God because in them we get an intimate look at Christ with His twelve disciples in the final hours before His death. These words are recorded only in John's Gospel; none of the other three Gospels records them. In fact, 92% of the subject matter in John's Gospel isn't found in the other three Gospels, which makes the Gospel of John quite different from the other three Gospel accounts. In these chapters, we will find not only great encouragement but also great motivation for living in holiness. If you have a desire to know the Lord in a more intimate way, and if you will study with an open heart and mind, with a view to applying what you learn, you will grow to be more in love with the Savior when you have finished than when you started! I trust that is your deepest desire this day—to know, love, and obey Him more.

Before we take a look into the first five verses of this portion of God's Word, let's first take a brief look at a little background information about the Gospel of John as a whole as well as what has happened up to this point in John's account, so that we understand what has brought our Lord to His final hours. We'll begin by asking and answering several foundational questions about the book.

Who wrote the Gospel of John? John's Gospel was written by one of Jesus' twelve disciples, a man by the name of John (Luke 6:13-14). John was the son of Zebedee (Matthew 4:21) and was known as the beloved disciple, or the disciple whom Jesus loved (John 13:23). John was also the one we will see leaning on the breast of the Lord during the Last Supper (John 13:23). It was to this man that Jesus entrusted His own mother when He was dying on the cross (John 19:26-27). John was the first to believe in Jesus' resurrection and the first to recognize Him on the shore of the Sea of Galilee following His resurrection (John 21:7). And, along with Peter and James, John was one of the three disciples who were most dear to our Lord (Matthew 17:1; Mark 5:37; 9:2; 14:33; Luke 8:51).

Where and when was the Gospel of John written? John wrote his Gospel account sometime between AD 85 and 90, from the city of Ephesus.

Why was the Gospel of John written? John's purpose in writing his Gospel was to prove the deity of Jesus Christ—that He indeed is the Son of God—so that those who come to believe in Him would have eternal life. John gives his purpose statement in John 20:31 (LSB), where he says, "but these have been written so that you may believe that Jesus is the Christ, the Son of God; and that believing you may have life in His name."

I would like to take a brief look at the first 12 chapters of John so that we can see what has happened in the life and public ministry of our Lord to bring Him to these solemn and final hours with His disciples. Let's begin by looking at the first 12 verses of John 1:

> In the beginning was the Word, and the Word was with God, and the Word was God. He was in the beginning with God. All things were made through Him, and without Him nothing was made that was made. In Him was life, and the life was the light of men. And the light shines in the darkness, and the darkness did not comprehend it.
>
> There was a man sent from God, whose name was John. This man came for a witness, to bear witness of the Light, that all through him might believe. He was not that Light, but was sent to bear witness of that Light. That was the true Light which gives light to every man coming into the world.

> He was in the world, and the world was made through Him, and the world did not know Him. He came to His own, and His own did not receive Him. But as many as received Him, to them He gave the right to become children of God, to those who believe in His name.

Here, John records for us who Jesus is and why He came. John relates to his readers that there are going to be two reactions to Jesus' coming. The first reaction will be that Jesus came to His own but his own did not receive Him. The second reaction will be that those who did receive Him He made to be children of God. This distinction is vitally important to an understanding of John's Gospel because what we will see in the first 12 chapters of John is a rejection of Jesus by the nation of Israel. Then, when we reach chapters 13-17, we will see more intimately those who did receive Christ and His incredible love for them. The rest of John 1 deals with the testimony of John the Baptist, and then Jesus comes on the scene in verse 29. John the Baptist baptizes Jesus and Jesus' public ministry begins.

In chapter two of John's Gospel we find an interesting contrast. First, we see the first miracle Jesus performed, turning water into wine at a wedding. In this, Jesus demonstrates His love and mercy in verses 1-12. But then we see another side of Jesus, His holiness and justice, in verses 13-25, exhibited in the temple. Seeing those who have made His Father's house a house of merchandise, in His zeal for His Father's house Jesus casts them out. *He came to His own, and His own did not receive Him.*

John 3 records the wonderful story of Jesus sharing the gospel with Nicodemus in verses 1-21, and the verse that most of us have known from since childhood, John 3:16. The end of John 3, from verse 22 to verse 36, deals with John the Baptist's humility and that wonderful statement we all need to hear and apply: "He must increase, but I must decrease" (John 3:30 LSB).

In John 4:1-45, we're presented with yet another wonderful example of Jesus sharing the gospel. However, this time it's not with a man, but with a woman, and with a woman of Samaria. It was not customary for a man in Jesus' day to speak to a woman and certainly not a Samaritan woman, but Jesus transcends tradition and speaks not only to a woman but to a Samaritan woman. Because our Lord was willing to challenge tradition, many came to believe in Him, as we see in verse 39. The chapter ends in verses 46-54 with a second miracle of Jesus, the healing of a ruler's son.

Chapter five of John's Gospel deals with the healing of a man at the pool of Bethesda, in verses 1-16. And with this, persecution of Jesus by the Jews begins to escalate because He had once again healed on the Sabbath day (He broke tradition *again*). And if that wasn't enough, in verses 17-47, Jesus claims equality with God, talks about the resurrection and the fact that the Father sent Him, and even begins to put those who did not receive Him in their place, in verses 39-47:

> "You search the Scriptures, for in them you think you have eternal life; and these are they which testify of Me. But you are not willing to come to Me that you may have life.
> "I do not receive honor from men. But I know you, that you do not have the love of God in you. I have come in My Father's name, and you do not receive Me; if another comes in his own name, him you will receive. How can you believe, who receive honor from one another, and do not seek the honor that comes from the only God? Do not think that I shall accuse you to the Father; there is one who accuses you—Moses, in whom you trust. For if you believed Moses, you would believe Me; for he wrote about Me. But if you do not believe his writings, how will you believe My words?"

How would you feel if Jesus had said these words to you? You can see why the Jews would be filled with wrath and desire to kill Him. *He came to His own, and His own did not receive Him.*

In John chapter six we see the wonderful compassion of our Lord in the feeding of the 5,000, in verses 1-14. He walks on the water, in verses 15-21, to calm His fearful disciples, and the majority of the rest of the chapter, verses 22-59, deals with His discourse on the bread of life. Tension is mounting even more, things are getting difficult, some don't like the reality of what He has to say anymore, and in verse 66 we learn that from that time "many of His disciples went away and were not walking with Him anymore" (John 6:66 LSB). *He came to His own, and His own did not receive Him.*

Chapter seven of the Gospel of John begins with the Jews seeking Jesus so that they might kill Him. His brothers even begin to not believe in Him, in verse 5. But Jesus isn't affected by these things and He goes to the feast at Jerusalem. This causes an uproar among the people and they begin to murmur among themselves as to who He is, in verse 12. In verse 20, they accuse Him of having a demon and seek to take him but are unable to because His time has not yet come. The chapter ends with a divided opinion about who Jesus is, in verses 40-53. Verse 53 sounds a little like what we do when we don't get our own way: "Everyone went to his home" (John 7:53 LSB). *He came to His own, and His own did not receive Him.*

In John 8:1-11, we see the mercy of our Lord toward the woman taken in adultery and yet in His mercy He tells her to go and sin no more. Then, in the rest of the chapter, verses 12-59, Jesus gives His discourse on the fact that He is the Light of the World, what genuine faith is, and His ongoing appeal to the Jews that they were in spiritual bondage because of their enslavement to sin. The Jews accuse Him again of having a demon, in verse 48. And life isn't getting much easier for our Lord, either, because they continue to seek to kill Him, as we see in verse 59. Soon the public ministry of our Lord will come to an end. *He came to His own, and His own did not receive Him.*

John 9 is solely devoted to the healing of a man born blind, and Jesus' accusation in the final verses points to the reality that the Pharisees are blind because of their sin. He ends chapter nine with these words to them: "If you were blind, you would have no sin; but now that you say, 'We see,' your sin remains" (John 9:41 LSB). *He came to His own, and His own did not receive Him.*

In chapter ten of the Gospel of John is the wonderful discourse of Jesus as our Good Shepherd, in verses 1-18. Again, we see upheaval beginning in verse 19, and they accuse Jesus yet again of having a demon. The chapter ends with a discussion with the Jews again about Jesus' deity. In verse 31, they take up stones again to stone Him and try to seize Him, but He escapes out of their hands. *He came to His own, and His own did not receive Him.*

John 11 deals with the moving story and miracle of Jesus raising Lazarus from the dead, in verses 1-44. It also has one of the shortest verses in the Bible, "Jesus wept," verse 35, but one which gives us a touching glimpse into His humanity. In verse 45, we see that many believe in Him as a result of this miracle, but others go and report to the Pharisees (verse 46), and the disputing goes on again among them. The chapter ends with the all too familiar tone of the Jews encouraging others to seize Jesus, in verse 57. *He came to His own, and His did not receive Him.*

Finally, in chapter 12 of John's Gospel, verses 1-8, we find the beautiful story of Mary anointing the feet of Jesus. It is now six days before the Passover. In verses 12-18, we read of Jesus' triumphal entry into Jerusalem as King. Then, in verse 23, Jesus begins to tell them of his impending crucifixion, and yet we see in verse 37 that they still have hearts of unbelief. One final appeal is made by Jesus in verses 44-50:

> "He who believes in Me, believes not in Me but in Him who sent Me. And he who sees Me sees Him who sent Me. I have come as a light into the world, that whoever believes in Me should not abide in darkness. And if anyone hears My words and does not believe, I do not judge him; for I did not come to judge the world but to save the world. He who rejects Me, and does not receive My words, has that which judges him—the word that I have spoken will judge him in the last day. For I have not spoken on My own authority; but the Father who sent Me gave Me a command, what I should say and what I should speak. And I know that His command is everlasting life. Therefore, whatever I speak, just as the Father has told Me, so I speak."

Verses 44-50 are Christ's final words to this unbelieving nation. In his final words, He still is compelling them to believe in Him. *These are His own whom He came to save, but His own did not receive Him.*

With the close of John 12, we find Jesus' public ministry has ended. In fact, after this point, John records no more words spoken by Jesus to the multitudes. With the beginning of John 13, we turn from Jesus' public ministry to His private ministry among his twelve disciples. You might be wondering how Jesus and his disciples got to this upper room. We know from the other three Gospel accounts that Jesus had sent Peter and John to make preparations for this time together in a large upper room (see Matthew 26:17-19; Mark 14:12-16; and Luke 22:7-13). He is now alone with them, in the upper room, and separated for a brief time from those who had rejected Him. He is alone with those He loves for a little while before He drinks the cup of suffering, before He experiences the wrath of Almighty God, before He takes on the sins of the world. He's now in His final hours; it is the night before His arrest. He has some things to say, some things to do, and some prayers to pray. I can't think of any other portion of Scripture that will better let us in on the heart of the Savior than John 13-17, the Upper Room Discourse. J. C. Ryle writes, "In every age the contents of these chapters have been justly regarded as one of the most precious parts of the Bible. They have been the meat and drink, the strength and comfort of all truehearted Christians. Let us ever approach them with peculiar reverence. The place whereon we stand is holy ground."[2] It is truly a wonderful privilege you and I have to read and study these last blessed words of our Master in the upper room. Let's begin our study by reading verses 1-5 of chapter 13.

> Now before the Feast of the Passover, when Jesus knew that His hour had come that He should depart from this world to the Father, having loved His own who were in the world, He loved them to the end.
>
> And supper being ended, the devil having already put it into the heart of Judas Iscariot, Simon's son, to betray Him, Jesus, knowing that the Father had given all things into His hands, and that He had come from God and was going to God, rose from supper and laid aside His garments, took a towel and girded Himself. After that, He poured water into a basin and began to wash the disciples' feet, and to wipe them with the towel with which He was girded.

---

2 J. C. Ryle, *Expository Thoughts on the Gospels*, https://www.monergism.com/threshold/sdg/expository_web.html. Accessed 9/29/2023.

In this first chapter, we will see three of Christ's attributes on display: *Christ's Omniscience* (vv 1, 3); *Christ's Love* (vv 1-2); and *Christ's Humility* (vv 4-5). John begins by giving us a look at the Savior's omniscience as well as His love, in verse one.

Christ's Omniscience   *John 13:1*

> Now before the Feast of the Passover, when Jesus knew that His hour had come that He should depart from this world to the Father, (John 13:1a)

John begins by mentioning an event called *the Feast of the Passover*. This celebration was instituted to celebrate what took place in Exodus 12. If you recall, God told Moses to lead His people out of Egypt to the Promised Land. Of course, it wasn't that easy; Pharaoh, the ruler of Egypt at that time, was not about to let God's people go. So, the Lord sent a series of plagues to get Pharaoh's attention. One of the plagues which God had promised was the horrible killing of all of Egypt's firstborn. Israel's firstborn, however, were to be spared if the children of Israel would kill a lamb and spread its blood on the two side posts and the upper doorposts of their houses. God said that all the firstborn in the land of Egypt would be killed, man and beast. But if the blood was found on the houses of the Israelites, He promised to pass over those houses and not destroy their firstborn. In fact, the term *passover* means to leap over, to spare, show mercy. The Jews continued in New Testament times to celebrate Passover. According to God's law, it was to be continually carried out on the 14th day of Nisan, which was the first month of the Hebrew calendar. This would correspond to March or April in our calendar. Each Jewish family had to bring a lamb that was free from blemish and offer it as a sacrifice in remembrance of what God had done for His people. They also would have a meal together, and this Passover meal is what the disciples had prepared here in this upper room. It would be the last meal they would eat with their Lord. John very possibly is letting us know that this is the feast of the Passover because soon there would be no need for the Passover to be celebrated. Jesus would soon become the Passover Lamb. He would be the lamb sacrificed once for all. Paul says in 1 Corinthians 5:7b (LSB), "For Christ, our Passover lamb, also was sacrificed." This is the scene, the feast of the Passover.

John says that Jesus *knew that His hour had come*. The Greek emphasizes the full consciousness of Christ. Christ was not in the dark concerning His final hour. And notice, only He knew and the Father, but not the disciples. In fact, when you read the Gospel accounts, you're struck with the fact that the disciples never quite understood that the Lord was going to die. John says He knew that His hour had come *that He should depart from this world to the Father*. Jesus knew that in 24 hours He would hang from Golgotha's tree. Jesus knew! The *hour* is often a reference to the time of Christ's sufferings and death (see John 7:30 and 8:20). Then, His hour had not yet come, but now it had. Jesus was getting ready to *depart from this world* and go to the Father. *This world* is a reference to this dark, wicked, hostile world. Jesus was going home, where He had come from. The Lord was going home and, you know, going home is what death is to any true believer. John says Jesus was going home *to the Father*, who we know is the first person of the Trinity. But before Jesus goes home, He has some work to do.

Christ's Love   *John 13:1-2*

> having loved His own who were in the world, He loved them to the end.
> (John 13:1b)

Foremost on Jesus' mind is His twelve disciples, as John says, *having loved His own who were in the world, He loved them to the end*. He loved His own who were in a world that was hostile toward Him. And He loved them to the end! The Greek word for *love* is *agape*, which indicates a direction of the will and finding one's joy in something. It is spoken of God's love toward man. According to this definition, God finds joy in loving us! Imagine that! This love, John says, is for *His own*, which denotes property or special relationship. John is referring to the Twelve here, even though we know that Christ loves all those who are His own, as we will see when we get to chapter 17. John says He loved the Twelve *to the end*. The Greek literally says that He loved them to perfection. He loved them as far as the limits of love could go. And in verses 4 and 5 we will see the extent of that love. This is a time when Jesus could have been preoccupied with Himself, but He wasn't. He's facing the awful death of crucifixion, betrayal by Judas, and denial by Peter, and yet He shows humility by letting absolutely none of that move Him to self-pity. The Passover Lamb is stooping to wash some disciple's dirty feet. But before we get to the foot washing, John adds a note here about one of the loved ones who was a hypocrite—Judas! And we see our Lord's love again, even to the betrayer.

> And during supper, the devil having already put into the heart of Judas Iscariot, the son of Simon, to betray Him (John 13:2 LSB)

Some Bible translations say here that the supper was *ended*, which is an unfortunate reading here because the actual translation of the Greek, as seen in the LSB, indicates the meal was still going on. It was actually while they were still eating that Jesus washed the disciples' feet. John indicates that the *devil* had *already put it into the heart of Judas Iscariot, Simon's son, to betray Him*. The devil *put it*, threw or cast it, as the Greek would read, into the heart of Judas to betray the Lord. This was not a surprise to our Lord; Jesus said way back in John 6:70, "Did I not choose you, the twelve, and one of you is a devil?" We need to keep in mind that Judas was one of the Twelve. Christ Himself chose Judas after spending a night praying about it. Judas walked with Christ for three years, he saw the miracles, he heard the gospel many times, and had seen Jesus love him again and again. And yet Satan possessed Judas. What a warning to you and me! J.C. Ryle says regarding Judas, "He shows us what length a man may go in religious profession, and yet turn out a rotten hypocrite at last, and prove never to have been converted .... Privileges alone without grace save nobody ... and he shows us the uselessness of mere head knowledge."[3] In many years of ministry, I have unfortunately seen some who proved themselves to have the same kind of spirit as Judas. It is a sobering warning and a deep heartbreak. Judas is a stark contrast to Jesus, who will soon demonstrate humility and love even while Judas demonstrates pride and hatred.

Now, Satan had cast a seed in Judas' heart to *betray* Christ, which means to deliver Him up. We cannot know when the devil first injected the thought of betrayal into the heart of Judas. It must have occurred sometime before this meal. The perfect tense signifies that the thought

---

3 Ibid, 4.

continued as thrown into his heart; it indicates that Judas harbored the thought for some time, entertained it, and played with it until he finally acted it out. According to Matthew 26:14-16, we know he acted upon that thought when he went to the chief priests and bargained with them to deliver Jesus to them for 30 pieces of silver. Matthew says that from that moment Judas sought an opportunity to betray Christ. How the Lord's heart must have ached! One of His own would deliver Him up! But John moves on to another thing the Lord knew. He not only knew His hour had come, but He knew three other things, according to verse 3.

Christ's Omniscience   *John 13:3*

> Jesus, knowing that the Father had given all things into His hands, and that He had come from God and was going to God, (John 13:3)

The word for *knowing* that John uses is the same word that he used in verse one, which means a full consciousness. What did Jesus know? He knew three things. First, *that the Father had given all things into His hands*. This means the totality of everything belongs to Him, as Paul says in Colossians 1:16 (LSB), "For in Him all things were created, both in the heavens and on earth, visible and invisible, whether thrones or dominions or rulers or authorities—all things have been created through Him and for Him." Second, Jesus knew *that He had come from God*. And, third, Jesus knew that He *was going to God*. Imagine, Jesus knew all this, that everything was His, that He had come from God, that He was going back to God, and yet we find Him in the following verses washing the disciple's feet with the full awareness that He Himself was God in the flesh. Just imagine if you were some prominent person. It would be quite tempting to expect others to serve you and certainly not easy for you to serve them. But this is exactly what our Lord did. And as we move into verses 4 and 5, we turn from seeing His love and omniscience to seeing His humility.

Christ's Humility   *John 13:4-5*

> rose from supper and laid aside His garments, took a towel and girded Himself. (John 13:4)

Jesus *rose from supper and laid aside His garments*. These garments would be large and loose outer garments that were so large that a man would sometimes sleep in it. Jesus took off that garment, *took a towel and girded Himself*. The act of *girding* would involve taking up any loose parts of that garment and tying it around one's waist. It was large enough that even while tied around Jesus' waist, the ends could be used to wipe the disciple's feet. In biblical times, this act of girding would indicate one was getting ready to do some sort of work. Jesus was now dressed like a slave. Peter, perhaps, was thinking of this incident when he penned the words of 1 Peter 5:5 (LSB), where he states that we should "clothe" (or gird) ourselves "with humility toward one another." In the upper room, Peter is seeing his Lord literally clothe Himself with humility by washing the disciple's feet.

> After that, He poured water into a basin and began to wash the disciples' feet, and to wipe them with the towel with which He was girded. (John 13:5)

Jesus first *poured water into a basin*, which would already have been in the room for that very purpose. The basin was usually kept at the entrance to a home, and it was there so that when guests would arrive, the slaves would wash the guests' feet. Foot-washing, they say, was especially needful in Palestine because the streets were dusty and many times even muddy. People didn't wear socks, only sandals. It was the hospitable thing to do to wash a guest's feet. We see an example of this in 1 Samuel 25:41 as Abigail expressed a willingness to wash the feet of David's servants. History tells us that wives would wash their husbands' feet and children would usually wash their parents' feet. 1 Timothy 5:10, in laying out the qualifications of a widow being put on the widow's list, states that such a woman must have washed the saints' feet. We will discover in our next chapter whether or not we should actually be washing one another's feet today. (Perhaps you should get a bucket and some soap before our next chapter!)

Since there was no servant present in the upper room to wash the disciples' feet, Jesus, God in the flesh, stooped to wash their feet. One of the disciples should have gotten up and done the foot washing, but none did. Jesus poured the water, *began to wash the disciples' feet* and to *wipe them with the towel with which He was girded*. All of this would have been the duty of a slave to his master. Yet the Savior has reversed that order. The Master is washing the feet of the servants. That's humility. As Jesus said in Matthew 20:28 (LSB), "just as the Son of Man did not come to be served, but to serve, and to give His life a ransom for many."

Some say that the order in which Jesus washed the disciples' feet would have been the order in which they sat, which would mean that Judas was likely first. The one who was going to betray Jesus was the first in line to have his feet washed! How do you think the disciples must have felt by now? Why weren't they washing their Master's feet? Why weren't they washing the feet of the one who was about to suffer and die for their sins? Perhaps they were too preoccupied with their own self-pity and sorrow over losing their dearest friend. We know from Mark 9:33-34 that they were preoccupied with who was going to be the greatest in the Kingdom of Heaven. They were doing what we often do, thinking of ourselves even when others are hurting. Were their hearts not pricked at their selfishness? Did they not realize the King of Kings and Lord of Lords was stooping to wash their dirty feet?

Summary

◊ We see Christ's love in verses 1 and 2. Having loved, He loves again! He loves His own to the end and His love is extended even to Judas.

◊ We see Christ's omniscience in verses 1 and 3. He knows His hour has come; He knows everything belongs to Him; He knows He has come from God; and He knows He is going back to God.

◊ We see Christ's humility in verses 4 and 5. He humbles Himself to wash his own disciples' feet.

Jesus Christ has come to His final hours. What does He do? He humbles Himself to wash some dirty feet! He draws no attention to Himself, though He is soon to die. He serves, and He loves those whom He loves to the end.

Let's suppose you knew that you were going to leave this earth tomorrow. What would you do? What would you say? If this were your last day, would it be your best day, as the Puritans prayed? Would you humble yourself and sacrifice to meet the needs of others? Or would you draw a crowd around you to pour out your stories of self-pity? It is a provoking thought, is it not? When you and I are tempted to wallow in self-pity, when you and I start demanding our rights from others, maybe we should peer into John 13 and let the humility of Christ sink into our souls. May we learn humility and love by meditating on the love of Jesus toward His disciples in washing their dirty feet, knowing all the while that tomorrow He would hang from Golgotha's tree.

QUESTIONS TO CONSIDER

1. (a) Read the entire Gospel of John this week (three chapters a day), especially taking note of the Lord's public ministry in chapters 1-12. (b) What words does Christ use to describe Himself and what He offers to an unbelieving world? (Example: From John chapter 6, "I am the bread of life ... if anyone eats of this bread he will live forever.") (c) In looking over these descriptions of our Lord, how have they proven to be true in your own life?

2. Memorize John 13:1.

3. What facts do you learn from Matthew 26:17-19; Mark 14:12-16; and Luke 22:1-13 regarding the events which led up to the Passover meal that Christ and His disciples shared in the upper room?

4. (a) John says of the Lord, "having loved His own who were in the world, He loved them to the end." According to John 13:1-5, who is John talking about? (b) What are the ways the Lord showed His love to His own in the previous chapters in John? EXTRA CREDIT: In what ways does the Lord manifest His love to the twelve disciples in chapters 13-17?

5. What do you observe about the Father, Christ, the disciples, and Judas from John 13:1-5?

6. (a) What did Christ do as He prepared to wash the disciples' feet? (b) How would you describe the act of our Lord washing the disciples' feet?

7. (a) What does Jesus say about Himself in Matthew 20:26-28 and Luke 22:27? (b) How does He demonstrate that in John 13:1-5? (c) Is your life characterized by a desire to serve or a desire to be served?

8. If you knew your final hour had come, what do you think you would do and say?

9. What do you hope to gain from our study, *With the Master in the Upper Room*? (Hold on to your answer until the end of the book!)

10. (a) What have you learned from the example of Christ washing the disciples' feet? (b) What is your prayer based on what you have learned?

Are You Washing the Saints' Feet?

John 13:6-17

THE greatest and most beloved leaders throughout history have been those who are willing themselves to be servants. One writer has put it this way:

> The great leaders of men in all fields have not been the arrogant and the greedy, but the servants. The real servants are the true nobility. The greatest of all, the Son of God Himself, declared that He had come not to be served but to be a servant, and to give His life a ransom for many.[1]

As we come to our next portion of Scripture we will see one of the most astonishing acts of humility from our Lord. Let's read it together in John 13:1-17.

> Now before the Feast of the Passover, when Jesus knew that His hour had come that He should depart from this world to the Father, having loved His own who were in the world, He loved them to the end.
>
> And supper being ended, the devil having already put it into the heart of Judas Iscariot, Simon's son, to betray Him, Jesus, knowing that the Father had given all things into His hands, and that He had come from God and was going to God, rose from supper and laid aside His garments, took a towel and girded Himself. After that, He poured water into a basin and began to wash the disciples' feet, and to wipe them with the towel with which He was girded. Then He came to Simon Peter. And Peter said to Him, "Lord, are You washing my feet?"
>
> Jesus answered and said to him, "What I am doing you do not understand now, but you will know after this."
>
> Peter said to Him, "You shall never wash my feet!" Jesus answered him, "If I do not wash you, you have no part with Me."

---

1 Quote by John E. Mitchell, in Paul Lee Tan, ed., *Encyclopedia of 7700 Illustrations* (Rockville: Assurance Publishers; 1985), 570.

> Simon Peter said to Him, "Lord, not my feet only, but also my hands and my head!"
>
> Jesus said to him, "He who is bathed needs only to wash his feet, but is completely clean; and you are clean, but not all of you." For He knew who would betray Him; therefore He said, "You are not all clean."
>
> So when He had washed their feet, taken His garments, and sat down again, He said to them, "Do you know what I have done to you? You call me Teacher and Lord, and you say well, for so I am. If I then, your Lord and Teacher, have washed your feet, you also ought to wash one another's feet. For I have given you an example, that you should do as I have done to you. Most assuredly, I say to you, a servant is not greater than his master; nor is he who is sent greater than he who sent him. If you know these things, blessed are you if you do them."

As we began our study of Jesus' ministry to the disciples in the upper room in our last chapter, we saw that Christ demonstrated three amazing attributes in the first five verses. We saw Jesus' omniscience in verses 1 and 3. He knew His hour had come; He knew everything belonged to Him; He knew He had come from God; and He knew He was going back to God. We also saw His love demonstrated in verses 1 and 2. We noted that He loved His disciples to the end, and His love was extended even to Judas. And we saw Jesus' humility expressed in verses 4 and 5 by the washing of His disciples' feet. In this chapter, we continue on with the Lord washing the disciples' feet and, as we do, we learn of four significant roles in the text: *The Inquirer: Peter* (vv 6-9); *The Betrayer: Judas* (vv 10-11); *The Receivers: Christ's Disciples* (v 12a); and *The Server: Christ* (vv 12-17). Let's begin with a look at the Peter the Inquirer.

The Inquirer: Peter   John 13:6-9

> Then He came to Simon Peter. And Peter said to Him, "Lord, are You washing my feet?" (John 13:6)

In our last chapter, we learned that Jesus, knowing fully that He was God in the flesh, knowing that His hour had come, knowing that everything was His, knowing that He had come from God and was going back to God, begins to do something that is utterly astonishing. He rises from supper and lays aside His garment, wraps Himself with a towel, and then begins to wash His disciples' feet. We also saw that not one of Jesus' disciples offered to do such a task, but their Lord, the King of Kings, began to wash their feet. As we come now to verse 6, we see Christ come to Peter. We're not sure where Peter was in the line of foot-washing, though we mentioned in our last chapter that it was probable that Jesus washed Judas' feet first. We know from verses 23-24 that John was next to Jesus and it appears that Peter may have been next to John. So, it's possible that Peter was second to the last in this order of foot washing. Regardless, the Lord, John says, *came to Simon Peter*. It is interesting that up until this point there appears to have been no other conversation—until Peter speaks. Perhaps the others were puzzled at what the Lord was doing, or too ashamed to say anything because they knew they should have been the ones washing the feet. We really don't know why there seems to be silence up until this point. But Peter, of course, breaks that silence. Peter asks the question, *Lord, are You washing my feet?* Peter doesn't question the washing of any other disciples' feet, but only his own, which is evidenced by the words *my feet*. Note that Peter calls Jesus *Lord*, which means master or owner. And every word of this question here is emphatic in the Greek; it's as though Peter is asking, "Do you, the Son of God, the Messiah, perform the humble office of a servant toward me, a sinner?!" The Greek shows Peter's humility but, at the same time, his refusal to let the Lord wash his feet. It is supposed by some that Peter drew up his feet at this moment, in essence declaring, "I can't allow this, Lord!" But notice that Jesus doesn't really answer Peter's question in verse 7, which is something we often see our Lord doing in the Gospel accounts.

> Jesus answered and said to him, "What I am doing you do not understand now, but you will know after this." (John 13:7)

Both times the pronoun *you* is used here, it is emphatic in the Greek, which conveys to us that this is a rebuke to Peter. It is a tender rebuke, however, and a lesson that we all need to learn (Galatians 6:1). Peter was certainly short on discernment, but Christ was long on patience. Jesus says to Peter *what I am doing you do not understand now*. *Understand* means to perceive with the outward senses, particularly with physical sight. Peter, you can't understand now what I'm doing, but, Jesus says, *you will know after this.* Peter, you will *know* later what I have done, and you will know it by experience. *After this* means after the death and burial and resurrection and glorification of Jesus. After all of these things, greater light will be shed on Peter and the other disciples. They will come to understand what Christ was doing in the upper room. They will come to understand more about what humility really is when they see their Lord humble Himself and become obedient in death on the cross. Isn't this true in our own lives? Sometimes, the Lord does things in our lives that we don't understand at the moment, but later on we say, "Oh, that's why the Lord did that!" Regardless, each of us has a responsibility to allow the Lord to do what He deems best in our lives. Peter failed here and withdrew his feet. And so we find him opening his mouth again. Notice what he says.

> Peter said to Him, "You shall never wash my feet!" Jesus answered him, "If I do not wash you, you have no part with Me." (John 13:8)

You shall never wash my feet is said in the strongest Greek negative you can use. It's as though Peter is saying, "No, never, never will you wash my feet, in all eternity; you will never wash my feet! You, Lord, will never wash my feet." This is a strange statement from a man who has just called Jesus Lord in verse 6. By Peter's reaction to Jesus, Peter is now acting like he is lord. But Jesus replies to him *if I do not wash you, you have no part with Me.* Jesus replies to Peter with an if-then statement. While the word "then" is not explicitly in the text, the syntax of the sentence in Greek implies it: *Peter, if you don't let me wash you, then you can have no part with Me.* What is Jesus saying? He isn't telling Peter that he must have his feet washed to be a part of Jesus, but that Peter must let Jesus wash the whole of him. In the Scriptures, water is a symbol which pictures spiritual washing; Jesus is talking about a spiritual cleansing. He's saying, "Peter, if you aren't washed by Me, you cannot be a part of Me." In 1 Corinthians 6:9-11, Paul lists numerous sins that the Corinthians had committed in their lives before Christ, but then he says to them in verse 11, "And such were some of you; but you were washed, but you were sanctified, but you were justified in the name of the Lord Jesus Christ and in the Spirit of our God" (LSB). The washing here is a reference to regeneration. Unless Christ purified Peter by the washing of spiritual cleansing, Peter could have no evidence that he was Christ's disciple. Whoever refuses to receive a spiritual washing has no part with Christ. None of us can be saved apart from the washing away of our sins by Christ's atoning blood. And notice that it is Jesus who has to do the washing; He is the only way to spiritual regeneration.

Now when Jesus says to Peter *you have no part with Me,* the word for *part* means fellowship. Peter, you don't have partnership with Me if you are not washed by Me! John makes this same truth very clear in his first epistle, where he mentions that we cannot have partnership with God apart from that washing. Consider his words in 1 John 1:6-7: "If we say that we have *fellowship* with Him and yet walk in the darkness, we lie and do not do the truth; but if we walk in the Light as He Himself is in the Light, we have *fellowship* with one another, and the blood of Jesus His Son cleanses us from all sin" (LSB, emphases mine). John is present in the upper room observing all that the Lord is saying to Peter, and he writes regarding the same thing in 1 John. Peter, however, seems to be a little frightened at the Lord's statement, so he goes to the other extreme in verse 9,

> Simon Peter said to Him, "Lord, not my feet only, but also my hands and my head!" (John 13:9)

We know from the Gospel accounts and the book of Acts that Peter was characterized as being a man of extremes. When we look at Matthew 14:28-30, we see a man who is courageous enough to walk on water but then cries for help as he starts to sink. In Matthew 16:16-23, we see a man who proclaims that Jesus is the Christ and then rebukes the very Christ he just confessed. In John 13:37 and 18:17-27, we see a man who is willing to lay down his life for His Lord but then turns around and denies that same Lord three times! And now, here in John 13, we see a man who first didn't even want his feet washed and now wants a bath! Peter still isn't getting it. He's still thinking in the physical realm. Peter would one day come to understand the spiritual washing that the writer to the Hebrews mentions in Hebrews 10:22: "let us draw near with a sincere heart in full assurance of faith, having our hearts sprinkled from an evil conscience and our *bodies* washed with pure water" (LSB, emphasis mine). Christ is ever so patient with Peter, and He is ever so patient with another disciple as well—the betrayer, Judas. And so, we move from the inquirer, Peter, to the betrayer, Judas, in verses 10 and 11.

The Betrayer: Judas *John 13:10-11*

> Jesus said to him, "He who is bathed needs only to wash his feet, but is completely clean; and you are clean, but not all of you." (John 13:10)

This is interesting wording Jesus uses here in verse 10. It's interesting because in biblical times guests would typically bathe prior to coming to a feast; naturally, then, when they arrived at the feast, only their feet really needed to be washed. The shoe of the day was typically a sandal, and most streets were very dirty, since they did not have pavement like we do in our day. Jesus is telling Peter that the one *who is bathed*, or has been spiritually cleansed, *is completely clean* and doesn't need his whole body washed; he *needs only to wash his feet*. But Jesus follows that statement by saying *and you are clean, but not all of you.* Jesus isn't talking about physical washing here, because he says *not all* are clean, which is a clear reference to Judas. Jesus is essentially saying, "Peter, if you have been cleansed once and for all by the blood of Christ, then all you need after that is to have your feet washed. Your feet get dirty, Peter, and they need to be washed." Peter is thinking in the physical realm; Jesus is thinking in the spiritual realm. Jesus is talking about spiritual purity. He is referring to spiritual cleansing, which is needful for any true disciple of Jesus Christ. What does Jesus mean by the phrase *needs only to wash his feet*? He means that after salvation all that is needed is confession of sin, or the washing of your feet, so to speak. Once you are washed you don't need to be washed again, speaking figuratively of salvation, but you do need to get the dust off your feet, so to speak, by ongoing confession of sin, and that is where 1 John 1:9 comes in. There, John states, "If we confess our sins, He is faithful and righteous to forgive us our sins and to cleanse us from all unrighteousness" (LSB). A genuine believer will confess their sins. In John 15:3, Jesus mentions this cleansing we receive from the Word when he says, "You are already clean because of the word which I have spoken to you." We need daily cleansing by the Word of God and by daily confession of our sins. I personally don't know how a believer gets through a day without both of these elements, the Word and prayer! We get dirty with sin every day and while we never need to be saved again, we do need daily cleansing. A. W. Pink says, "Our daily contact with the evil all around causes the dust of defilement to settle upon us so that the mirror of our conscience is dimmed and the spiritual affections of our heart are dulled .... How deep is our daily need of putting our feet in the hands of Christ for cleansing, that everything which hinders communication with Him may be removed, and that He can say of us 'Ye are clean'!"[2]

Sadly, Jesus follows this encouraging word by saying that all the disciples are clean except one. And we know that our Lord is speaking of Judas, who is not spiritually clean in any sense. Judas was the betrayer! John elaborates on our Lord's comment in verse 11.

> For He knew who would betray Him; therefore He said, "You are not all clean." (John 13:11)

Jesus, being all knowing, knew who would betray Him. Jesus has mentioned this tragedy twice before. First, in John 6:64, He said, "'But there are some of you who do not believe.' For Jesus knew from the beginning who they were who did not believe, and who would betray Him." Then, in verse 70 of that same chapter, we read, "Jesus answered them, 'Did I not choose you, the twelve, and one of you is a devil?'" It's amazing that Jesus knew Judas would betray Him and yet He loved Judas anyway. If you knew that one of your dearest and most intimate friends was going to turn their back on you this time next year, even playing a part in your unjust death, would you still love him? Jesus did.

I really wonder what Judas was thinking at this point. He knew he was the betrayer. Did he bow his head in shame? Did he gloat over the evil he was soon to perform? Isn't it interesting that none of the disciples knew who the betrayer was, according to verses 21 and 22? Ladies, we must keep in mind that there are betrayers among us, and sometimes we are totally unaware of it. Paul mentioned this very thing to the elders of the

---

[2] A. W. Pink, *Exposition of the Gospel of John*, https://www.monergism.com/threshold/sdg/pink/AnExpositionGospelJohnAWPink.pdf. Accessed 10/5/2023.

Ephesian church, in Acts 20:29. He says, "For I know this, that after my departure savage wolves will come in among you, not sparing the flock." And then he goes on to say in verse 30 that these savage wolves will be men (elders) from among them! I have been in ministry long enough to have had my life marked by those who profess to be a disciples of Christ while possessing the same spirit of betrayal as Judas. It is a grief unlike any other. How this impending betrayal by Judas must have grieved our Lord at this moment in His life!

So, the dialogue ends between Jesus and Peter. And I just imagine that the disciples are trying to comprehend all of this and what it all means; not one of them is saying anything, though. Having seen the role that Judas the betrayer has among the disciples, we move into verse 12 to take a brief look at the receivers, the disciples, and then we'll take a longer look at our Lord, the server!

The Receivers: Christ's Disciples *John 13:12*

> So when He had washed their feet, (John 13:12a)

John makes it clear that Jesus had washed all the disciples' feet. The phrase *He had washed their feet* indicates that Jesus had, indeed, washed the feet of all 12 of the disciples, 24 dirty feet in all, including Judas'. In my humble opinion, I think we read over these words too quickly. Let's stop and think about this. Think about the time it took Jesus to do this. Think of those dirty, ugly, calloused, smelly feet, that our Lord was willing to wash. Think about the fact that this was the last physical act Jesus would do for His disciples before His death. Ladies, that is humility! Would you do that if you knew your death was around the corner? The disciples were the receivers of this humble act, but John goes on to elaborate on who the real receiver is—our Lord, the server.

The Server: Christ *John 13:12-17*

> So when He had washed their feet, taken His garments, and sat down again, He said to them, "Do you know what I have done to you?" (John 13:12)

After Jesus washed the disciples' feet, *He took His garments, and sat down again.* The word for *sat down* means to fall back, to lie down, to recline. The disciples weren't sitting around a table, as we might do for dinner; they were reclining on couches, usually three, that were situated in the form of a U-shape. This was the custom of the day, and it made it easier for those who were dining to lean on their left sides and use their right hands to eat with. I know it sounds more difficult for us, but it was the practice of the day.

Sitting was also the custom of teaching in our Lord's day, so the fact that Jesus now sits down indicates that He is getting ready to teach the disciples—and indeed He does! (We see an example of this in Jesus when he delivered His Sermon on the Mount in Matthew 5:1) So Jesus begins His teaching time with a question, as often He does in the Gospels. After giving the disciples a live example of humility, Jesus turns to asks them a question: *Do you know what I have done to you?* It would not have been nearly as effective if the Lord had just said, "Be humble." Instead, He showed them by His own example. We learn so much more by example; discipleship is truly caught more than it is taught. Ladies, your children learn more by your example than they do by what you say. Jesus says, "Do you know the meaning of what I've just done?" He doesn't necessarily ask this question to get an answer but to get their attention. He goes on to say:

> "You call Me Teacher and Lord, and you say well, for so I am." (John 13:13)

You know, we never find in the Gospel accounts that the disciples call the Lord, "Jesus." They always refer to Him as Lord or Teacher. *Lord* is a term that indicates ownership, and *Teacher* is a term that means Rabbi or Master. Indeed, Jesus was their teacher, but he wasn't only a teacher; He was also Lord. In fact, Peter has just referred to Jesus as Lord twice, in verses 6 and 9. Christ reminds them that even though He had humbled Himself in washing their feet, He still was their Lord and Master. He had not given up His authority. Jesus says, essentially, in affirmation of their belief, "You're right in saying that I am these things." But He goes on to say,

> "If I then, your Lord and Teacher, have washed your feet, you also ought to wash one another's feet." (John 13:14)

He uses yet another if-then statement. *If I, your Lord and Teacher, have washed your feet, then you also ought to wash one another's feet.* Think of it: their Master and Lord has just washed their feet! The One who was getting ready to lay down His life for the disciples has just washed their feet. The word *ought* is a very strong term that indicates obligation. Jesus is telling them that it is their duty and debt to wash one another's feet.

Is Jesus telling us that we should literally wash each other's feet? If this is what He is saying, it's curious that we don't have any other recorded incidents of customary foot washing in the New Testament, except in 1 Timothy 5:10, which refers to widows who had washed the saints' feet. But, again, that was the custom in those days, because of dirty roads and traveling conditions, most of which were traveled by foot. Some churches today do practice literal foot washing ceremonies, but what Jesus is saying here is that we need to be meeting each other's needs in a self-sacrificing way. (Maybe it would be a good foot washing or foot rub!) Our Lord is illustrating a death to oneself for the sake of others. He is endeavoring to impress upon the hearts of His disciples, in His final hour, that no act of service should be beneath them. The disciples certainly needed this lesson in humility; they had just been arguing over who would be the greatest in the Kingdom of Heaven (Mark 9:34). And, ladies, if they needed this lesson, how much more do you and I need it? We need to be living our lives in a sacrificial way. No task of service should be beneath us. Nothing! In fact, just the day before I wrote this chapter, I was tested with an inquiry to help someone with something I really did not want to do. My conscience was so pricked because I had been studying this passage that I had to say, "Yes I will do that for you!" How sad that I had to be studying John 13 for my heart to be obedient! Serving one another sacrificially should be the norm for all who profess the name of our Lord. Elaborating, Jesus goes on to say,

> "For I have given you an example, that you should do as I have done to you." (John 13:15)

Jesus says *I have given you an example.* The word *example* means an exhibit for illustration or warning. In fact, another Greek term used here (*kathos*) means like or as. Jesus could have used a different Greek word like the word *ho*, which would have meant "that which" and would have indicated an ordinance. When Jesus says *you should do as I have done to you,* He isn't saying, "Do what I do." He's saying, "Do like I do." This is another reason we know that Jesus isn't calling for a literal foot washing. It is not the outward ordinance that Jesus is after, but the inward attitude of humility. Remember, up until now Jesus had been repeatedly rebuking the Scribes and the Pharisees for all their outward acts of religion, which had left them with a heart of hypocrisy. The disciples were going to be on their own soon, and Jesus wanted them to live lives very different than those of the Scribes and Pharisees, lives characterized by humility.

You might be wondering, "If the Lord is not saying that we should literally wash each other's feet, then how do we practically 'wash each other's feet' as Jesus washed the disciples' feet?" I believe there are two ways we can sacrificially serve one another in a foot-washing sort of way. The first is physical, and the second is spiritual. First, let's take the physical. I think we wash each other's feet by doing just what Christ did, by being a servant and not being concerned about what kind of a job it is or how your reputation might be marred by doing it. It might be cleaning the church, volunteering in the nursery, taking out the trash, making a meal for someone or sending a card of encouragement. Serving is not about you; it's about others. Find out what the physical needs are among the people around you and then go meet those needs. Oswald Chambers says, "But, if we do not steadily minister in everyday opportunities, we will do nothing when the crisis comes."[3]

The second way we can wash each other's feet is in the spiritual sense. Ministering the Word of God is a great way to wash each other's feet. In Ephesians 5:26, husbands are commanded to follow the example of Christ in cleansing their wives by the washing of the Word. In John 15:3, Jesus says that we are clean by His Word. The writer to the Hebrews

---

[3] Taken from *My Utmost for His Highest*, updated edition © 1992 by Oswald Chambers Publications Association, Ltd., Original edition © 1935 by Dodd, Mead & Company, Inc. Copyright renewed 1963 by Oswald Chambers Publications Association, Ltd. All rights reserved., 225.

says, "But encourage one another day after day, as long as it is still called 'Today,' so that none of you will be hardened by the deceitfulness of sin" (Hebrews 3:13, LSB). One of the best foot washing ceremonies we can experience is to be refreshed and renewed by the teaching and admonition of the Word in our lives. And, we are to do this gently, in a spirit of meekness, as Paul explains in Galatians 6:1. Christ doesn't wash the disciples' feet harshly or with scalding water; He wipes them with a towel and He does so tenderly. When we are washing others' feet with the Word of God, we need to remember the compassion and mercy of Christ. I don't know about you, but it refreshes me! Christ, the server, continues to teach His disciples about humility, by saying,

> "Most assuredly, I say to you, a servant is not greater than his master; nor is he who is sent greater than he who sent him." (John 13:16)

Jesus says *Most assuredly, I say to you.* This means verily, truly, or amen, and it serves to confirm something. It was used to give one's assent to something and, in the Gospel accounts, it is used only by Jesus and always as a precursor to significant statements. So, this is something important Jesus is getting ready to say to the disciples. And what is He getting ready to say to them? *A servant is not greater than his master; nor is he who is sent greater than he who sent him.* A *servant* would be a slave, one who is in a permanent relation of servitude to another, his will being altogether consumed in the will of the other. Jesus is saying, "If I, your Lord, do not consider washing your feet a task beneath my dignity, then neither should you regard any act of service beneath your dignity!" Ladies, if you ever find yourself thinking or saying, "Let someone else do that task, it's too troublesome for me," then beware! We need to remind ourselves of what our Lord is saying here and remind ourselves of the One who stooped to wash two dozen dirty feet. Jesus is saying something so simple, but so profound, and He ends His admonition by saying:

> "If you know these things, blessed are you if you do them." (John 13:17)

This is Jesus' third if-then statement: *If you know these things, then blessed are you if you do them.* The phrase *if you know these things* implies that they did know, but they needed to act upon what they knew. Isn't that the way it is with all of us? We know what we should be doing, we know the responses we should be having, we know the words we should and should not be saying, we know all these things, but it is the doing we so often neglect. Jesus says by doing *these things*, you will be blessed. By doing what things? The things that are in the context: washing one another's feet and the humility that must accompany those kinds of actions. Just knowing does not bring happiness. Happiness is found in the doing, and not just doing once, but doing again and again, as evidenced by the Greek tense here; it means that we are to keep on doing. If we keep on doing these things, we will be *blessed*. This means we will be superlatively blessed, fully satisfied. James also mentions this in his epistle, in James 1:22-25. He tells us that it is the doers of the Word who are blessed and not those who are merely hearers only. The doers are the ones who are happy! The world knows nothing of this kind of happiness, but the believer who is living a life obedient to Christ knows exactly the kind of blessedness the Lord is talking about. You can meet a lot of Christians with a lot of knowledge, and yet they may not necessarily be happy. The happiest Christians are the ones who are doing the Word for others and for God, not considering themselves at all. Think about the Christians that you know who are happy and examine their lives, and I guarantee you will find this to be true. The unhappiest Christians are the ones who are constantly thinking of themselves and their problems, and not giving of themselves for others.

Summary

What does your life exemplify this day? Are you an inquirer, like Peter? Are you a betrayer, like Judas? Are you a receiver, a taker, like the disciples? Or are you a server, like our Lord? Ladies, do you want to be really happy? Do you want to be blessed this day? I guarantee you won't find happiness in asking questions like Peter did, and you won't find happiness in betraying Christ like Judas did. You won't find happiness by being on the receiving end only, always taking from others. Genuine happiness comes from being a humble servant like our Lord. That's where joy comes from! My recommendation to you is that you follow the example of our Lord in His final hours by finding 24 dirty feet and giving them a good foot washing, in the biblical sense!

QUESTIONS TO CONSIDER

1. (a) Read John 13:6-17, making note of all the "if-then" statements. How many are there? (Example: verse 8: "If I do not wash you, you have no part with Me.") (b) What do you think Jesus meant by these statements?

2. Memorize John 13:13-14.

3. List observations of Christ, Peter, Judas, and the disciples in 13:6-17.

4. Read Mark 8:31-33 and Mark 9:2-6. (a) What do these passages and John 13:6-9 tell you about Peter? (b) What do you learn about the importance of our speech from these passages?

5. (a) Jesus tells Peter, in John 13:7, that what He is doing now Peter will understand later. According to John 2:18-22 and John 12:12-16, what other things did Jesus do or say which the disciples did not understand at the time but understood later? (b) What comfort does this give you today for circumstances that you do not understand? EXTRA CREDIT: What do you think Jesus meant when He told Peter that he would understand later? Prove your answer biblically.

6. (a) Do you think we should be literally washing each other's feet today? (b) Why or why not? (c) What are some of the ways we could be figuratively "washing the saints' feet," so to speak? (d) Do you allow others to "wash your feet," or are you like Peter, saying, "You shall never wash my feet"? (e) What do you need to do to change your attitude?

7. (a) What do Matthew 6:9-13 and 1 John 1:9 say regarding a believer's confession of sins? (b) How often do you come to the Lord for confession and cleansing of your sins? (c) According to Psalm 51, what should be a believer's attitudes when confessing his or her sins? (d) Are these your attitudes?

8. Assignment: Wash someone's feet this week—in the biblical sense!

9. (a) How has God spoken to you through this chapter? (b) Please write a prayer request to share.

Judas, the Betrayer
John 13:18-30

OVER the years, I've visited with countless professing Christians who don't attend church for one reason or another. When I have inquired as to why they don't attend, I've gotten a myriad of reasons—or excuses—to justify their disobedience. But you know the number one reason I hear? It's this: "I don't come to church because there are too many hypocrites in the church." My flesh almost always wants to respond with something like, "So... by your disobedience you're *also* proving to be a hypocrite." But I typically respond by saying, "Yes, there are hypocrites in the church and there always will be," and then I compel them to be obedient. Ladies, this is a sobering fact: there are hypocrites in the church. But should we expect it to be any different today when there was a hypocrite among Jesus' own twelve disciples? In our study of the Upper Room Discourse, we've come to a sobering passage regarding Judas the betrayer, the great pretender, the hypocrite. Let's read about him together in John 13:18-30.

> "I do not speak concerning all of you. I know whom I have chosen; but that the Scripture may be fulfilled, 'He who eats bread with Me has lifted up his heel against Me.' Now I tell you before it comes, that when it does come to pass, you may believe that I am He. Most assuredly, I say to you, he who receives whomever I send receives Me; and he who receives Me receives Him who sent Me."
>
> When Jesus had said these things, He was troubled in spirit, and testified and said, "Most assuredly, I say to you, one of you will betray Me." Then the disciples looked at one another, perplexed about whom He spoke.
>
> Now there was leaning on Jesus' bosom one of His disciples, whom Jesus loved. Simon Peter therefore motioned to him to ask who it was of whom He spoke.
>
> Then, leaning back on Jesus' breast, he said to Him, "Lord, who is it?"

> Jesus answered, "It is he to whom I shall give a piece of bread when I have dipped it." And having dipped the bread, He gave it to Judas Iscariot, the son of Simon. Now after the piece of bread, Satan entered him. Then Jesus said to him, "What you do, do quickly." But no one at the table knew for what reason He said this to him. For some thought, because Judas had the money box, that Jesus had said to him, "Buy those things we need for the feast," or that he should give something to the poor.
>
> Having received the piece of bread, he then went out immediately. And it was night.

We leave the humility of Jesus exemplified in His washing of the disciples' feet to look upon the pride of Judas exemplified in his betrayal of Jesus. From the purest to the vilest; from the perfect to the worst. In our last chapter, we examined four types of individuals: the inquirer, Peter; the betrayer, Judas; the receivers, the disciples; and the server, Christ. Christ finished the task of washing His disciples' feet and then sat down to teach them a lesson in what it means to be a servant. We left off that chapter with verse 17 and the promise that the disciples would find happiness as they followed Christ's example of doing any task with an attitude of humility.

In this chapter, we will learn seven facts regarding hypocrites. My friend, this is a vital lesson because Jesus will make clear that no hypocrite will have a part in eternal life but only in hell's torment. Yet, many on that day will think they're going to be granted entrance into the Kingdom, only to find that Jesus will tell them to depart because He never knew them. Let's begin this sobering lesson in verse 18 with the first fact regarding hypocrites.

> "I do not speak concerning all of you. I know whom I have chosen; but that the Scripture may be fulfilled, 'He who eats bread with Me has lifted up his heel against Me.'" (John 13:18)

If you recall from our previous chapter, Jesus had just told the disciples in verse 17 that they would be happy if they understood the things He was doing and followed His example. What we have here in verse 18 is very much a continuation of Jesus' words in verse 17. In other words, Jesus is telling them that they are happy, but not all of them: *I do not speak concerning all of you.* There is one among you, Jesus is saying, who does not do the things I do; there is one who is not blessed, that being Judas. I know this, Jesus says, because *I know whom I have chosen. Here we see our first fact regarding hypocrites: Hypocrites are known by God.* God knows those who are His and those who are not His. Why? Because He knows whom He has chosen. The word *chosen* indicates choosing for oneself, and this choosing involves preference and choice from among many. Jesus knew what He was doing when He chose Judas as one of the Twelve. Jesus did not choose His twelve lightly; Luke records in his Gospel (Luke 6:12-16) that Jesus spent all night in prayer to God before He chose them. Remember, Jesus Himself said in John 6:70, "Did I not choose you, the twelve, and one of you is a devil?" This was not an accident. I have to say that if I knew ahead of time that a woman in whom I was going to invest my life was going to prove herself to be a hypocrite, I would have a difficult time taking her on as a disciple. I've discipled several women who have proved to be hypocrites, but I certainly didn't know that at the beginning. Why then would Jesus choose Judas? Jesus says *that the Scripture may be fulfilled, "He who eats bread with Me has lifted up his heel against Me."* What *Scripture* is Christ talking about that was fulfilled? He is speaking of Psalm 41:9 (LSB), which says, "Even my close friend in whom I trusted, who ate my bread, has lifted up his heel against me." Psalm 41 was written by David when he was ill. Let's read it together:

> How blessed is he who considers the poor;
> Yahweh will provide him escape in a day of calamity.
> Yahweh will keep him and keep him alive,
> And he shall be blessed upon the earth;
> And do not give him over to the desire of his enemies.
> Yahweh will sustain him upon his sickbed;
> In his illness, You restore him to health.
>
> As for me, I said, "O Yahweh, be gracious to me;
> Heal my soul, for I have sinned against You."
> My enemies speak evil against me,

"When will he die, and his name perish?"
And when he comes to see me, he speaks worthlessness;
His heart gathers wickedness to itself;
When he goes outside, he speaks it.
All who hate me whisper together against me;
Against me, they devise for me calamity, saying,
"A vile thing is poured out upon him,
That when he lies down, he will not rise up again."
Even my close friend in whom I trusted,
Who ate my bread,
Has lifted up his heel against me.

But You, O Yahweh, be gracious to me and raise me up,
That I may repay them.
By this I know that You delight in me,
Because my enemy makes no shout in triumph over me.
As for me, You uphold me in my integrity,
And You make me stand firm in Your presence forever.

Blessed be Yahweh, the God of Israel,
From everlasting to everlasting.
Amen and Amen.
(LSB)

David acknowledges in this Psalm that his illness is a result of his own sin (verse 4). Evidently, his enemies secretly wanted him to die (verses 5-8). And, in verse 9, he speaks of this close friend who had lifted up his heel against him. Many scholars believe this is a reference to Ahithophel, who had been one of David counselors—one of the best, in fact. In 2 Samuel 16:23, we read: "Now the advice of Ahithophel, which he gave in those days, was as if one had inquired at the oracle of God." From 2 Samuel 16:20-17:23, we learn that David had been forced to flee from Jerusalem. His son, Absalom, was trying to seize power from David and as Absalom did so he sought counsel from Ahithophel, who advised Absalom to have sex with his father's concubines in front of all of Israel. If that wasn't enough, Ahithophel then went on to tell Absalom to pursue David and kill him. (Sounds like strange counsel from a man whose counsel had been considered to be like the oracle of God!) Absalom, evidently, began to wonder about this counsel of Ahithophel, so he called another counselor, Hushai, who warned that the counsel Ahithophel had given was not good and gave his reasons in 2 Samuel 17:5-13. Absalom agreed that Hushai's counsel was better than Ahithophel's, so when Ahithophel saw that his counsel wasn't followed, he saddled his donkey and went to his house, got it in order, and hanged himself. In the same way that David was betrayed by his trusted table companion, Ahithophel, who then went out and hanged himself (2 Samuel 17:23), so Judas, Jesus' close companion, betrayed Him and then hanged himself. What happened to David in the Old Testament is now happening to David's Son in the New Testament! The Scripture is being fulfilled! Psalm 55:12-14 (LSB), which is David's lament regarding Ahithophel, is also applicable to Christ and Judas: "For it is not an enemy who reproaches me, then I could bear it; nor is it one who hates me who has magnified himself against me, then I could hide myself from him. But it is you, a man my equal, my close companion and my familiar friend; we who had sweet counsel together walked in the house of God in the throng."

Judas' betrayal was indeed a fulfillment of prophecy, but Judas was nonetheless still responsible for his actions. Man is always responsible for his actions; God is sovereign, yes, but man is responsible. Jesus says *he who eats bread with me has lifted up his heel against me*. To *eat bread* at the table of a superior was to offer a pledge of loyalty and was a proof of friendship. This one who has eaten with Christ is now going to *lift up his heel against* Him. This act would be like a stubborn and vicious horse, who suddenly turns around and kicks at his master. It was a gross breach of hospitality to eat bread with anyone and then turn against that one. Jesus had just washed Judas' feet, including his heel, and now Judas was going to lift up that heel against Him. Jesus comforts His disciples by saying,

> "Now I tell you before it comes, that when it does come to pass, you may believe that I am He." (John 13:19)

Jesus is telling the disciples now about Judas' coming betrayal so that they may believe that He is who He says He is. In fact, the word for *believe* means that you may keep on believing. The other eleven were not to think when this tragedy occurs that Jesus was somehow deceived by Judas; knowing this would help them to believe that Jesus was who He said He was. The disciples could have been seriously shocked and their faith shattered had Christ not forewarned them of Judas' betrayal. Ladies, this is a reminder to us that we should not be surprised at the Judases in our midst. Very similar types of things have happened numerous times in my life and it is always heartbreaking, but now that I am older in the faith I almost expect it. We must beware lest we too become disillusioned with hypocrites and abandon our Lord. Christ's statement here shows His compassion and love; He takes the time in His final hours to tell His disciples what is yet to come, just as a dying parent would take the time in their final hours to lovingly explain certain things to their children. Also, it's worthy of noting that Jesus says *I am He*. Literally, Christ is saying, "I AM." Remember that the Gospel of John was written for the purpose of authenticating the claim that Jesus is God, and here Jesus calls Himself the very name of God, I AM. He is saying, "I AM GOD." Jesus wants the disciples' faith to be strengthened, not weakened, when they see this coming betrayal. After Judas' plan has been carried out, the disciples must remember who they are, who has sent them, and that God is still ruling on His throne. In the next verse, verse 20, Jesus goes on to tell the disciples a second fact about hypocrites:

> "Most assuredly, I say to you, he who receives whomever I send receives Me; and he who receives Me receives Him who sent Me." (John 13:20)

Jesus says *most assuredly, I say to you*. In other words: Listen up, guys! This is important! Anyone who had accepted or received the disciples, in reality, had accepted or received Jesus, and whoever would accept or receive Jesus would be accepting or receiving the Father. When the disciples see what Judas will come to do in a few short hours, they might be tempted to think that their work is over. But this is a reminder to them that the betrayer will not affect their apostleship; no matter what Judas does, the work of the Lord will go on by the One who sent them.

Fact number 2 regarding hypocrites: They do not stop the work of Christ. What an encouragement that is to you and me as well! No matter what

Satan does through the Judases in the world, the One who sent us and the work He sent us to do remain unaffected. Satan is at work among the Lord's people, and we must not be discouraged by that. John tells us in 1 John 4:4 that the One who is in us is greater than the One who is in the world! Where there are true Christians, there will also be hypocrites, but that should not affect our calling or our commission. After this word of encouragement to the disciples, Jesus becomes troubled in spirit, in verse 21.

> When Jesus had said these things, He was troubled in spirit, and testified and said, "Most assuredly, I say to you, one of you will betray Me." (John 13:21)

To be *troubled in spirit* means to be stirred or agitated. This is one of the strongest expressions used to describe the sorrows of Christ. The same verb is used in John 11:33, when Jesus comes to Lazarus' tomb and sees Mary weeping and the Jews weeping, and it says that He groans in spirit and is troubled and weeps. To be *troubled* is to have an inner disturbance that affects one's entire being. Here, we see our Lord in His humanity. Jesus wasn't stoic; He hurt and He grieved as a real man. Why was He troubled in spirit? Because He knew that Judas would betray Him.

Fact number 3 about hypocrites: They grieve our Lord. Verses like this should cause us to realize how very deeply Christ loves sinners. They also should encourage us that when we are forsaken by friends and family because of our connection with Christ, He knows exactly how we feel because He has been touched with the feelings of our infirmities. When women I have discipled forsake the faith or turn against me in some way, it grieves my soul like nothing else can. But what comfort I can take in the knowing that my Lord has gone through the same heartache and He has been touched with the feelings of my infirmities!

Being troubled, Jesus goes on to say to his disciples *most assuredly, I say to you, one of you will betray Me.* This is a solemn announcement, as exemplified by the prefix *most assuredly*. Notice that Jesus does not mention who His betrayer is. If he had, the other eleven would probably have clobbered him! 1 out of 12 was going to betray Him; why should we think the ratio will be any different today? Could it be possible that 1 out of 12, or even more, in our own churches today are betrayers? Didn't Jesus say that there would be few who would find eternal life? This solemn statement by our Lord causes the disciples to react as we see them react in verse 22.

> Then the disciples looked at one another, perplexed about whom He spoke. (John 13:22)

The disciples *looked at one another* in bewilderment. Luke 22:23 records that they began to inquire among themselves about who among them would do this thing. They were *perplexed*; they were puzzled. Not one of them knew it was Judas.

Fact number 4 about hypocrites: They can be unknown by believers. Judas looked just as religious as Peter, James, and John. This shows us that a hypocrite will go to great lengths to hide his or her hypocrisy. The disciples didn't know that it was Judas and yet they'd been with him day after day. This also indicates that Jesus had treated Judas with the same kindness and love for three years that He treated the other disciples. Matthew 5:44, "But I say to you, love your enemies, bless those who curse you, do good to those who hate you, and pray for those who spitefully use you and persecute you." Of course, upon hearing this disturbing news from Jesus, one of the disciples just has to probe a little more with a question—and guess who it is? Peter!

> Now there was leaning on Jesus' bosom one of His disciples, whom Jesus loved. (John 13:23)

We need to understand the position here of the disciples. It is not like the Last Supper painted by Leonardo de Vinci! That really gives us a false picture. The disciples would be reclining on their sides on couches, which were arranged in the shape of a U, their left arms resting on a cushion, which was on the table, and their right hands free to take food. Their feet would be stretched out behind them. The host or principle person would be reclining in the center, and the place of honor was above him. The person to the right of the host would be placed so that his head would be close to the host's breast, and it would be easy therefore to say a word to him confidentially, which we see in verse 25. From verse 23, we know that John was positioned to the right of Jesus. We know John was this disciple because he is referred to as the one whom Jesus loved. Some say he was closest to the Lord and yet did you know he was the youngest? Church history tells us he was about 22 at this time. It is very probable that Judas was reclining immediately to the left of Jesus, since he was the treasurer. This would have meant that Jesus would have been leaning on Judas' breast and would have washed his feet first, as we brought out in our first chapter. And, an interesting side note, the person to the left of the host was considered the guest of honor, which in this case would have been Judas. Evidently, Judas was next to Jesus, as Jesus dips the sop and speaks to Judas, as we see in verse 27. It is truly amazing that Jesus loved Judas to the end! It appears that Peter was next to John and of course he has something to say in verse 24.

> Simon Peter therefore motioned to him to ask who it was of whom He spoke. (John 13:24)

Inquisitive Peter says, "Hey, John! Ask Jesus who it is! Who would do such a thing?!" (Sounds like something I would say!) It's possible that Peter did not want to ask the Lord directly because of his previous questions during the foot-washing. So, John leans over and asks Jesus who it is.

> Then, leaning back on Jesus' breast, he said to Him, "Lord, who is it?" (John 13:25)

In verse 23, John was leaning on Jesus' bosom, and now he's *leaning back on Jesus' breast*. In verse 23, it simply means that he was sitting next to Jesus in that reclining position which now makes it easy for him to fall back on Jesus' breast and speak privately so that the others cannot hear. So John asks for Peter, *Lord, who is it?* Jesus answers in verse 26.

> Jesus answered, "It is he to whom I shall give a piece of bread when I have dipped it." And having dipped the bread, He gave it to Judas Iscariot, the son of Simon. (John 13:26)

It was a token of intimacy to allow a guest to dip his bread in the common dish. It was a sign of friendship. In fact, this is one of the gracious acts that Boaz did for Ruth; he said to her, "Come here, that you may eat of the bread and dip your piece of bread in the vinegar" (Ruth 2:14a LSB). The sop would probably be a piece of bread that one would dip into a vessel filled with a mixture of vinegar, figs, nuts, dates, and other fruit, that together would form a thick mass. This is what Jesus did for Judas, who was probably reclining to the left of Jesus. It was such a usual courtesy that it escaped the notice of the other disciples. If John did understand who Christ was referring to, he must have refrained from telling the others. And so, Jesus *dipped the bread* and *gave it to Judas*. We see here that Jesus had not exhausted His effort to call Judas to repent. He is still reaching out to Judas to the end: "Judas, it is you, don't you know that I know what you are getting ready to do?" You have to wonder what Judas was thinking of at this time. Was his heart not pricked at all as Jesus' hand touched his with the bread and sop? Jesus' act of friendship to Judas was the final act which caused Judas to betray the friendship. Notice, too, that John is careful to say which Judas it was who was getting ready to do this horrendous deed, as he says *Judas Iscariot, the son of Simon*. John then records something very sobering that we all should take notice of, in verse 27.

> Now after the piece of bread, Satan entered him. Then Jesus said to him, "What you do, do quickly." (John 13:27)

It's interesting that in John 13:2 the devil put it into Judas' heart to betray Jesus, and now we see Satan entering into Judas. This is not so much bodily possession as complete spiritual possession. This is the only time the word *Satan* is mentioned in John's Gospel. He *entered* into Judas' very being. *Fact number 5 about hypocrites: They are controlled by Satan.* Jesus then says to Judas, *what you do, do quickly*. This literally means do it more quickly, do it as fast as possible, carry out your plans even more quickly than you had proposed. But the disciples still seem to have no clue as to what is going on, as we see in verses 28 and 29.

> But no one at the table knew for what reason He said this to him. (John 13:28)

No one knew still what was going on and why Jesus had *said this*; they were clueless. *This is the 6th fact about hypocrites: Many times, they look like the real thing.* It appears that only John had heard what Jesus said in verse 26, though he may have told Peter. But none seemed to understand what Christ meant by telling Judas to do it quickly, as verse 29 indicates,

> For some thought, because Judas had the money box, that Jesus had said to him, "Buy those things we need for the feast," or that he should give something to the poor. (John 13:29)

They thought Jesus meant one of two things by His statement. First, they thought that Judas may have been buying things for the feast. This scene in the upper room was occurring prior to the feast of the Passover (verse 1), and it was probably about 24 hours before it was to be celebrated, so Judas would have ample time to purchase what they needed for the feast. The second thing they thought Christ may have meant by His statement was that Judas should give something to the poor. He was the treasurer, even though he was also a thief. Consider John 12:3-6 (LSB),

> Mary then took a litra of perfume of very costly pure nard, and anointed the feet of Jesus and wiped His feet with her hair; and the house was filled with the fragrance of the perfume. But Judas Iscariot, one of His disciples, who was going to betray Him, said, "Why was this perfume not sold for three hundred denarii and given to the poor?" Now he said this, not because he was concerned about the poor, but because he was a thief, and as he had the money box, he used to take from what was put into it.

The disciples thought that Judas may have been aiding a poor household, perhaps even to provide a Paschal lamb for the Passover, which would take place the next day.

One thing to note, before we go on, is that it appears Judas could not handle the temptation of money; he betrayed our Lord for 30 pieces of silver, according to Matthew 26:15, and was a thief, according to John 12:6. Judas is a fulfillment of what Paul warned Timothy of in 1 Timothy 6:10 (LSB): "For the love of money is a root of all sorts of evils, and some by aspiring to it have wandered away from the faith and pierced themselves with many griefs." Judas erred from the faith, and what grief he has even this day. We end with verse 30 and a very sobering message for us all:

> Having received the piece of bread, he then went out immediately. And it was night. (John 13:30)

Judas mocks Jesus to the end, as he takes food from the hand of the One he is soon to betray. "He who eats bread with Me has lifted up his heel against Me." Judas appears to be the vilest of hypocrites; not even the washing of his feet by our Lord softened his heart. And John says that when Judas went out it was night. We know this is literally nighttime, as John 18:1-3 indicates that after the Upper Room Discourse they came with lanterns and torches to arrest Jesus—it was nighttime. The rest of the Upper Room Discourse takes place at night. But it was also night spiritually for Judas as well. Judas went out into the darkness. John uses this symbolic meaning for a reason: Judas was leaving the light of the world and was choosing to go out into the blackness of darkness forever. Jude 1:13 talks about false teachers in hell and writes that the blackness of darkness forever is reserved for them. Jesus describes hell in Matthew 8:12 as "outer darkness" where "there shall be weeping and gnashing of teeth." And for Judas, it is still night. He who might have judged one of the 12 tribes of Israel is now to become the child of hell. In this, we have the final and 7th fact about a hypocrite, that their end is eternal damnation.

Summary

This is a very sobering lesson and one from which I think we can glean a lot of personal application. There are seven facts regarding hypocrites in these verses:

1. Hypocrites are known by Christ (vv 18-19). If you are aware that you are a hypocrite, you might be fooling others, maybe even your spouse or closest friend, but never will you fool our Lord. Everything is naked and open unto the eyes of Him with whom we have to do, as Hebrews 4:13 (LSB) tells us, "And there is no creature hidden from His sight, but all things are uncovered and laid bare to the eyes of Him to whom we have an account to give."

2. Hypocrites don't stop the work of Christ (v 20). Have you been discouraged by those you know who have proven to be false? Don't be discouraged, dear friend! The work of the Lord will go on. He is not in Heaven wringing His hands wondering how His plan will be carried out. His will *will* be done!

3. Hypocrites grieve our Lord (v 21). This is a wonderful encouragement as we see our Lord loving even His enemies to the end, even though they were grieving Him. Should you and I not follow that example by endeavoring to love those who seem to be false? This does not mean we don't confront their sin, but it does mean that we love them.

4. Hypocrites can be unknown by others (vv 22-26). In Matthew 13, true and false believers are likened to wheat and tares that grow up together until the time of harvest when they are gathered up together and the tares are then burned up. In many instances, you and I will not know who the Judases are in our midst.

5. Hypocrites are controlled by Satan (v 27). We are either children of God or children of the devil. There is no in-between. Those who are hypocrites are controlled by Satan, not by God.

6. Hypocrites may look like the real thing (vv 28-29). Ladies, it happens all the time. I have seen it often; in many instances, I never would have guessed. They looked just like you and me and looked and acted outwardly just like a follower of Christ. Second Corinthians 11:14-15 (LSB) states: "And no wonder, for even Satan disguises himself as an angel of light. Therefore it is not surprising if his ministers also disguise themselves as ministers of righteousness, whose end will be according to their deeds."

7. Their end is eternal damnation (v 30). All hypocrites will have their place in the lake of fire. In fact, Jesus says in Matthew 24:51 that hypocrites will spend all eternity weeping and gnashing their teeth. Jesus says that it would have been better if Judas had not been born.

Hypocrisy is very serious, and I hope each of you will examine yourselves thoroughly so that you will not be among those in the end whom Jesus will say He never knew. What is the cure for hypocrisy? How might you and I avoid hypocrisy? Guard your motives carefully, walk in the Spirit each day, and immediately confess even the slightest hint of hypocrisy. Someone once said, "Sacrificing a lasting relationship with an eternal God for a brief dance of promised pleasure is deadly to the progress of my soul."

QUESTIONS TO CONSIDER

1. (a) Read Matthew 26:20-25; Mark 14:17-21; Luke 22:21-23; and John 13:18-30. In which of these accounts is the betrayer identified? (b) What differences and similarities do you notice between these passages? (c) From the John passage, write down the things you notice that characterize hypocrisy.

2. Memorize John 13:21.

3. (a) Read Matthew 26:14-25; 26:47-50; and 27:1-10. What were the signs of Judas' betrayal? (b) What was Judas' reaction when he heard that Jesus had been condemned?

4. (a) Read John 12:1-8. How did Mary demonstrate her love for Christ? (b) What objection did Judas raise? (c) What was his motive? (d) What do you learn about Judas?

5. What do you learn about Jesus, Judas, Peter, John, and the other disciples from John 13:18-30?

6. The quote from John 13:18 comes from Psalm 41:9, which is a reference to David's friend, Ahithophel. Read 2 Samuel 16-17, and write a summary paragraph of what was going on in these chapters and why David would say this regarding his friend. (Feel free to use outside helps, if needed.)

7. (a) Do you know someone who lives a life of hypocrisy? (No names, please!) (b) Will you lovingly warn them today of the danger they are in? (Matthew 23:27-28; Mark 14:21; and Acts 1:25 give sobering reminders of the danger they are in.) (c) What are some ways we as believers can lovingly warn those we know who are living a double life?

8. (a) How would you define hypocrisy? (b) What are some ways that God's children manifest hypocrisy? (c) Is there any hypocrisy in your life, dear friend? I beg you to root it out this day as it could be a matter of life or death!

9. As you consider question 8c, write down a prayer request for your own life regarding any area of hypocrisy.

The Glory of God as Seen in His Son and in His Children
John 13:31-35

WHEN our children were growing up, there were times when one or more members of our family were behaving in a less-than-loving manner. When this would occur, it was often stopped by some other member of the family singing a song about how love is the preeminent attribute of believers. And, most of the time, that would be enough to bring the ungodly conduct to a sudden halt. "They will know we are Christians by our love" is a truth our Lord expressed to the disciples in the upper room. And yet we know that even though He said it directly to them, they, just like us, had difficulty living it out.

We have come to a very difficult portion of the Upper Room Discourse. It is not difficult in the sense of explaining its meaning; it's difficult in the sense of living it out! Loving others is sometimes the hardest thing to do, and yet Jesus says in the text we'll cover in this chapter, that loving others is how all men will know that we are His disciples. Let's read this portion of God's Word together from John 13:31-35:

> So, when he had gone out, Jesus said, "Now the Son of Man is glorified, and God is glorified in Him. If God is glorified in Him, God will also glorify Him in Himself, and glorify Him immediately. Little children, I shall be with you a little while longer. You will seek Me; and as I said to the Jews, 'Where I am going, you cannot come,' so now I say to you. A new commandment I give to you, that you love one another; as I have loved you, that you also love one another. By this all will know that you are My disciples, if you have love for one another."

In this text, we will examine two basic themes: *The Glory of God as Seen in His Son* (vv 31-32); and *The Glory of God as Seen in His Children* (vv 33-35). In our last chapter, we took a sobering look at Judas and discovered seven facts regarding hypocrites: they are known by Christ; they don't stop the work of Christ; they grieve our Lord; they can be unknown by other believers; they are controlled by Satan; they look like the real thing; and their end is eternal damnation. Let's now turn from the grievous topic of hypocrisy to the glorious topic of our Savior and especially how His glory is seen in His Son.

The Glory of God as Seen in His Son *John 13:31-32*

> So, when he had gone out, Jesus said, "Now the Son of Man is glorified, and God is glorified in Him." (John 13:31)

John begins by saying *so, when he had gone out*, which we know is a reference back to verse 30 and the mention of Judas going out. Judas is now gone out from the presence of Jesus and the other disciples, and the rest of what Jesus says from now through chapter 16 will be critical for these eleven disciples as these are Jesus' final words to them. He begins by saying to them *now the Son of Man is glorified, and God is glorified in Him*. What does it mean that *the Son of Man is glorified*? To *glorify* means to recognize, honor, praise, or to bring honor to. The term *glory* or *glorified* is mentioned five times in the next two verses. When Jesus says *the Son of Man is glorified*, He means that His innate glory is brought to light. When Jesus is glorified, God is glorified. We already saw in verse 20 that, whoever receives Jesus, receives the Father, as they are one. And now Jesus says that to glorify the Son is to glorify the Father. What is done to one is done to the other. Jesus says *now* the Son of Man is glorified, indicating that the going out of Judas was a sign that the betrayal and death of the Son of Man was at hand. The action of Judas going out to betray our Lord was an indication that soon Jesus would go to the cross. He had waited at least 33 years for the time that He would be glorified. The series of events that would lead to the cross was beginning and it began by Judas going out to betray Jesus. Does this mean Jesus was not glorified before? No. Jesus glorified the Father while He was on earth, and He will mention that in His prayer in John 17:4: "I have glorified You on the earth. I have finished the work which You have given Me to do." But Jesus will also pray for the glory He had with the Father to be restored to Him, in John 17:5: "And now, O Father, glorify Me together with Yourself, with the glory which I had with You before the world was."

So, what is Jesus saying here? J. C. Ryle helps us: "Now has the time come that I, the Son of Man, should be glorified, by actually dying as man's substitute, and shedding my blood for the sins of the world. Now has the time come that God the Father should receive the *highest glory* by my sacrifice on the cross."[1] Notice, too, that Jesus refers to His own death not as a dreaded thing but as a time in which the Son and Father would be glorified. Wouldn't it be great if we all would think of our own deaths as opportunities to glorify the Father and not as occasions for self-pity? I have watched some Christians approach death by bringing immense glory to God, and yet I have seen others go through the dying process in exactly the opposite manner. What an opportunity we have to glorify our Lord even in the valley of the shadow of death! He is with us; what do we have to fear? Death can be a time for His glory to be shown powerfully in us!

The eleven remaining disciples probably did not yet understand what Jesus was saying. At this moment, which seems to be so disastrous, the Son of Man is glorified? They would witness Him tomorrow hanging on a cross between two thieves and perhaps feel great shame and disappointment. How could such an experience glorify God? A.W. Pink gives us some good insights as to why the death of Christ would bring glory to the Father. I'll paraphrase his thoughts here:

1. Jesus performed the greatest work, which the whole history of the entire universe ever witnessed, or ever will witness. Think of it: no one else has ever died on a cross for the sins of the world. That brings glory to God!

2. Because on the cross, Christ reversed the conduct of the first man, Adam. Paul says in Romans 5:18 that as by the offense of one (Adam) judgment came upon all men to condemnation, even so by the righteousness of one (Jesus) the free gift came upon all men unto justification of life. That brings glory to the Father!

---

[1] J. C. Ryle, *Expository Thoughts on the Gospels*.

3. Because through death Jesus destroyed him who had the power of death, that is the devil. The writer to the Hebrews puts it this way: "Inasmuch then as the children have partaken of flesh and blood, He Himself likewise shared in the same, that through death He might destroy him who had the power of death, that is, the devil" (Hebrews 2:14). Destroying Satan brings glory to the Father!

4. Because at the cross Christ paid the ransom-price, which purchased for Himself all the elect of God. And that brings glory to God the Father!

5. By virtue of the work on the cross, a glory was acquired by the Mediator: there is now a glorified Man at God's right hand. 1 Timothy 2:5-6 (LSB) tells us, "For there is one God, and one mediator also between God and men, the man Christ Jesus, who gave Himself as a ransom for all, the witness for this proper time." That brings glory to the Father.[2]

When you think about it, at the cross the attributes of God were displayed thus bringing God glory. We can't mention them all, but almost every attribute of God was displayed at the cross—the power of God, the justice of God, the holiness of God, the faithfulness of God, and the love of God, to name just a few. John expounds a little more on this truth in verse 32.

> "If God is glorified in Him, God will also glorify Him in Himself, and glorify Him immediately." (John 13:32)

There is now no postponement in the Lord being glorified. Judas has gone out to betray the Son of Man. The glory will take place immediately at the cross, and then at the resurrection and the ascension. J. C. Ryle again helps us: "If the Son, on the one hand, specially glorifies the Father's attributes of holiness, justice, and mercy, by satisfying all His demands with His own precious blood on the cross, so, on the other hand, the Father specially glorifies the Son, by exalting Him above all Kings, raising Him from the

---

[2] A. W. Pink, *Exposition of the Gospel of John*.

dead, and giving Him a name above every name."[3] Jesus knows that all these things will mean glory for His Father, to whom He is soon to return, but now, in verse 33, He turns His thoughts toward how this will affect His disciples, and He refers to them as little children. He addresses them as Head of the family and in the tenderness of a Father. So, we turn from the seeing the glory of God in His Son to seeing the glory of God in His children.

The Glory of God as Seen in His Children *John 13:33-35*

> "Little children, I shall be with you a little while longer. You will seek Me; and as I said to the Jews, 'Where I am going, you cannot come,' so now I say to you." (John 13:33)

The term *little children* is a term of affection used by a teacher of his disciples. This is the only place in the Gospel of John where this term occurs. It is also the only time the Lord refers to the disciples as little children. The apostle John uses this term often in his first epistle, and perhaps that's because he heard his Lord use it. A disciple will be like his teacher. This is a truth I've seen manifested in my own life as I take on the characteristics of those who pour their lives into me. Only now can Jesus refer to his disciples as little children, because Judas, the betrayer, has gone out from their midst. Judas was not a child of God; only Christians can be referred to as Christ's little children. But now that Judas has left, Jesus can with confidence call the remaining eleven His little children. He can also begin to expound on some very important and intimate subject matters that they will need to know going forward. I'm sure it would be the same with most of us; I know I would have difficulty opening up to my enemies but certainly not to my trusted friends. Also, by Jesus using the term little children, He is confirming that He is their Father and they are in need of His teaching and guidance, just as earthly children need the teaching and guidance of an earthly father.

After calling the disciples His little children, Jesus says *I shall be with you a little while longer*. He wasn't trying to hide the fact that He was indeed leaving them; He wanted to be candid with them regarding the fact that

---

[3] J. C. Ryle, *Expository Thoughts on the Gospels*.

the time of His departure was approaching and He would be soon gone. In fact, it would be only a few hours away. The disciples probably had no idea that He would be taken from them that quickly. He already said this once in John 12:35, and He will tell them again in John 14:19; 16:16; and 16:19. He's saying, "I am leaving, little children, so listen to what I am going to say. Give me your undivided attention." We can understand this as parents. If we knew we had only a few days left with our earthly children, we would want them to listen intently as we share our final thoughts with them.

Jesus lets them know: *You will seek Me; and as I said to the Jews, "Where I am going, you cannot come," so now I say to you.* What does Jesus mean by this statement? Most likely, He is referring to the time after His death; they would be seeking Him and wondering where He had gone. Just like little children would do if suddenly their father disappeared, they would seek him. He says you are going to *seek Me* but *as I said to the Jews, "Where I am going, you cannot come," so now I say* the same thing *to you*. When did Jesus say this statement to the Jews? First, in John 7:33-34 (LSB), He said to them, "For a little while longer I am with you, then I go to Him who sent Me. You will seek Me, and will not find Me; and where I am, you cannot come." He also said this in John 8:21 (LSB): "I am going away, and you will seek Me, and will die in your sin. Where I am going, you cannot come." Notice that to the Jews He states that they will not find Him. Why? Because of the hardness of their hearts and their unbelief, they will not be going where He was going, to Heaven. The seeking of Jesus from the unbelieving Jews will end in them dying in their sins. They will be weeping in hell. The disciples will also be troubled and weep, as Jesus tells them in John 14:1-2 and 16:20, but their tears will be because their Master is gone and their hearts will be sad. Jesus goes on to tell them that where He is going they *cannot come*. Where He is going, that is, to Heaven, they cannot come now, but they will afterwards, as He will mention in verse 36.

The thought of having their Master, their friend, their discipler, their teacher taken from them was probably frightening to the Eleven, to Jesus' little children. Perhaps that is why now Jesus leaves them with the commandment to love one another, in verse 34. After He is gone, they will still have one another, and they are to love one another. This is how His little children will glorify Him, by loving one another.

> "A new commandment I give to you, that you love one another; as I have loved you, that you also love one another." (John 13:34)

A new commandment implies freshness. It is fresh because the commandment given in the Old Testament, Leviticus 19:18 (LSB), which says, "You shall not take vengeance, and you shall not keep your anger against the sons of your people, but you shall love your neighbor as yourself; I am Yahweh," did not have this new element: *as I have loved you*. This commandment to *love one another* was new because it had the fresh and new meaning of Jesus' love in it, which was not seen in the Old Testament concept. Believers are now motivated to love others because Christ loved us first and modeled for us how we are to love one another. And, remember, this is right after He has exemplified love by washing the disciples' feet. This new commandment Jesus gives narrows the range and is inspired by a new motive, which is Jesus Himself. This kind of love empties itself for the sake of those it loves. This love is the highest standard of love and one that is challenging at times for any of God's little children. The Greek word for love here is *agapao*, which indicates a direction of the will and finding one's joy in anything. It is used of God's love toward man.

How did Jesus manifest this love to the disciples? He showed His love for them in many ways, but I want to share with you four ways.[4] First, He certainly loved them *selflessly*. When you think about it, did Christ ever do anything for Himself? Matthew tells us that "the Son of Man did not come to be served, but to serve, and to give His life a ransom for many" (Matthew 20:28). He has just displayed His selflessness by washing the disciples' feet, but when you look at the whole of Christ's time with them, you see a selfless man. He ministered to them, prayed for them, calmed their fears in a boat, showed them how to minister to others, answered their endless questions, and the list goes on and on. It is a rare thing to encounter a child of God who is truly selfless. We love ourselves, preserve

---

4 William Barclay, *The Gospel of John: Volume 2* (Louisville: The Westminster Press; 1956), 174-175.

ourselves, talk about ourselves, promote ourselves, and yet we are called to forget ourselves!

Secondly, Jesus loved the Eleven *sacrificially*. He was getting ready in the upper room to lay down His life for them and for the world. He did not hold on to His life. He said in John 10:15 (LSB), "even as the Father knows Me and I know the Father; and I lay down My life for the sheep." Some bristle at the thought of helping another out by running errands for them, cooking a meal for them, babysitting for them, helping them move, but sacrificial love is what marks a genuine child of God.

Thirdly, Jesus loved the disciples *understandingly*. What tenderness we see in these verses! He was patient with their endless questions, and He was compassionate toward them on numerous occasions. Even when they didn't understand the things He was saying, He was understanding. He did not call them names or become frustrated with them. Oh, how we need to grow in being more understanding of others and less judgmental! We need to seek to understand why people do what they do and stop assuming others' motives.

Lastly, Jesus loved His disciples *forgivingly*. Judas had already betrayed them, and the rest are going to soon forsake Him and flee. In fact, Matthew and Mark record that after Judas' betrayal all the disciples forsook Jesus and fled. Christ knew their frame, He knew they were but dust, and so His heart of forgiveness reached out to them in numerous ways. Oh, that we would forgive others in the same proportion that our Lord has forgiven us! That we would put off bitterness and resentment and put on forgiveness and love!

These are but a few of the ways our Lord loved the disciples. And this is how they would be known from now on, by the same type of love He had shown to them. Ladies, you and I are commanded to love in the same way Christ loved! The love here is in the present tense, which means that we are to keep on loving. We are to love at all times, not just when we feel like it or when the person is lovely, but always. The Jews were known by their external works; Christians are to be known by their love. As Albert Barnes says, "This was a new expression of love; and it shows the strength of the attachment which we ought to have for Christians, and how ready we should be to endure hardships, to encounter dangers, and to practice self-denial, to benefit those for whom the Son of God laid down his life."[5] This command to love one another is very important; it is the identifying mark of every true believer in Jesus Christ. Jesus puts it this way, in verse 35,

> "By this all will know that you are My disciples, if you have love for one another." (John 13:35)

By this, in this way, Jesus says, *all will know that you are My disciples*. The term *disciple* is used only in the Gospels and in Acts. A disciple is one who attaches himself to a master for the purpose of learning and obeying what his or her master says. A disciple accepts the instruction given to him and makes it his rule of conduct. It's a foreign concept to us in the 21st century—we don't like to follow anyone—but, my friend, true biblical discipleship is what Paul says in many places in the New Testament: be followers of me, follow me as I follow Christ. When I was being formally discipled by two different women, I would have never considered not carrying out their instructions, unless those instructions were unbiblical. But things have changed quite a bit in our culture; now discipleship is, more often than not, just getting together and chatting and maybe following through on something my discipler suggested.

Well, how will all men know that we are His disciples? If we *have love for one another*. *Love* here is *agape*, which is a benevolent kind of love that does what the one who loves deems is needed by the one loved. It's a little bit different meaning from the term for love that is used in verse 34. But it, too, is in the present active tense, which means that we are to keep on loving in this way. Hatred of one another is a sign that we are not Christ's disciples. It is well known that the heathen would say of the early Christians, "See how they love one another!" One of the marks of a true disciple of Jesus Christ is our love for God and for one another. It is said that John, the writer of this Gospel account, in his old age, never ceased to repeat, "Little children, love one another!" In fact, in

---

5 Albert Barnes, *Barnes' Notes on the Old and New Testaments: The Gospels* (Grand Rapids: Baker Book House, 1983), 323-324.

his first epistle, 1 John, he gives the exhortation numerous times to his little children that they should love one another; he even explains that hatred for another is a sign that one is an unbeliever and a murderer (1 John 3:15). Chrysostom once said that in his day Christians showed little love; he said, "Even now, there is nothing else that causes the heathen to stumble, except there is no love …. Their own doctrines they have long condemned, and in like manner they admire ours, but they are hindered by our mode of life."[6] It behooves us, dear friends, to think about our own lives and how we are representing Christ in our world. Too many of God's children, are ruining the testimony of our Lord with social media fights regarding good men and women of God and issues that are simply not worth slandering people over. Keep in mind that on judgment day, no partiality will be given to anyone who uses social media to sow discord among the brethren. When we do that, we are behaving no differently than the lost world that spews forth their hatred!

Summary

We have seen the glory of God as seen in His Son, in verses 31-32. In just a few short hours from this scene in the upper room, God will be glorified as His Son Jesus Christ hangs on Golgotha's tree.

We have also seen the glory of God as seen in His children, in verses 33-35. God is glorified when His children love each other with the same love that His Son Jesus Christ has exemplified.

In these few verses we have seen our Lord once again loving His own. He instructs them as a dying Father would instruct his children who are soon to be left behind. He speaks of His glory. He gives them a new commandment, that they should love just as He has exhibited before them in the upper room as He washed their feet, even demonstrating that love to His betrayer, Judas.

As we draw this chapter to a close, I want to zero in on the new commandment Christ has just given to the Eleven, to love one another

---

[6] John Chrysostom, quoted in Leon Morris, *The Gospel According to John* (Grand Rapids: William B. Eerdmans Publishing Company, 1995), 563.

as He has loved them. Since we are to be known by our love for one another, I would ask you, "Would others characterize you by your love?" Would they say, "There goes Becky! Behold how she loves the brethren!" or, "There goes Stephanie! See how she loves!"? What does love look like? Paul tells us in 1 Corinthians 13 what genuine love looks like. So, with that passage of Scripture in mind, let's consider the following self-examination questions:

◊ Do you love the brethren? Do you *really* love the brethren?

◊ Are you patient with people, especially your husband and your children and those in your family? Love is very patient.

◊ Are you kind to others? Does it show in your tone of voice and in your body language? Love is kind.

◊ Are you jealous of other people, wanting what they have? Do you envy their position, their looks, or their material possessions? Love is never jealous or envious.

◊ Do you boast around others about how great you are or what you have accomplished? Do you secretly think you are better than others and judge others in your heart? Love is never boastful, proud, or haughty.

◊ Do you always insist on your own way? Do you pout when you don't get your own way? Do you resent the time or energy that you give to others? Love is not selfish, nor does it demand its own way.

◊ Do you cut people off in traffic? Do you treat your children or husband as second-class citizens? Are you abrupt on the phone with others? Love is not rude.

◊ Are you agitated and frustrated with others or circumstances that God allows? Do others know it is that "time of the month" by your behavior? Love is not irritable or touchy.

- ◊ When someone hurts your feelings, do you bring it up to them? Do you remember all the mistakes your husband has made? Love does not hold grudges and will hardly even notice when others do it wrong.

- ◊ Do you secretly or even openly gloat when an enemy of yours gets their due? Do you rejoice when others excel, especially in the things of Christ? Love is never glad about injustice but rejoices whenever truth wins out.

- ◊ Are you loyal to your marriage, to your children, to your friendships, to the leaders in your church? If you love someone, you will be loyal to him no matter the cost. You will always believe in him, always expect the best of him, and always stand your ground in defending him.

It is not by wearing crosses around our necks that others will know we are Christ's disciples. It's not by carrying our Bibles that others will know we are His disciples. And it is not by having a religious bumper sticker on our cars that men will know we are His disciples. It certainly is not by having the fish sign on our business cards that others will know we are His disciples. It's not by our good-looking churches that all men know that we are His disciples. And, I'm sorry to say, it's not by our works and acts of service that men will know we are His disciples. It is by our love, and by our love only, that men will know we are His disciples.

Jesus is soon leaving and some of His final words are: "Love each other as I have loved you. By this love the world will know you belong to Me." Does the world we live in know that *you* belong to God by your love for others?

QUESTIONS TO CONSIDER

1. Read John 13:31-35. (a) What two words or phrases are repeated in this passage? (b) In what ways do you think the death of the Son brought glory to the Father? (c) What did Jesus mean by the phrase, "a new commandment I give unto you," in verse 34?

2. Memorize John 13:34-35.

3. (a) What do the following passages say about the Son of Man being glorified? Isaiah 53:10-12; John 17:4-6; John 17:20-24; Hebrews 1:1-3; 1 Peter 3:22; Revelation 21:22-23. (b) In what ways do you and I bring glory to the Father, according to the following passages? John 14:13; Romans 15:6-9; 2 Corinthians 3:18; Ephesians 1:12; Philippians 2:11; 1 Peter 4:9-11. (c) In what ways should these be evident in a believer's life?

4. (a) Read 1 Corinthians 13. (b) What does love look like, according to this chapter? (c) How does the type of love that Paul defines in 1 Corinthians 13 describe the love that Jesus had for the twelve disciples? Skim through the Gospel accounts and list the references where Christ exemplified each quality of love. (d) Where are you falling short in demonstrating this kind of love? (e) What will you do about it?

5. (a) What do the following passages teach regarding love? Romans 12:9-10; Galatians 5:22-23; 1 Peter 1:22; 1 Peter 4:8; 1 John 4:7-10. (b) How can you apply these things in your own life?

6. Look around for opportunities this week to express agape love to others. Perhaps you could babysit for a needy mom, take a meal to someone, do laundry or housework for someone, or visit an elderly person. Be creative. Come prepared not necessarily to share *what you did*, but the blessings you received.

7. Come with a prayer request after prayerfully considering question number four.

A Shocking Prophecy
John 13:36-38

IT goes without saying that most Christians at one time or another in their pilgrimage have made a promise to the Lord. Promises like, "Lord, I promise I am going to witness to my neighbor or my family member who is lost." Or, "Lord, I promise I am going to read or study or memorize your Word more." "God, I am going to spend more time in prayer." "God, I am really going to be more submissive to my husband and love him the way I should." "God, I promise, I will not yell at my kids anymore," or, "I really will be more consistent with disciplining my children, Lord." Or, "Lord, I will really try and love that unlovely person in my life; I really am going to overcome evil with good." On and on goes our list of promises to the Lord. And yet, how many of those promises do we really fulfill? Some of us might be embarrassed if we had to give an account to one another of the actual number of promises we've made to the Lord and how many of those promises we have actually fulfilled.

As we finish John chapter 13, we will discover that we are not alone in making promises to the Lord that we do not fulfill. The apostle John, through the Holy Spirit, records a promise made by Peter. It is a promise that Peter doesn't fulfill, and his failure to keep it is recorded for all of us to see. But ladies, it is recorded for us so that we might learn from Peter's example—and the lessons we will learn in this portion of God's Word are *not* about how to make promises we never intend to keep. What was the promise Peter made, and what lessons can you and I learn from it? Let's consider these questions together as we finish chapter 13 of John's Gospel in John 13:36-38.

> Simon Peter said to Him, "Lord, where are You going?" Jesus answered him, "Where I am going you cannot follow Me now, but you shall follow Me afterward."
> Peter said to Him, "Lord, why can I not follow You now? I will lay

down my life for Your sake.

>Jesus answered him, "Will you lay down your life for My sake? Most assuredly, I say to you, the rooster shall not crow till you have denied Me three times."

In this chapter, we'll discover three proclamations: *Jesus' Startling Proclamation* (v 36); *Peter's Spontaneous Proclamation* (v 37); and *Jesus' Shocking Proclamation* (v 38). In our last chapter, we saw the glory of God as it is seen in His Son, in verses 31 and 32. God will be glorified as His Son Jesus Christ hangs on Golgotha's tree. We also saw the glory of God as it is seen in His children, in verses 33-35. God is glorified when His children love each other with the love of His Son, Jesus Christ. Let's turn now from looking at how our Lord is glorified to a startling proclamation He makes in verse 36.

Jesus' Startling Proclamation — John 13:36

>Simon Peter said to Him, "Lord, where are You going?" Jesus answered him, "Where I am going you cannot follow Me now, but you shall follow Me afterward." (John 13:36)

Before John records the question Peter asks, John uses Peter's old name: *Simon Peter*. It is interesting to note when John has used Simon Peter's name thus far. We see it used in verses 6, 9, 24, and now in 36. We can only guess as to why John does this, but it appears to be used when Simon Peter is acting in a fleshly rather than godly manner. It's possible that it is used here in verse 36 because he seems to be ignoring the Lord's admonition to love the brethren in verses 34 and 35. For some reason, Peter's mind is still fixed on the statement in verse 33: "where I am going, you cannot come." Peter seems to have missed the point about loving the brethren.

I don't know about you, but I can identify with Peter; I've been in conversations with people when something is said and, as I'm thinking of what I want to ask or how I'm going to respond, they're moving on to another topic. This may be what has happened here. Peter seems to be fixed on the fact that His Lord is leaving, as was mentioned in verse

33, and the fact that he doesn't want to be separated from the Lord. So, Peter asks yet another question: *Lord, where are You going?* The fact that the Lord was going somewhere would be very upsetting to Peter and probably to all the disciples. They loved their Lord and didn't want to be separated from Him; they wanted dearly to be with Him. May I say that a true disciple of Jesus Christ longs to be with Him? We should long to be with our Lord, and there is usually something amiss when we don't long for His presence. And, by the way, I think this is true also in the physical realm with those who disciple us; there's usually a longing to be with them, to learn from them. I think of those who have invested in my life, who have discipled me—I dearly long to be with them, to learn from them. I also long to be with those whom I disciple because ours is precious time together.

Notice that Peter begins his question by calling Jesus *Lord*, a term that means master or owner. Now, this is not the first time that Peter has asked the Lord a question. In fact, in John's Gospel alone I found Peter asking questions seven times, three of them in this chapter alone. In verse 6, he asked Jesus, "Lord, are you washing my feet?" In verse 24, he asked John to ask Jesus who was going to betray Him. And now, he's asking where Jesus is going.

But Peter is not the first one to ask the Lord this question. Consider John 7:33-36 and John 8:21-22. In John 7:33-36 (LSB), we read, "Therefore Jesus said, 'For a little while longer I am with you, then I go to Him who sent Me. You will seek Me, and will not find Me; and where I am, you cannot come.' The Jews then said to one another, 'Where does this man intend to go that we will not find Him? Is He intending to go to the Dispersion among the Greeks and teach the Greeks? What is this statement that He said, "You will seek Me, and will not find Me; and where I am, you cannot come"?'" In John 8:21-22 (LSB), we read, "Then He said again to them, 'I am going away, and you will seek Me, and will die in your sin. Where I am going, you cannot come.' So the Jews were saying, 'Surely He will not kill Himself, since He says, "Where I am going, you cannot come"?'"

We see from these passages that the Jews were also curious about where Jesus was going. We will see in our next chapter that Thomas also was curious about this, in John 14:5 (LSB): "Thomas said to Him, 'Lord, we do not know where You are going. How do we know the way?'" And when we get to chapter 16, we will see that all the disciples chimed in wanting to know where Jesus was going. John 16:17 tells us, "Then some of His disciples said among themselves, 'What is this that He says to us, "A little while, and you will not see Me; and again a little while, and you will see Me"; and, "because I go to the Father"?'" And yet, we know from the Gospel accounts that the Lord had been preparing them all along that He was leaving them. It appears as if the disciples did not comprehend what the Lord had been telling them. They just didn't get it. Ladies, you and I are no different than the disciples. How many times does the Lord repeat the same truth over and over to us, and we still don't get it? We are slow to understand, are we not? How thankful I am for the patience of the Lord!

The Lord answers Peter's question with a startling proclamation: *Where I am going you cannot follow Me now, but you shall follow Me afterward*. Now, Jesus gives a hint as to where he is going in John 14:2; He's going to glory, to Heaven. But he says to Peter *you cannot follow Me now*, but you will follow later. It is interesting that to Peter Jesus says he will be able to come later, but to the Jews in both of passages we read, in John 7 and John 8, he tells them that where He is going, they cannot come. Why? They would not be able to go where He was going, because of their unbelief; they were hardened in their sin and would not be spending eternity with Him but in hell.

What does Jesus mean when He says to Peter *you will follow Me afterward*? Some hold that Jesus is referring to what He will later say to Peter, in John 21:18-19 (LSB), "'Truly, truly, I say to you, when you were younger, you used to gird yourself and walk wherever you wished; but when you grow old, you will stretch out your hands and someone else will gird you, and bring you where you do not wish to go.' Now this He said, signifying by what kind of death he would glorify God. And when He had spoken this, He said to him, 'Follow Me!'" In other words, Peter can't go to the cross with the Lord now, but soon his time for martyrdom will come.

Indeed, it came and it happened just as Jesus said it would, as Peter's hands were stretched out. Peter was martyred during the persecution which took place under Nero in 64-67 AD. He was about 70 at the time of his persecution and he requested that he be crucified upside down because he did not feel worthy to die as his Lord did. Peter wasn't in the dark about his death; not only did Jesus tell him here and in John 21, but Peter himself says in 2 Peter 1:14 (LSB), "knowing that the laying aside of my earthly dwelling is imminent, as also our Lord Jesus Christ has indicated to me." So, one possibility of what Jesus is saying here is that Peter will follow Christ later in dying by crucifixion.

However, Jesus could be referring to the fact that Peter can't go to Heaven, to His Father's house, just yet, but that he will indeed follow later. That seems to me to be the clearer answer, because of what Jesus will say next in John 14:1-3: "Let not your heart be troubled; you believe in God, believe also in Me. In My Father's house are many mansions; if it were not so, I would have told you. I go to prepare a place for you. And if I go and prepare a place for you, I will come again and receive you to Myself; that where I am, there you may be also." In fact, as soon as Peter is crucified, he will go directly to Heaven to be in the presence of the Lord!

Both these interpretations are legitimate. Whichever of these views seems to you to more accurately describe what Jesus meant by His statement, it was clearly a startling prediction to Peter. "I can't go where you are going? Are you kidding?!" Peter doesn't seem to be satisfied with Jesus' answer, so in verse 37, he poses another question, along with his own spontaneous proclamation.

Peter's Spontaneous Proclamation *John 13:37*

> Peter said to Him, "Lord, why can I not follow You now? I will lay down my life for Your sake." (John 13:37)

It is interesting to note that Peter calls Christ *Lord* a second time. The very one that he has called Lord twice, he will soon deny, however. So, Peter turns from the question of where Jesus is going to a *why* question: *Why can I not follow you now?* (All he needs now are the who, when, and how questions and Peter would make a good Bible Study student!) Peter asks, "Why? Why can't I follow you, Lord?" A good translation of this question would be, "Why can't I follow you right now, this minute?" Peter's question shows that he lacked patience as well as understanding of what was going on. And, of course, Peter continues on in his impulsive way by making his own spontaneous proclamation. He says *I will lay down my life for Your sake*. Perhaps Peter was recalling yet another stumbling with his mouth and the Lord's response to it. Consider Matthew 16:21-26:

> From that time Jesus began to show to His disciples that He must go to Jerusalem, and suffer many things from the elders and chief priests and scribes, and be killed, and be raised the third day.
>
> Then Peter took Him aside and began to rebuke Him, saying, "Far be it from You, Lord; this shall not happen to You!"
>
> But He turned and said to Peter, "Get behind Me, Satan! You are an offense to Me, for you are not mindful of the things of God, but the things of men."
>
> Then Jesus said to His disciples, "If anyone desires to come after Me, let him deny himself, and take up his cross, and follow Me. For whoever desires to save his life will lose it, but whoever loses his life for My sake will find it. For what profit is it to a man if he gains the whole world, and loses his own soul? Or what will a man give in exchange for his soul?"

Perhaps, in the back of Peter's mind, he's thinking that he needs to make up for this failure by boldly declaring that he's willing to lay down his life for his Lord. Jesus told the disciples in Matthew that they needed to take up their crosses and follow Him and be willing to lose their lives for His sake. Peter seems, at this point in John, to be willing to do just that. Now, in case you find yourself coming down hard on poor Peter, take a look at Matthew 26:35 (LSB): "Peter said to Him, 'Even if I have to die with You, I will not deny You.' All the disciples said the same thing too." It appears that the other 10 chimed in as well, "Yes, Lord, we will too! We'll die with You and never deny You!" They all said they would lay down their lives for the Lord's sake, and yet they all forsook him and fled, according to Matthew 26:56. We can't be too hard on Peter; all the disciples were guilty of denying their Lord by forsaking Him at His most crucial hour. We must take heed because we are all guilty at times of denying our Lord, too.

Now, what does Peter mean when he says *I will lay down my life for Your sake*? The word *life* literally means soul. He's saying, "I will lay down my very physical life for you, Lord." Remember, this was the mark of the good shepherd, according to Jesus' words in John 10:11 (LSB): "I am the good shepherd; the good shepherd lays down His life for the sheep." Perhaps Peter has now remembered that the Lord had said this, and he now wants to lay down his own life. Remember Thomas, in John 11, upon hearing of Lazarus' death? He said, "Let us also go, so that we may die with Him" (John 11:16b LSB). The disciples seemed to already understand that laying down one's life is a sign of genuine love, something Jesus will tell them in John 15:13: "Greater love has no one than this, than to lay down one's life for his friends." But Peter and the other disciples still seem in a fog regarding the fact that it will be Christ who will be laying down His life for them very soon. None of them will be laying down their lives for Him, at least not yet. So, the Lord decides to answer Peter's question with a question, in verse 38, and here we see a rather shocking proclamation.

Jesus' Shocking Proclamation *John 13:38*

> Jesus answered him, "Will you lay down your life for My sake? Most assuredly, I say to you, the rooster shall not crow till you have denied Me three times." (John 13:38)

Jesus answers Peter's second question with a question. Throughout the Gospels, we see the Lord answering individuals' questions with questions of His own. And I think that is a great discipleship method. I have done this many, many times, and it allows the person you are discipling to think through the issues before them. Jesus says *Will you lay down your life for My sake?* "Will you really and truly, Peter, lay down your life for Me? Will you?" Then, He gives Peter a shocking proclamation, and says those solemn words: *Most assuredly, I say to you, the rooster shall not crow till you have denied Me three times*. Jesus says *most assuredly*, which is essentially Him saying, "Peter, this will indeed happen." What will indeed happen? *The rooster shall not crow till you have denied Me three times*. The words *the rooster shall not crow* refer to the time before the day dawns; before the day dawns, Peter will deny Christ. Mark's account (Mark 14:30) adds that this will happen before the rooster crows twice.

The *rooster* was accustomed to crowing twice, once at midnight and the other just before the break of day. So sometime between 12 midnight and morning the denials will take place. Now, the word for *deny* means to remove oneself, to say no, to disown. Peter will completely disown Jesus as though he never had anything to do with Him! And, indeed, it did happen. This was a shocking proclamation from our Lord's lips, and one that would soon take place, probably sooner than Peter ever imagined. J. C. Ryle gives us a good translation of this verse: "I tell thee in the most solemn answer, that this very night, before the cock crow, before sunrise, thou, even thou, wilt deny three times that thou knowest Me. So far from laying down the life, thou wilt try to save thy life by cowardly denying that thou hast anything to do with Me."[1] Let's look at the account of this betrayal together from Luke's account.

> Having arrested Him, they led Him and brought Him into the high priest's house. But Peter followed at a distance. Now when they had kindled a fire in the midst of the courtyard and sat down together, Peter sat among them. And a certain servant girl, seeing him as he sat by the fire, looked intently at him and said, "This man was also with Him."
>
> But he denied Him, saying, "Woman, I do not know Him."
>
> And after a little while another saw him and said, "You also are of them." But Peter said, "Man, I am not!"
>
> Then after about an hour had passed, another confidently affirmed, saying, "Surely this fellow also was with Him, for he is a Galilean."
>
> But Peter said, "Man, I do not know what you are saying!" Immediately, while he was still speaking, the rooster crowed. And the Lord turned and looked at Peter. And Peter remembered the word of the Lord, how He had said to him, "Before the rooster crows, you will deny Me three times." So Peter went out and wept bitterly. (Luke 22:54-62)

Here we see Jesus' prediction coming to pass exactly as He said it would—Peter denying Him three times. Can you imagine what Peter must have felt as the rooster crowed and then the Lord turned and looked at him? Can you imagine the awful guilt? Luke records for us that Peter went out and wept bitterly. Instead of laying down his life for the Lord, Peter

---

1 J. C. Ryle, *Expository Thoughts on the Gospels*.

denies him three times. (Interestingly, in John 21, he vows that he loves the Lord three times.) Instead of giving his life for Jesus, Peter saves his life to deny Jesus. And Peter doesn't do this by just remaining silent, which is the way most of us do it, but he does it with his mouth, and with oaths and curses. Peter completely disowns Jesus as though he never had anything to do with him. Instead of Peter laying down his life for the Lord, it will be the Lord who will soon lay down his life for Peter.

Ladies, there is great comfort in the fact that the Lord loves Peter even to the end; even though He knows Peter is soon to deny Him, He loves Peter. Amazing Love! Forgiving Love! I just imagine that this convicting statement by his Lord silenced Peter, especially when Jesus began His warning by saying, "Most assuredly, this will happen, Peter." It would silence me! In fact, it does silence Peter until chapter 18, verse 10. Inquisitive Peter finally stops asking questions. We'll hear from some of the other disciples, but not Peter. You might be wondering, "What are the other disciples thinking at this time? Do they think that Peter is perhaps the one Jesus referred to in verse 21? After all, Judas hasn't betrayed him publicly yet." The question might also have come to your mind, "Is there a difference in the betrayal of Judas and the soon denial of Jesus by Peter? Yes, there is a difference. Judas' betrayal was premeditated, thought out, and carried to action. He had already been paid 30 pieces of silver for what he was going to do. He was cold and heartless. Peter, on the other hand, was an impetuous disciple acting on a whim. He's like many of us, I'm afraid, with the foot-in-the-mouth disease. After Judas betrayed the Lord, he went out and hanged himself. Peter, however, went out and wept bitterly. Judas will spend eternity in hell. Peter will spend eternity in Heaven. There is a vast difference between Judas and Peter.

Summary

◊ We have seen Jesus' startling proclamation in verse 36: "Where I go you can't come now, but you will follow me later,"

◊ We have seen Peter's spontaneous proclamation in verse 37: "I will lay down my life for you,"

◊ We have seen Jesus' shocking proclamation in verse 38: "The rooster shall not crow until you have denied me three times."

What do we learn from Peter? Why would Peter so quickly say he would lay down his life for the Lord and then so quickly deny Him? What happened? What can you and I learn from Peter so that we don't deny our Lord? Do you want to know how to stay loyal to Jesus Christ? Do you want to know how to keep yourself from ever denying the Lord who bought you with His own blood? Do you want to know how to keep all those promises you have made to Him?

Realize that you do not have full understanding of everything the Lord has said in His Word. Peter did not. He was limited in understanding what the Lord had been saying about leaving and going somewhere. This caused him to make a rash promise.

Realize that making rash promises without thinking and praying through them could cause you to sin by not fulfilling them. It appears that Peter did not think or pray before he opened his mouth and said. "I'll die for you, God! I will!" This statement caused him much grief later and he went out and wept bitterly because of it.

Realize the mercy of our Lord when you do fail Him. Peter did. He writes often of it in 1 and 2 Peter. He learned much from his failed promise.

J.C. Ryle once said, "Like Peter, we may think we can do wonders for Christ, and like Peter, we may learn by bitter experience that we have no power and might at all. The servant of Christ will do wisely to remember these things. 'Let him that thinketh he standeth, take heed lest he fall.' (1 Cor. x. 12.) A humble sense of our own innate weakness, a constant dependence on the Strong for strength, a daily prayer to be held up, because we cannot hold up ourselves,—these are the true secrets of safety."[2]

---

2 Ibid.

QUESTIONS TO CONSIDER

1. (a) Read John 13, making note of all the times Peter's name is mentioned. Also, make note when his old name, Simon Peter, is mentioned. (b) Why do you think John calls Peter "Simon Peter" at times?

2. Memorize John 13:38.

3. (a) How many questions does Peter ask the Lord in John 13, and how does the Lord answer each one? (b) What quality of love do you see our Lord displaying toward Peter during these "questioning" times?

4. (a) What do the following passages teach you about making rash vows? Ecclesiastes 5:1-7; Matthew 5:33-37; James 5:12. (b) How could Peter have applied these truths before making his rash vow in John 13:37?

5. In addition to what is recorded in John 13:36-38, read the other accounts of Jesus foretelling Peter's denial, in Matthew 26:30-35; Mark 14:27-31; and Luke 22:31-34. What are the differences and what are the similarities among all of these accounts?

6. (a) What did Jesus mean in Luke 22:31-32 when He declared, "Simon, Simon! Indeed Satan has asked for you, that he may sift you as wheat"? (b) What did Jesus mean by the phrase, "and when you have returned to Me, strengthen your brethren"? (c) What comfort do you take in these verses?

7. Read *either* 1 Peter or 2 Peter and write down all the ways that Peter "strengthens the brethren" through his writings.

8. (a) In what ways do Christians deny the Lord? (b) In what ways do you deny the Lord? (c) Are you willing to literally lay down your life for Christ today?

9. Please bring a prayer request to share based on your answers from question 8.

Five Cures for a Troubled Heart
John 14:1-6

WE all have seasons of life in which we go through troubling times. I don't know about you, but I've noticed in my own life that those troubling times seem to include more than one "trouble" at a time, if you know what I mean. We may learn that a friend has a life-threatening disease and, at the same time, our husband loses his job, one of our parents dies, and our teenage son or daughter makes a poor choice with consequences that affect the entire family.

In John 14, we find the disciples in similar circumstances. They're very troubled, and they're troubled about many things. Jesus has just humbled Himself and washed their dirty feet; that is troubling. He has announced Judas' betrayal; that also is troubling. He has told them He is going to die; that is very troubling. And Matthew's Gospel tells us that Jesus has also told the disciples that they will all fall away; this, too, is troubling. And now, Jesus has just told Peter that he was going to deny Him, which is troubling as well, especially to Peter. All these things are weighing very heavily on the disciples. They're probably by now beginning to understand that indeed their Lord is leaving them and that also frightens them. I imagine, by now, they are sitting in the upper room looking at one another and saying, "What is going on here? Jesus is leaving us! We've enjoyed three years of bliss and now everything seems to be turning upside down." Of all the disciples present, Peter would probably need the most comfort, since Jesus has just announced his coming denial.ABs not only reads the troubled looks on their faces, but He reads His disciples' troubled hearts, and says in John 14:1-6:

> "Let not your heart be troubled; you believe in God, believe also in Me. In My Father's house are many mansions; if it were not so, I would have told you. I go to prepare a place for you. And if I go and prepare a place for you, I will come again and receive you to Myself; that where I am,

> there you may be also. And where I go you know, and the way you know."
>
> Thomas said to Him, "Lord, we do not know where You are going, and how can we know the way?"
>
> Jesus said to him, "I am the way, the truth, and the life. No one comes to the Father except through Me."

Martin Luther called these verses "the best and most comforting sermon preached by Christ while on this earth ... a jewel and a treasure not purchasable with the world's goods."[1] In fact, in the many funeral services I've attended in which my husband has preached, I believe this text rates as the one most frequently used by him.

In our last chapter, we learned of three proclamations in the text: Jesus' startling proclamation (v 36), in which He said, "Where I am going you cannot follow me now, but you shall follow me afterward." Peter's spontaneous proclamation (v 37), in which Peter declares, "I will lay down my life for Your sake!" And Jesus' shocking proclamation (v 38), in which He responds to Peter by saying, "The rooster shall not crow till you have denied me three times." In the six verses we are going to study in this chapter, we will discover five cures for a troubled heart, and I will give them to you in the form of an acrostic, spelling the word **QUIET** (note: they will not occur in this order). I thought this word to be appropriate for this chapter since quiet is the opposite of troubled. Let's begin by looking at verse 1 and the first cure for a troubled heart.

> "Let not your heart be troubled; you believe in God, believe also in Me." (John 14:1)

There isn't any kind of break here between Christ's solemn words to Peter at the end of chapter 13 about his soon denial of Him and Christ's words here at the beginning of chapter 14. The chapter and verse divisions were added to the text long after it was originally written. The discourse here in chapter 14 is simply a continuation of what was being said in chapter 13. Jesus has turned from Peter and here addresses the eleven disciples and says *Let not your heart be troubled*. The meaning here is:

---

1 Martin Luther, quoted in John MacArthur, "The Solution to a Troubled Heart," *Grace to You*, www.gty.org/library/articles/_P24/the-solution-to-a-troubled-heart. Accessed 9/21/2023.

"Stop letting your heart be troubled." This is a command which forbids what the disciples had begun to do, to be troubled in their hearts. *So, the number one cure for a troubled heart, according to Jesus, is the **Q** on your acrostic—**Quit being troubled!*** The word *troubled* means to stir or agitate, to be tossed, to be thrown into a state of confusion and perplexity. This verse is a command which means to go on not being troubled.

When Jesus refers here to the *heart* that is being troubled, He is not talking about the physical organ that's pumping inside each of us right now; He is speaking about the mind. He's going to repeat this same command in John 14:27. Now, ladies, Jesus is not speaking from a calloused heart here; He knew what it was like to be troubled. Consider John 11:33, which takes place just after Lazarus' death, when Jesus has come upon the scene and found Mary and Martha and the Jews crying: "When Jesus therefore saw her crying, and the Jews who came with her also crying, He was deeply moved in spirit and was troubled" (LSB). Consider also John 13:21: "When Jesus had said these things, He was troubled in spirit, and testified and said, 'Most assuredly, I say to you, one of you will betray Me.'" This is a passage we just considered a few chapters ago; Jesus' troubled spirit in this passage is in reference to Judas' coming betrayal—that reality greatly troubled the Lord! There isn't a sin in being troubled in and of itself, but there is a sin in continuing to stay in that troubled state. King Jehoshaphat, in 2 Chronicles 20, when he was facing an enormous army, is an excellent example of not staying in a troubled state. He immediately was afraid, but he didn't wallow around in panic; instead, he set himself to seek the Lord with prayer and fasting.

Jesus tells the disciples here to stop it, to stop being troubled. The disciples are very troubled; their world, as they know it, is turning upside down, and they are terrified at the thought of Jesus leaving them. If you've ever been permanently separated from someone you love very dearly, especially by death, then you know the turmoil the disciples are feeling at this point. But notice Jesus' concern over His troubled disciples; He isn't absorbed in Himself, in His own hurts, but in the hurts of others. This is a time when Jesus could have been consumed with His own hurts, because the cross was ever before Him. But He isn't, and in this, ladies, He is a wonderful example for you and me to follow.

Notice that the Lord didn't end with the command to stop being troubled. If we are going to put off something, we need to put on something, in its place, right? So, Christ tells His disciples what to put on! The command to let not your heart be troubled is a negative command, but Jesus follows it up with a positive command: *you believe in God, believe also in Me. The second cure for a troubled heart is the **T** on your acrostic—Trust in God and Christ!* Jesus is saying, "You believe in God; then, believe also in Me. You trust in God; now, also trust in Me." To *believe in God*, to trust in God, means to put confidence in, to rely on for support and consolation. This is a command which means to keep on believing in God and in Christ. It is a command that they should believe in Jesus the same way they believe in God, and that such belief should continue. Why would Jesus need to say this at this time? During troubling times, we might find ourselves tempted to doubt God. James speaks regarding this type of person in James 1:6; he speaks of an individual who is going through trials and is doubting, and he describes them like a wind-driven sea with waves going back and forth! One minute they trust in God, and the next minute they don't. That is not the posture we should have, ladies, when going through troubling times. We should trust in God and trust in Christ. The disciples will have a big challenge before them, as their Lord is getting ready to be crucified and eventually leave them and go to Heaven. And yet, they are commanded to continue to believe in Him in their darkest hour. And in our darkest hour, we are to believe in Him, even though we can't see Him. The Psalmist puts it this way, as he goes through his troubling time in Psalm 27:13 (LSB): "I would have despaired unless I had believed that I would see the goodness of Yahweh in the land of the living." Proverbs 3:5-6 (LSB) says, "Trust in Yahweh with all your heart and do not lean on your own understanding. In all your ways acknowledge Him, and He will make your paths straight." Peter picks up on this as well, in his first epistle, in 1 Peter 1:6-8:

> In this you greatly rejoice, though now for a little while, if need be, you have been grieved by various trials, that the genuineness of your faith, being much more precious than gold that perishes, though it is tested by fire, may be found to praise, honor, and glory at the revelation of Jesus Christ, whom having not seen you love. Though now you do not see Him, yet believing, you rejoice with joy inexpressible and full of glory.

The disciples were certainly going through a major trial, and Peter says in his epistle, "Stick with it for the glory of God; even though you don't see Him, you love Him." And that will soon be the case for each of the disciples; they won't see Him.

Before we move on to the next verse, I want to clarify that believing in Jesus is not something additional to believing in God; Jesus is the revelation of God. You hear people say they believe in God, but what do they mean? Do they believe that Jesus is God? Do they believe verse 6, which clearly states that Jesus is the way to God? Speaking of God, Christ begins to talk about His Father's house in verse 2, where we find our third cure for a troubled heart.

> "In My Father's house are many mansions; if it were not so, I would have told you. I go to prepare a place for you." (John 14:2)

Notice that Jesus calls God His *Father*. God and Jesus are one, yet we see Christ here in His role of Son. What is Jesus referring to when He mentions His *Father's house*? He is referring to Heaven. Heaven, we know, in various Scriptures is called a country (Hebrews 11:16), a city (Hebrews 11:10), a kingdom (Matthew 4:17), and Paradise (Luke 23:43). But probably the most intimate name the Scriptures use for Heaven is the one right here, *My Father's house*. In the earthly realm, what do most of us think of when we think of going to our Father's house? We must admit when we think of going to our Father's house, we think of going home, a place where we are loved, where we are always welcomed, and where we can relax and get away from the cares of the world. It is—or should be—a place of peace.

Jesus says that in His Father's house *are many mansions*, which means many permanent abiding places, resting places, apartments. This may refer to individual places for families, even as they lived on earth. In the Jewish world, when a son got married, the father would add a wing to his house. When another son married, yet another wing would be added. Eventually, the original dwelling would become a set of dwellings that enclosed a patio in the middle; all the relatives lived around that patio. Ladies, we will live in a dwelling place that is attached to the Father's house, right in the same house with the Father. *When we think on this incredible truth, we can bank on the third cure for a troubled heart—**E***yes fixed heavenward. This is the **E** on your acrostic.* If we would fix our eyes on Heaven and do it more often, then it really wouldn't matter what troubles we have here. Who cares?! We are going home one day, and we are going to live in the Father's house! We are to be setting our affections on things above, not on things here on earth. This is not our home; we are simply pilgrims passing through.

Now, is Jesus telling the disciples some fabricated story to give them false hope? No, He says *if it were not so, I would have told you*. The Lord is assuring His disciples that what He is saying is the truth: "If there was the least uncertainty about it, I would tell you." Nothing that Jesus Christ has ever said has been a lie, as He is truth. He is telling them the truth.

Next, Jesus states one of the reasons that He is going back to Heaven: to prepare a place for them. *I go to prepare a place for you*. The words *I go* are referring to His ascent into Heaven. The figure is taken from one who is on a journey, who goes before his companions to provide a place to lodge in, and to make the necessary preparations for his companions' arrival. This was a customary practice; Mark 14:13-16 tells us that Peter and John had been sent ahead to make ready for the Passover meal. *A place for you* seems to indicate just the right room for each individual person. That's pretty exciting, is it not? You might be wondering, "How are we all going to fit in there?" Well, according to Revelation 21:16, Heaven is a pretty big place; John says, "And the city is laid out as a square, and its length is as great as the width; and he measured the city with the rod, 12,000 stadia; its length and width and height are equal" (LSB). This description gives us a cube, with equal sides that are approximately 1500 miles in every direction. Heaven could hold more than 30 times the population of our world right now and still have plenty room to spare! Imagine! The Lord is saying that in Heaven there is room for all. If that isn't exciting enough, He goes on to say:

> "And if I go and prepare a place for you, I will come again and receive you to Myself; that where I am, there you may be also." (John 14:3)

The first statement Jesus gives here is a purpose clause; that is, this is the purpose of the departure and the return of Christ. The purpose is so that He can come and take us home. Some have pictured the preparation that Jesus is doing in a human realm, just like we might prepare a room for a guest who is coming to stay with us; we might put all the things in their room that they would like, and we might embellish and decorate it for their delight. Jesus is preparing a place for us, for each one of us. We can only imagine what those dwelling places will be like! Have you ever pondered what Christ is making for you? If preparing a place for each of us isn't enough, He now says that He will come again and receive us unto Himself: *I will come again and receive you to Myself; that where I am, there you may be also.* The words *receive you to Myself* literally read: and I shall take you along to my own home. This is a wonderful promise for all who die before the Rapture; Jesus comes for us at the moment of our death. Remember, the disciples obviously would not have been taken up in the Rapture, so the promise to them is that Christ will receive them when they come to glory! We get a glimpse of this in Acts 7, when Stephen was being stoned; in verse 59 (LSB), it says, "They went on stoning Stephen as he was calling out and saying, 'Lord Jesus, receive my spirit!'" Jesus came and received Stephen unto Himself at the moment his spirit left his body. Here, in John 14, Jesus is telling His troubled disciples about this wonderful truth so that they will know that they too will come where He is going. He's saying that His departure is not permanent, just temporary; soon, they will have a glorious reunion. And when each one of the disciples did eventually die, Jesus was there to receive them into glory—what a glorious thought! Hearing this truth now should ease their troubled hearts; it should ease our troubled hearts as well, especially when we have a saved loved one who goes on before us. The separation is only temporary. Of course, for those who do not die before the Rapture we have the wonderful promise of His coming again and receiving us in a different way. Paul puts it this way in 1 Thessalonians 4:16-17 (LSB): "For the Lord Himself will descend from heaven with a shout, with the voice of the archangel and with the trumpet of God, and the dead in Christ will rise first. Then we who are alive and remain will be caught up together with them in the clouds to meet the Lord in the air, and so we shall always be with the Lord."

You might be asking, "Why is Jesus coming for us?" He answers that question when He says *that where I am, there you may be also.* You know, we can dream and wonder all we want about Heaven and what it will be like, but the best part about Heaven will be that we will be where Jesus is forever. When we really love someone, we want to be with him or her, do we not? If we love Christ, we should desire to be with Him. And while we can be with Him even now, what we experience now is a mere shadow of what it will be like to be with Him in Heaven. There won't be any more prayers asking Him for a sense of His presence, because we will be in His presence forever and ever. *This brings us to the fourth cure for a troubled heart, and it is the **U** in your acrostic—**U**nderstand that Christ is Coming!* There will be a day when Christ will either receive you as you die, or He will come Himself and take you home in the Rapture. Meditating on this truth will most certainly help you during troubling times. Christ now turns from the thought of coming to receive the disciples back to the thought of leaving them and assures them by saying,

> "And where I go you know, and the way you know." (John 14:4)

Jesus just told them where He was going in verses 2-3, but here he adds *and the way you know.* What does Jesus mean by this statement? It refers to *the way* the Eleven must take to reach their destination, the Father's house, that Jesus has just spoken about. Jesus will explain the way in verse 6, but before he does, Thomas is prompted by Jesus' statement to ask a question that all the disciples were likely wondering.

> Thomas said to Him, "Lord, we do not know where You are going, and how can we know the way?" (John 14:5)

You might be wondering if Thomas has a hearing problem or something. Didn't he hear what Christ just said, that He was going to the Father's house to prepare a place for them? At first, it may seem to us that Thomas' question is rather silly, especially because Jesus has just said where He is going. But let's not be so hard on Thomas. Think about it: when our hearts are troubled, it is a confusing time, and sometimes we can ask some really dumb questions, questions that we already know the answers to. One writer put it this way: "Believers in the frame of Thomas are like people who hunt for their keys and purses, when they have got them in their pockets."[2] I don't think we should feel ashamed during troubled times when we ask questions. What we have to be careful of is despairing and getting angry with God because of our circumstances. Remember, the disciples did not fully comprehend until *after* the resurrection all that was going on and all that Jesus had said to them. They presumed that He was an earthly King who was going to set up His earthly Kingdom, and they didn't comprehend the reason for which He was to die. The Holy Spirit had not yet come to show them the things to come, so things were not quite clear to them yet. Jesus doesn't answer Thomas harshly or call him ignorant; He just very simply answers him in verse 6.

> Jesus said to him, "I am the way, the truth, and the life. No one comes to the Father except through Me." (John 14:6)

*We have here in this amazing statement by our Lord the fifth cure for a troubled heart. It is the **I** on your acrostic—**I**dentify the Way.* My dear sisters, you must know where you are going after death and how you are getting there in order for your heart to be trouble-free. Nothing is more comforting than to know you have assurance of salvation and life hereafter, and nothing is more troubling than to not know where you are going after death.

Why does Christ call Himself *the way*? Because we can only reach the Father by going through Jesus. The Father's house can only be reached by believing in the right way. The Way is the connection between God and man, which is Jesus. As Paul would say in 1 Timothy 2:5-6 (LSB), "For there is one God, and one mediator also between God and men, the man Christ Jesus, who gave Himself as a ransom for all, the witness for this proper time."

Let's suppose we are getting ready to go on a trip. Usually, we get directions on how to get to our destination via a map, GPS, or some other means. We're dependent on those services to tell us how to get to where we are going. But suppose someone tells you, "You know, I'm going to the same

---

[2] Trapp, quoted in J. C. Ryle, *Expository Thoughts on the Gospels*.

place, why don't you follow me there, so you don't get lost. I know the way." We wouldn't miss our destination, would we? That's the way it is with Jesus. He just doesn't tell us about the way; He is the Way. There is only one way to Heaven, and it is Jesus. (And this way, Jesus tells us in the Sermon on the Mount, is a narrow way, which few will find.)

What does Christ mean when He says He is *the truth*? Jesus is truth, which is the opposite of types, emblems, or all that is false. Jesus is the source of truth. Jesus told the disciples He was going to die, and He did. He told them He was going to rise again, and He did. He told them He was going to Heaven, and He did. He told them they were going to be persecuted, and they were. We could go on and on with all the things that Jesus said would happen and did! He is truth! Men can teach truth, but there is only One who can say He is the Truth, and that is Jesus Christ. Men search for truth in science, history, philosophy, religion, and even in the daily newspaper, but few search for truth in the Word of God.

What does Jesus mean when He says He is *the life*? He means that He is life as opposed to death. In John 10:10b (LSB), He says, "I came that they may have life, and have it abundantly." Jesus is the source of life to those who are dead in their trespasses and sins. He is the source of both physical and spiritual life. There is no spiritual life apart from Jesus.

The terminology here, *the way, the truth, and the life*, is interesting because Jesus is soon going to be showing the disciples *the way* to Heaven as He hangs on a cross. Soon others will lie against Him and falsely testify against Him, but He will show Himself to be *truthful*. And soon He will be hanging between Heaven and earth giving up His *life* for mankind. The way, the truth, the life—all three of these are active, when you think about it. The way brings us to God, the truth sets us free, and the life produces fellowship.

Jesus ends with this: *no one comes to the Father except through Me*. There is no exception here! No man, no woman, no one can get to Heaven except through Christ! Period! *Through me* literally means by me, as a door, a gate, a road, a path, an entrance. It is an expression that would be known by the Jews because it had been taught from their childhood.

They would be taught to draw near to God through the priests. We can only draw near to God by going through Jesus Christ. This means that we come in His name and depend on His merits. There are a lot of religions and cults in our world that tell us that there are many ways to get to Heaven. But, ladies, Christ is the only way. Acts 4:12 (LSB) says, "And there is salvation in no one else, for there is no other name under Heaven that has been given among men by which we must be saved." Someone once said "Take away Jesus, and the way, the truth, and the life are gone; no way, no truth, no life are left."[3]

Summary

Do you find yourself troubled this day, dear sister? Where have you gone for the solution to your trouble? Or, to whom or to what have you turned during your troubles? I trust that the next time you go through troubling times, you will fix your heart on John 14:1-6 and the five cures for a troubled heart we've discovered there. Instead of being troubled in your spirit, be **QUIET** in your spirit.

1. *Quit being troubled.* Instead of turning to medication, people, sleep, food, or entertainment to forget your sorrows as the world does, just stop letting your heart be troubled (Matthew 6:31-34).

2. *Understand that Christ is coming.* Don't hope for some inheritance to come your way to get you out of all your troubles; hope for the day the Lord will usher you into His presence (Psalm 73:23-24).

3. *Identify the Way.* Don't find a way of escape through sleep or a vacation, but make sure you know the way, the truth, and the life (John 14:6).

4. *Eyes fixed heavenward.* Instead of keeping your eyes fixed on your circumstances or the people in your life who are troubling you, why not fix your eyes on Heaven (Colossians 3:1-4)?

---

[3] R. C. H. Lenski, *The Interpretation of St. John's Gospel 11-21* (Minneapolis: Augsburg Fortress, 2008), 981.

5. *Trust in God and Christ.* Don't trust in friends for the answers, or your Christian upbringing, or your good works, or religious activity, or a pill, but trust in a person—Jesus Christ (Psalm 146:3-7).

Having a heart free from trouble is a wonderful gift and it is possible even in a troubling world, which presents us with troubling circumstances almost daily. May we adopt the quote from a country preacher and all ask the Lord to "Heap on others the gift of richness, but give to me the gift of the untroubled heart."

QUESTIONS TO CONSIDER

1. (a) Read John 14:1-6. Why would the disciples' hearts be troubled? (b) How does the Lord comfort them?

2. Memorize John 14:1.

3. (a) How do John 14:1-6 and 1 Peter 1:6-9 relate to one another? (b) What comfort do these verses give you during troubled times?

4. (a) What is the cure for a troubled heart, according to the following passages? Psalm 42:5-11; 43:5; 77:2-14; 2 Corinthians 12:9-10. (b) To whom or to what does the world turn in times of trouble? (c) To whom or to what do you turn when your heart is troubled?

5. (a) Jesus says in John 14:2 that He has gone to prepare a place for us. How does John describe that place in Revelation 21 and 22? (b) Who will be there and who will not be there? (c) What is the best thing about Heaven to you?

6. (a) Jesus says in John 14:6 that He is the way, the truth, and the life. What do those three things mean? (b) Look up the following verses and note what else Jesus says He is and what He means by each of these statements: John 6:48; 8:12; 10:9; 10:11; 11:25; 15:1.

7. (a) What are some ways in which unbelievers are hoping to gain eternal life? (b) How could you use what Jesus says in John 14:1-6 as well as other passages, to confront their false security?

8. How is Jesus the way, and the truth, and the life to you personally?

9. Is your heart troubled? Come prepared with a prayer request for how we might pray for you during this troubled time.

Jesus and the Father Are One
John 14:7-12

AS we begin this chapter, I want ask you to do something that might seem a little strange at first, but I hope it will come to make sense. What I would like for you to do is lift up your hand and hold it out before your eyes. Now, between your eyes and your hand are three separate things that also are one. Do you see them? Each one of these things may be studied separately, but it is impossible to have one without the others. Do you know what they are? They are light, heat, and air. Your eye can right now see your hand because of the light waves that are present there. Also, in the light that you now see, there is also air. If you blow on your hand you can feel that air. But there is also heat between your eyes and your hand. If you had a thermometer you could measure that heat. Scientists tell us that we cannot have heat, light, or air without having each of these things in some relationship in our atmosphere. Science can use any one of them apart from the others but can never separate them totally. They are three, yet they are one.

You might be thinking, "Thanks for the science lesson, Susan, but what does this have to do with this chapter?" Well, what we have here is a good illustration of what you and I believe as Christians. We do not believe there are three Gods; rather, we believe there is one true God who is three persons, the Father, the Son, and the Holy Spirit. This is the wonderful truth that our Lord communicates in this lesson as He imparts some last words to His dear disciples. In these verses are some of the most amazing things that our Lord said in His last hours, as He was actually claiming to be God! Let's listen it to what He has to say in John 14:7-12.

> "If you had known Me, you would have known My Father also; and from now on you know Him and have seen Him."
>
> Philip said to Him, "Lord, show us the Father, and it is sufficient for us."
>
> Jesus said to him, "Have I been with you so long, and yet you have

> not known Me, Philip? He who has seen Me has seen the Father; so how can you say, 'Show us the Father'? Do you not believe that I am in the Father, and the Father in Me? The words that I speak to you I do not speak on My own authority; but the Father who dwells in Me does the works. Believe Me that I am in the Father and the Father in Me, or else believe Me for the sake of the works themselves.
>
> "Most assuredly, I say to you, he who believes in Me, the works that I do he will do also; and greater works than these he will do, because I go to My Father."

In this chapter, we will learn of three ways in which Christ claims to be God; He says *To Know the Son is to Know the Father* (v 7); *To See the Son is to See the Father* (vv 8-9); and *To Believe the Son is to Believe the Father* (vv 10-12). In our last chapter, we discovered five cures for a troubled heart and remembered them by using the acrostic **QUIET**: **Q**uit being troubled; **U**nderstand that Christ is coming; **I**dentify the way; **E**yes fixed heavenward; and **T**rust in God and in Christ. In this chapter, Christ continues on with His discourse with His eleven disciples, giving them three valid proofs that He is God, and all three have to do with His relationship to the Father. Let's look at the first one.

To Know the Son Is to Know the Father   John 14:7

> "If you had known Me, you would have known My Father also; and from now on you know Him and have seen Him." (John 14:7)

Jesus begins by saying *if you had known Me, you would have known My Father also*. The word *known* is used four times in verses 7-9, and it has the same meaning each time it is mentioned. It means to know experientially, as opposed to knowing intuitively (which means to perceive or understand immediately and without reason). The disciples had known Jesus experientially; they were His disciples and had left all to follow Him. So Jesus is not saying here that they don't know Him in the sense of not being His disciples; He's saying that they did not yet know Him in His full significance. They did not fully understand all things about Him, just as you and I do not fully understand all things about the Godhead. It is a mystery indeed! What Jesus is clarifying here is that no one can rightly know Him without knowing the Father, because He and the Father are one. This fact had already been declared early in the Gospel of John when Jesus said in John 1:18, "No one has seen God at any time. The only begotten Son, who is in the bosom of the Father, He has declared Him." Ladies, have you ever desired to know God better? Jesus is saying, "You can know God through Me, His Son." Perhaps we would all do well to read and study the Gospel accounts more often, that we might get a deeper glimpse of God our Father as seen in Jesus His Son.

The disciples didn't fully know Jesus, just as you and I do not fully know Him—yet, we do know Him. That is, we have a relationship with Him, just as the disciples did. It seems as if Jesus is seeking here to reaffirm to His disciples who He is. Remember, this was a confusing time for the disciples; they had fears and doubts about what was going on, they were troubled about many things, and they wanted to make sure that they had not put their trust in someone other than the Messiah. And Jesus has just lovingly told them, a few sentences back, to stop being troubled.

But now, Jesus says to them *and from now on you know Him and have seen Him*. This is a reference to a time in the future when the disciples will begin to understand who Jesus is and who the Father is. The Holy Spirit will help them with that process when His ministry begins with them. This, of course, will begin after Jesus dies and is raised from the dead and ascends into Heaven. Specifically, it will begin on the day of Pentecost, when a series of events will begin to occur that will enable the disciples to see more clearly. Christ will mention this later on in the upper room, in John 14:25-26, when He says, "These things I have spoken to you while being present with you. But the Helper, the Holy Spirit, whom the Father will send in My name, He will teach you all things, and bring to your remembrance all things that I said to you."

I would like to bring out an important principle here, if I may. Many times, in our own lives, while we're going through troubling times, we, too, do not see things clearly, but later the Holy Spirit helps us to see those things in a clearer way, does He not? In a way, that is what Jesus is saying here: "Sometime soon, you will understand that to know Me is to know the Father. In the last three years, while you have seen Me here on earth, you have been seeing the Father." Now, that profound statement raises a question from Philip, in verse 8, and in Christ's response, He gives His second valid proof that He is God.

To See the Son Is to See the Father   *John 14:8-9*

> Philip said to Him, "Lord, show us the Father, and it is sufficient for us." (John 14:8)

This is the first time we hear from *Philip* in the upper room. You might be asking yourself, "Who is Philip?" The first mention we have of Philip is in John 1:43-46 (LSB): "On the next day, He desired to go into Galilee, and He found Philip. And Jesus said to him, 'Follow Me.' Now Philip was from Bethsaida, the city of Andrew and Peter. Philip found Nathanael and said to him, 'We have found Him of whom Moses in the Law and also the Prophets wrote—Jesus of Nazareth, the son of Joseph.' And Nathanael said to him, 'Can any good thing come out of Nazareth?' Philip said to him, 'Come and see.'" Philip obviously was a student of the Old Testament because He understood that this was the One who was spoken of in it. Another account we have of Philip is found in John 6:4-7 (LSB): "Now the Passover, the feast of the Jews, was near. Therefore Jesus, lifting up His eyes and seeing that a large crowd was coming to Him, said to Philip, 'Where should we buy bread, so that these people may eat?' And this He was saying to test him, for He Himself knew what He was going to do. Philip answered Him, 'Two hundred denarii worth of bread is not sufficient for them, for everyone to receive a little.'" Here we see Jesus testing Philip's faith in Him. Jesus wanted to know if Philip really believed that He was all-powerful. The last account we have of Philip is found in John 12:20-22 (LSB): "Now there were some Greeks among those who were going up to worship at the feast; these then came to Philip, who was from Bethsaida of Galilee, and began to ask him, saying, 'Sir, we wish to see Jesus.' Philip came and told Andrew; Andrew and Philip came and told Jesus." In this account, we see that Philip was the one the Greeks inquired of regarding Jesus and the one to whom they communicated their desire to see Him. These are the three mentionings of Philip in John's Gospel. Not much more is really known about Philip and his family.

Here, in John 14, Philips asks Jesus a question. And you'll notice that Philip uses the same word Peter and Thomas used to address Jesus: *Lord* or Master. This is the way a true disciple of Jesus Christ views his or her Lord—as Master or owner of their life. Our lives no longer belong to us, but to another, to our Lord. Now, Philip's request is not all that uncommon: *Lord, show us the Father, and it is sufficient for us.* The word *show* means to demonstrate. He's saying, "Lord, demonstrate to us the Father and it will be enough for us." When you think about it, we are a lot like Philip in that when we go through troubling times we want the Lord to show Himself to us, right? "Lord, just make it clear what you want; write it on the wall! That will satisfy me! Show me your presence." Did you know Moses made the same request in Exodus 33:18 (LSB)? "Then Moses said, 'I pray You, show me Your glory!'" Moses, like the disciples, was also going through troubling times. Those children of Israel just wouldn't cooperate. They had murmured and complained and even made a golden calf while he was on Mount Sinai receiving the ten commandments. I'm sure Moses had just about had it, but God tells him he has to continue on with the journey and that His presence will go with him. Moses just wanted to catch a glimpse of God's glory. Both Philip and Moses were going through troubling times, and both were wanting some manifestation of God for strength, comfort, assurance, and guidance. I am afraid Moses and Philip are just like you and me in the sense that many times we want to substitute sight for faith. But Hebrews 11:1 (LSB) teaches us that "faith is the assurance of things hoped for, the conviction of things not seen." We walk by faith, not by sight, right? Faith is what the Christian life is all about. Paul says in Romans 1:17b (LSB), "the righteous will live by faith." We must to be careful during troubling times, because sometimes our difficulties can seem so intense that they can shatter our faith or cause us to doubt. You and I are much like Philip: "Lord, show us the Father! This will satisfy me right now!" This request from Philip must have deeply troubled the Lord:

> Jesus said to him, "Have I been with you so long, and yet you have not known Me, Philip? He who has seen Me has seen the Father; so how can you say, 'Show us the Father'?" (John 14:9)

Here we see Jesus rebuking Philip. Jesus is saying, "Have I been such a long time with you, and yet you still don't know who I am, Philip?" Jesus had been with the disciples for three years now. In fact, we just read in John 1:43-46 that Philip was one of the first disciples the Lord called. He had been with Jesus probably longer than any of the others. He had seen Jesus for three years doing miracles and healings and hearing His teaching and instruction. Three years of intense discipling, and yet Philip is still in uncertain as to who Jesus is. I'm sure the Lord must have been somewhat discouraged by this; it was the night before He was to leave them, and now one of the Twelve was questioning who He is. Philip probably had no idea how this disturbed the Lord's heart, just as you and I have no idea how our doubts grieve our Lord. "Susan, you have been a believer for over 30 years now, and is this all you know about Me?" How our lack of spiritual understanding must grieve the heart of God!

Did you notice that Jesus uses Philip's name when speaking to him? I bring this out because it is a great discipling technique. I have a friend who did this during our discipling times, and it certainly made me more attentive and many times was used to prick my conscience.

Jesus goes on to say to Philip *He who has seen Me has seen the Father*. To see the Son is to see the Father. What does this mean? We know from John 1:18 that no man has seen God at any time. What Jesus is referring to here is that the manifestation of God is seen in Christ. The Father has been manifested to us in the incarnation of Christ as well as in His works and in His teachings. To perceive who Jesus is, is to perceive who the Father is. Jesus had already made this claim back in John 12:45 (LSB): "And he who sees Me sees the One who sent Me."

Jesus has already said in verse 7 that to know Him is to know the Father. He has also said in John 13:31 that to glorify the Son is to glorify the Father, and in John 13:20 that to receive the Son is to receive the Father. He's also going to tell the disciples in John 15:24 that to hate Him is to hate the Father. By now, the disciples are hopefully seeing the picture. Jesus and the Father are one and the same; to see Jesus is to see the Father. In fact, Jesus ends this question with a continued rebuke: *how can you say,"Show us the Father?"* It's as though He's asking, "What do you mean by this 'show us the Father'? Don't you have a clear understanding of who I am?" This must have been a real heartache for the Lord, and yet He was very patient with Philip. This is again another good example for us to follow. A discipler will be patient with those they disciple, even when they waver in their faith, and even when they hurt us. We must follow the example of our Lord, who having loved, loved the disciples to the end. Philip asks for a visible sign, for some proof, but Jesus answers him not with a visible sign, but with a challenge to believe that He is who He said He is: God in the flesh! And that is the third valid proof that Jesus is God: to believe the Son is to believe the Father.

To Believe the Son Is to Believe the Father *John 14:10-12*

> "Do you not believe that I am in the Father, and the Father in Me? The words that I speak to you I do not speak on My own authority; but the Father who dwells in Me does the works." (John 14:10)

Jesus continues on with His rebuke to Philip: *Do you not believe that I am in the Father, and the Father in Me?* "Philip, the Father and I have a fellowship of unity that is comparable to none. Don't you believe this?" This was not a new revelation to the disciples, and yet they were having difficulty understanding it. I imagine that Jesus expected greater faith from these men; after all He had been with them for three years. I like the fact that Jesus doesn't cater to their whims or give them some sign; He simply says, "Believe." He goes on to say *The words that I speak to you I do not speak on My own authority; but the Father who dwells in Me does the works.* Christ had been endeavoring to get this fact to sink into their minds and hearts. Consider John 7:16 (LSB), "So Jesus answered them and said, 'My teaching is not Mine, but from Him who sent Me.'" And John 8:26 (LSB), "I have many things to say and to judge concerning you, but He who sent Me is true; and the things which I heard from Him, these I am saying to the world." And also John 12:49-50 (LSB), "For I did not speak from Myself, but the Father Himself who sent Me has given Me a commandment—what to say and what to speak. And I know that His commandment is eternal life; therefore the things I speak, I speak just as the Father has told Me." Every word that Jesus speaks is from the Father. Does this mean that the Father is controlling everything that Jesus says, like a puppet? No, Jesus speaks the mind of His Father because it is also Jesus' mind. The two speak as one because they are one. Notice from this phrase that Jesus is claiming to be God in two ways: First, in His words, and second, in His works. He's saying, "What I *speak*, He speaks, and what I work, He *works*." Jesus does His speaking and His working by the Father who *dwells* in Him. This literally means that the Father remains in Jesus; He stays in a given place. Ladies, this indicates a most intimate union between the Father and the Son. The Father who remains with Jesus, that Father speaks the words and does the works. Jesus has already spoken of this previously in John 10:37-38 (LSB): "If I do not do the works of My Father, do not believe Me; but if I do them, though you do not believe Me, believe the works, so that you may know and continue knowing that the Father is in Me, and I in the Father." Now, in verse 11, Jesus says the same thing, only He doesn't pose a question but gives a statement.

> "Believe Me that I am in the Father and the Father in Me, or else believe Me for the sake of the works themselves." (John 14:11)

Up until this point, it appears that Jesus has been addressing Philip. The way we know Jesus is now addressing all the disciples is that the Greek word *believe* here is in the plural, indicating that Jesus is now addressing all of them. It reads like this: "Once more, I say, believe, *all of you,* my words, when I say that I and the Father are so closely united that I am in Him and He in Me." And, again, there were two grounds on which they should believe. First, was His word, His testimony. Jesus is trying to tell Philip and the others that they should believe that He is God because He says He is. And we know He cannot lie. He's saying, "I am who I say I am. And if you can't accept that, then at least believe Me for the works' sake." This is the second ground on which they should believe Him: for the things that He has done, the works. The disciples had seen Him do numerous miracles—how could they deny that He was God? They had seen Him heal the sick, cleanse lepers, raise Lazarus from the dead, feed 4,000 people on one occasion and 5,000 people on another, with only a few loaves and fishes—and that's just a few of the miracles He did. We are often just like the disciples in that we read Jesus' words in the Bible, and we see Him working in our lives, and yet we still sometimes doubt.

Now, this is a claim that Jesus has already made in John 5:36 and John 10:25. In John 5:36 (LSB), Jesus said, "But the witness I have is greater than the witness of John; for the works which the Father has given Me to finish—the very works that I do—bear witness about Me, that the Father has sent Me." And in John 10:25 (LSB), we read, "Jesus answered them, 'I told you, and you do not believe; the works that I do in My Father's name, these bear witness of Me.'" Now, the Lord closes this section with the wonderful promise of verse 12.

> "Most assuredly, I say to you, he who believes in Me, the works that I do he will do also; and greater works than these he will do, because I go to My Father." (John 14:12)

Jesus says, solemnly, *I say unto you, he who believes in Me* (that is, keeps on believing), *the works that I do he will do also*. What *works* is Jesus referring to here? His miraculous works, the same works He just mentioned in the two preceding verses, the works which He stated were the proof of who He is. This was addressed to the disciples and had direct reference to them only; consider Luke 10:19 (LSB), "Behold, I have given you authority to tread on serpents and scorpions, and over all the power of the enemy, and nothing will injure you." And Matthew 10:1 (LSB), "And summoning His twelve disciples, Jesus gave them authority over unclean spirits, to cast them out, and to heal every kind of disease and every kind of sickness." The promise here was to the disciples for the apostolic age. You and I do not have the power to do the miracles that Jesus did; otherwise we would be clearing out the hospitals! But the disciples had those powers. And Jesus says *and greater works than these he will do, because I go to My Father*. What does Jesus mean by *greater works than these he will do*? How can anyone do *greater works* than Jesus? What Jesus is saying is that when the Holy Spirit comes the disciples will be able to do greater works than Christ. This does not mean that they will have greater power, but that because of the indwelling Holy Spirit, they will possess the ability to do greater works. What a promise to them!

You might be wondering, "Well, how were their works greater?" They were greater in that the extent of the disciple's ministry was much greater than that of Christ while He was on earth. Their works were not necessarily greater in quality but in quantity. They were greater in effect. The disciples would go places that Christ had not gone. For example, the gospel had never gone outside of Palestine in Jesus' day, but after He was gone, it did, and the Spirit began working mightily everywhere. One of the greater works that was done occurred when Peter preached to the crowd in Acts 2 and 3,000 people were born again. Did that ever happen in Jesus ministry? No. Also, the gospel didn't go to the Gentiles until Acts 10, after Christ's ascension into Heaven. These, my dear sisters, are greater works.

Now, how is it that the disciples will be able to do these greater works? Jesus gives the answer: *because I go to my Father*. The Holy Spirit cannot come until Christ goes to the Father. He will tell them that later on, in John 16:7: "Nevertheless I tell you the truth. It is to your advantage that I go away; for if I do not go away, the Helper will not come to you; but if I depart, I will send Him to you." The disciples will have the power of the indwelling Holy Spirit who will enable them to do these greater works. Now, as I mentioned, this is a promise directly to the disciples, but when you think about it, because you and I have the indwelling Holy Spirit, we are able to do wonderful works for the Lord when we are controlled and yielded to Him. Think of John MacArthur's ministry, for example. How many millions of people have been reached with the gospel because of his efforts through the power and ministry of the Holy Spirit? Greater works you will do because I go to my Father! Think of Elisabeth Elliott and the millions of women she has helped through her radio ministry and books. Greater works will you do because I go to my Father! Millions have been reached by the works of John Calvin, Charles Spurgeon, Jonathan Edwards, Martin Luther, and countless others. Greater works you will do because I go to my Father! Are you doing those great works? Paul says in Ephesians 2:10 (LSB), "For we are His workmanship, created in Christ Jesus for good works, which God prepared beforehand so that we would walk in them." God has ordained ahead of time certain works for you and me to do. Do you know what good works you should be doing? Are you doing them? Are you fulfilling the job God gave you to expand His Kingdom? Are you occupying until He comes?

Summary

In these verses, we have learned that to know the Son is to know the Father (v 7); to see the Son is to see the Father (vv 8-9); and to believe the Son is to believe the Father (vv 10-12).

Ladies, do you know the Son? Do you have a personal relationship with Him? Is it consistent? Has it changed your life and the way you live? Do you believe the Son? Do you believe the words He has given us in His book? Do you believe He really did the works that are recorded for us in His book? How has it changed the way you live your life? If what you believe about God and His Son doesn't change how you behave, something is amiss. Perhaps some of you intellectually believe, but you've never embraced His Lordship; you can't call Him Lord as Philip, Thomas, and Peter have in the upper room. I appeal to you: don't put off embracing His Lordship!

These words of our Lord are full of mystery. The disciples, by now, are perhaps a little puzzled, as they cannot possibly understand the full meaning of what Christ is saying. But we must be content as they were, to believe even if we cannot fully explain and to stand in awe and reverence of the fact that the Father and the Son are one. They are two distinct Persons, yet one. This should cause us to bow in humble adoration that Jesus, who is God, humbled Himself to become a man and become a substitute for our sins. He made our sins, which once were scarlet, white as snow. Let us cast ourselves at His feet and determine to do those works that He has ordained for us to do!

QUESTIONS TO CONSIDER

1. (a) Read John 14 and write down all the commands that you see. (b) How are you doing in obeying these commands?

2. Memorize John 14:9.

3. Read John 14:7-12 and Exodus 33:18-23 and answer the following questions. (a) How are Moses' and Philip's questions similar? (b) How do the responses to their questions differ?

4. How does Hebrews 1:1-2 relate to John 14:10?

5. (a) What do the following passages in the Gospel of John say about the relationship between the Father and the Son and specifically the fact that they are one? John 1:18; 3:35; 5:19-30; 6:38, 57; 7:29; 13:31. (b) What have you learned by looking at these verses?

6. (a) What are some of the "works" (see John 14:11) that Christ did? (b) Why did the disciples have a difficult time believing in Him even though they had seen many of those works?

7. According to the following verses in Acts, what are some of the "greater works" which the disciples did? Acts 2:4-11, 41; 4:4; 5:14-16; 6:7; 19:11-12.

8. (a) What things do you know about Christ that help you to know the Father, and how do they help you to know the Father?

9. In simple terms, how would you explain to someone that Jesus is God?

10. Write a praise for the fact that Jesus is God!

The Method, the Motive, and the Miracle of Prayer
John 14:13-14

THERE is a method of prayer that is quite popular in many of our churches today, especially in Tulsa, Oklahoma, where I live. It is commonly known as the "name it and claim it" method (though some people call it the "blab it and grab it" method). From what I understand, it supposedly works like this: whatever you pray for, you get. For example, if I need $1,000 and I pray for it, then I'm guaranteed I will have it. If I pray for someone's healing in Jesus' name, then that person will be healed. I've even heard of such bizarre happenings as people praying for gas in their empty car tanks, the healing of kitchen appliances, gold fillings in people's teeth, and even asking God for gold dust to fall from Heaven. In fact, a woman I was counseling once told me of a preacher in my town, whose church she had visited, who once said, "You do not need to ask God for that job you're interviewing for tomorrow. You just need to tell God, 'I want that job I am interviewing for tomorrow.' You don't have to ask for His will; you just tell Him." Thankfully, my counselee walked out of that church, which is what we all should do, if we find ourselves in such a situation: we should not entertain such heresy!

One of the most bizarre happenings in my city occurred when a preacher's wife died in a local hospital and her preacher-husband would not allow anyone to remove her body while he called people to pray for three days that she would be raised from the dead! You and I might read that and think, "How sad!" Yet, the people who believe this are very serious about it. After all, in the Bible, Jesus said, "Whatever you shall ask in my name, I will do it." Have you and I misread the Word? What does praying in the name of Jesus really mean?

Before we answer those questions, we need to remind ourselves of where we are at in our study of Jesus' Upper Room Discourse. We need to look at the context of where we have been. We must remember that the disciples are going through troubling times. Jesus is leaving them. What will they do? Where will they go for their resources? For three years now, they have been discussing everything with their Lord, and soon He will be gone. Who will they talk to? How will they get answers for their problems? We have seen how Christ comforted them with five cures for a troubled heart in verses 1-6 of chapter 14. He also consoled them by reminding them that He and the Father are one—that to know Him is to know the Father, to see Him is to see the Father, and to believe in Him is to believe in the Father. In fact, we ended our last chapter with verse 12, which is the key to understanding and unlocking verses 13 and 14. Verse 12 says, "Most assuredly, I say to you, he who believes in Me, the works that I do he will do also; and greater works than these he will do, because I go to My Father." (John 14:12). Not only would Christ's return to the Father bring about the promise of greater works that they would be able to do, but one of those greater works would be prayer. Jesus reminds the disciples that His absence will unite them to Him in a more intimate way. Prayer will bring them into His presence at any time; it will be one of those greater works He had just spoken of. Just think, up until this point, the disciples really had no need to pray, because they talked and walked with Jesus throughout the day. But soon, He will be leaving, and they won't have that privilege. But, they will have a greater privilege of access to Him at anytime and anyplace. He will always be available to them, 24 hours a day, seven days a week. So, with these things fresh in their minds, Jesus comforts His troubled disciples with these words in John 14:13-14:

> "And whatever you ask in My name, that I will do, that the Father may be glorified in the Son. If you ask anything in My name, I will do it."

In these two short verses, we'll learn *The Method of Prayer* (v 13a); *The Motive of Prayer* (v 13b); and *The Miracle of Prayer* (v 14). Let's look first at the method of prayer, in verse 13.

The Method of Prayer *John 14:13*

> "And whatever you ask in My name, that I will do," (John 14:13a)

When Jesus says *whatever*, that is just what He means. However, that term must be taken along with the phrase *in My name*, which is not only mentioned here in verse 13, but also in verse 14. You can't take one without the other. But if we have carefully kept them together, we see that the phrase becomes very broad. It includes far more than just the spiritual, even though that is of utmost importance; it also includes the personal needs of the disciples—and of us. Sometimes, I am amazed at the simplest requests that the Lord answers. The word for *ask* here means to request or to beg; it is the seeking of something from a superior by an inferior. Often, those who are proponents of the prosperity gospel reverse this order, thinking that God should bow to their desires. But Jesus says whatever we ask in His name, He will do it. *This is the method of prayer: in His name.* Now, what does it mean to ask *in My name*? It means we ask for whatever is conformable to His character and to His purposes; it is to acknowledge all that He is and all that He did, and to ask on His account or for His sake. We must consider the person of Christ and the work of Christ when we pray in His name. That request you want the most in your life today, can you honestly say that it will further the work of Christ? Is it in agreement with the person of Christ, with who He is? Some people think that praying in the name of Jesus simply means ending our prayers with, "in the name of Jesus, Amen," or, "we ask this in Jesus' name, Amen." That is not what Jesus is talking about here. When we pray in the name of Jesus, it is as if Christ Himself were making the request. We must set aside our own wills and bow to the perfect will of God. This is actually a great comfort to the troubled disciples; it is a promise that, after He has gone, when they pray in His name He will answer. They will certainly need help, strength, support, and guidance after their Lord ascends into Heaven. And you and I need that same help, strength, support, and guidance as well. It is a great mystery to me how Christians can go through the day and not pray. How do they make it through the day?! Now, this is the first mention of praying in Jesus' name, but it is not the last mention of it. It comes up again in John 15:16 and 16:23-24, and 26.

The Motive of Prayer　　　　　　　　　　　*John 14:13*

"that the Father may be glorified in the Son." (John 14:13b)

What is the reason that we are to pray in Jesus' name? It is not to indulge us or to pamper us, but to glorify the Father. *This is the motive of prayer: that the Father may be glorified in the Son.* What does it mean that *the Father may be glorified in the Son*? To *glorify* means to recognize, honor, and praise. The whole purpose behind our praying is *that the Father may be glorified*, that He may be honored and praised and recognized, in the Son. Notice that the purpose is to glorify the Father, and yet the glory is *in the Son*. The two are inseparable; they are one. That is why prayer may be addressed to either God the Father, or God the Son, or God the Holy Spirit. Sometimes in our praying, we call out to our Father, who is our Abba, our papa-daddy, our protector and guide. Sometimes we call out to Jesus, as we are reminded of the fact that He was tempted like us and He can help us in our weaknesses. And, yes, sometimes we call out to the Holy Spirit to prick our hearts when we sin, to teach us truth as we read or study or memorize the Word, to not grieve or quench Him. Ladies, no matter which Person of the Godhead we address our prayers to, we must remember that all our praying is to be for the glory of God.

This poses a lot of questions about our prayer life, does it not? For example, if I am praying for a new car or a new house, I must ask myself if it will glorify God? It might glorify God, but it might not, and that's where we need to discern the motives of our hearts. Why do I want a new car or a new house? Is it to satisfy some fleshly desire of mine? Is it to impress my friends? Or will it truly bring glory to God? Many years ago, my husband and I were considering looking around to move, not because we needed a new house, but because our house was not conducive to having two offices, which was a growing need for us. I needed a quiet place to study and he needed more room for his books that were beginning to take over the house! The question for us became whether we should remodel what we already had or look for something that was ready and could be moved into immediately. And, believe me, the thought of moving was not desirable to me at all, but the thought of being able to study and do the work that God had called me to do in a better environment was very desirable.

Let's consider another prayer request, this time for someone who is lost and on their way to a Christless eternity in hell. We know that a prayer request for this person's soul to be saved is a request that is praying in Jesus' name and for His glory, because the Bible says that He is not willing that any should perish but that all should come to repentance (2 Peter 3:9). Certainly, a life transformed from darkness to light brings praise to God, does it not? Another prayer request that you might pray might be regarding your marriage. Perhaps your marriage isn't what you think it ought to be, and so you're praying for God to restore your marriage so that it looks like Christ and the church. This would certainly be a request for the glory of God. I believe we all need to examine our prayers in light of this verse, asking ourselves, "Is this request that I am making intended to satisfy my own personal desires and happiness only, or is it intended to bring glory to My Father in Heaven?" If we can honestly pray, "Father, I'm asking this because I know it will bring glory to You," then it is a pretty good indication that we are praying in His will. Prayers of revenge or personal ambition or selfishness cannot be said to be in the name of Jesus, and there is no promise in Scripture of an answer for those kinds of prayers. Perhaps, we should remind ourselves of James 4:1-3, which says to us,

> Where do wars and fights come from among you? Do they not come from your desires for pleasure that war in your members? You lust and do not have. You murder and covet and cannot obtain. You fight and war. Yet you do not have because you do not ask. You ask and do not receive, because you ask amiss, that you may spend it on your pleasures.

James says that we are to ask, but that there is a right way to ask and a wrong way to ask. James' readers were asking amiss, which means they were asking in a base or mean way. They were asking for things so that they could consume those things upon their lusts and spend what they received on their own pleasures. They were asking for things that would please the flesh. This is not asking in the name of the Lord or for His glory; anything that seeks to please the flesh or to gratify the flesh does not bring glory to our Lord. We are to glorify Him, not gratify ourselves! It might be interesting sometime to make note of our prayers that we pray to God and see what category they fall in—our desires or God's desires? Jesus now repeats what He has just said, but in a different way, in verse 14.

The Miracle of Prayer *John 14:14*

> "If you ask anything in My name, I will do it." (John 14:14)

The stress here is no longer on what the disciples shall ask, but on who it is that answers their prayers. Ladies, *this is the miracle of prayer: He will do it.* Jesus said this very thing, that if we *ask anything in My name, I will do it*, in verse 13 and now He says it again here in verse 14. If we are asking in His name, then the promise here is that we can ask for anything, and He *will do it*. This means He will give or grant your request. Jesus also makes this same promise in John 15:7 and 16 and 16:23-24. John the apostle also says this same thing in 1 John 3:22 and 1 John 5:14-15. Remember, John not only wrote this Gospel account that we are studying, but he picked up his pen later in life and wrote his first epistle, 1 John. In 1 John 3:22 (LSB), we read, "And whatever we ask we receive from Him, because we keep His commandments and do the things that are pleasing in His sight." And in 1 John 5:14-15 (LSB), John says, "And this is the confidence which we have before Him, that, if we ask anything according to His will, He hears us. And if we know that He hears us in whatever we ask, we know that we have the requests which we have asked from Him." In the upper room, John is sitting right next to the Lord, hearing Him say this, and then, many years later, John takes up his pen to remind his fellow believers at Ephesus of this same truth.

The promise is that God will answer, and we know He is a God who cannot lie. But again, the condition is that it must be asked *in His name*. Notice, it is the Son who answers the prayers; Jesus says, *I will do it*. This is an incredible promise! Ladies, these verses are wonderful promises to the disciples and to us. And so, I ask you, does God answer your prayers? If not, why not?

Before we draw this chapter to a close, I would like to give you five hindrances to prayer that perhaps might help some who are not seeing the Lord answer their prayers. *The first hindrance to prayer is not knowing the One to whom you are praying.* Prayer is a mystery and perhaps to some of you it is more of a mystery than to others. Perhaps it is because you don't know the One to whom we are to pray. It would be like trying to go to a bank and cash a check for 100 dollars and yet you don't have an account there. The teller would obviously look at you and tell you she can't cash your check because you don't have an account there. You might say to her, "I know I don't have an account here, but I want you to know that I sincerely believe in cashing checks." You may sincerely believe all you want in cashing checks, but unless you have an account in that bank, you might as well forget it. In the same way, it is not enough to pray in the name of Jesus, there must be the true deposit of saving faith. You must have an account in the bank; your name must be written in the Book of Life. That may be one of the biggest reasons some do not see God answer prayer. Make sure you have genuine saving faith, dear friend. If you're unsure of what the gospel is, please refer to the gospel presentation placed at the back of this book.

The second hindrance to prayer is unconfessed sin. David says in Psalm 66:18, "If I regard iniquity in my heart, the Lord will not hear." Also, Isaiah 59:1-2 (LSB) says, "Behold, the hand of Yahweh is not so short that it cannot save; nor is His ear so dull that it cannot hear. But your iniquities have made a separation between you and your God, and your sins have hidden His face from you so that He does not hear." You might say, "Well, I don't know of any sin that I am committing." Maybe we need to remind ourselves of some common sins that we commit and often overlook. Some of us may need to confess and repent of these sins in order for God to be willing to hear our prayers:

1. *An unthankful spirit:* 1 Thessalonians 5:18 (LSB) says, "in everything give thanks, for this is God's will for you in Christ Jesus." Do you worry about things? Do you give God thanks for everything, even the trials? Do you thank Him for the blessings as well as the disappointments of the day?

2. *A lack of witnessing:* Acts 1:8 (LSB) says, "but you will receive power when the Holy Spirit has come upon you; and you shall be My witnesses both in Jerusalem, and in all Judea and Samaria, and even to the end of the earth." In Matthew 28:19, we are commanded to go into all the world and preach the gospel. Have you failed to share the gospel with lost family members and neighbors? Do you think to yourself, "I'll

just live it before them and not witness with my mouth"? The Bible says, "And how will they hear without a preacher?" (Romans 10:14b LSB).

3. *A proud spirit:* James 4:6b says, "God is opposed to the proud, but gives grace to the humble." Are you proud of your accomplishments, your talents, and your family? Do you see yourself as better than others? Do you insist on your own way all the time? Do you rebel at the things in God's Word that you know He is asking you to do?

4. *A complaining spirit:* Philippians 2:14 states, "Do all things without complaining and disputing." Do you constantly complain, find fault, and argue? Do you have a critical spirit? Do you carry a grudge against others who do not see eye-to-eye with you on all things?

5. *Abusing your body:* Romans 12:1 (LSB) tells us, "Therefore I exhort you, brothers, by the mercies of God, to present your bodies as a sacrifice—living, holy, and pleasing to God, which is your spiritual service of worship." Are you careless with your body? Do you abuse it with drugs or alcohol? Do you feed it properly? Do you give it enough exercise and rest?

6. *Improper speech:* In Ephesians 4:29 (LSB), Paul reminds us, "Let no unwholesome word proceed from your mouth, but only such a word as is good for building up what is needed, so that it will give grace to those who hear." Do you speak words that are edifying, or do you use your mouth to tear others down? Do you use filthy language and tell off-colored jokes or tolerate others doing so in your presence? Do you gossip, slander, or flatter?

7. *Neglecting church attendance:* Hebrews 10:25 (LSB) reminds us that we should be "not forsaking our own assembling together, as is the habit of some, but encouraging one another, and all the more as you see the day drawing near." Are you irregular in your church attendance? Do you attend in body only? Do you daydream, talk to others, or read on your electronic device? Are you texting or checking your email in church or, worse—and yes, I've witnessed this—playing games on your phone?

8. *Lying:* Colossians 3:9 says, "Do not lie to one another, since you have put off the old man with his deeds." Do you ever lie, even "little white lies," whatever those are? I am amazed sometimes how even believers think it is okay to lie for surprise parties, or to their children, for one reason or another. Are you deceptive? Do you exaggerate, telling things the way you want them told, rather than the way they really are?

9. *Unwholesome entertainment:* 1 Peter 2:11 (LSB) admonishes us, "Beloved, I urge you as sojourners and exiles to abstain from fleshly lusts which wage war against the soul." Do you fill your mind with sexually-oriented television programs, movies, books, and internet searches? Are you lusting over a member of the opposite sex?

10. *A lack of love toward the brethren:* Jesus just mentioned earlier in the upper room, in John 13:35 , "By this all will know that you are My disciples, if you have love for one another." Are you guilty of being divisive in your church? Do you add fuel to misunderstandings? Are you showing partiality in your church by only loving those who love you? How have you loved the brethren this week?

11. *An unforgiving spirit:* Colossians 3:13 (LSB) tells us that we are to be "bearing with one another, and graciously forgiving each other, whoever has a complaint against anyone, just as the Lord graciously forgave you, so also should you." Have you failed to forgive anyone for anything they may have done against you? Are you holding grudges?

12. *Wasting time:* Paul admonishes us in Ephesians 5:16 (LSB) to be "redeeming the time, because the days are evil." Do you waste your time or the time of others? Are you late to functions, even church? Do you realize that doing so is stealing time from others and from God? Do you spend time lying around in front of the television when you should be about your daily chores as a homemaker? Do you work diligently throughout the day? Does your husband come home to a clean house and a warm meal on the table, or does he come home and find you still in your PJ's and consumed with your favorite social media site? Do you waste hours and days on things that you know have no eternal value?

13. *Love of money:* 1 Timothy 6:10 (LSB) warns, "For the love of money is a root of all sorts of evils, and some by aspiring to it have wandered away from the faith and pierced themselves with many griefs." Is your goal in life to make as much money as possible or to accumulate things? Do you give to the Lord's work or are you robbing God by not giving your tithe?

14. *Hypocrisy:* Matthew 23:28 (LSB) says, "In this way, you also outwardly appear righteous to men, but inwardly you are full of hypocrisy and lawlessness." Do you know in your heart that you are a fake, pretending to be a Christian? Are you someone different at church than you are at home?

15. *Wrong thinking:* Philippians 4:8 is a reminder to us of what we are to be thinking; "Finally, brethren, whatever things are true, whatever things are noble, whatever things are just, whatever things are pure, whatever things are lovely, whatever things are of good report, if there is any virtue and if there is anything praiseworthy—meditate on these things." Is your mind consumed by all the "what ifs" in life? Do you always think the worst of people and situations? Do you dwell on pure things? Do you think the best of others?

Obviously, there's no way we could take the time to list all the sins one could possibly be engaged in, given that there are over 600 commands in the Word of God, but I think you have the picture by now. Any kind of sin will hinder your prayers. In fact, I once read of a man who was so distressed about his relationship to God that he stayed up all night trying to discern which command he was disobeying. Are you that serious about obeying the Lord?

The third hindrance to prayer is praying with wrong motives. Let's remind ourselves again of James 4:1-3 (LSB), "What is the source of quarrels and conflicts among you? Is not the source your pleasures that wage war in your members? You lust and do not have, so you murder. You are envious and cannot obtain, so you fight and quarrel. You do not have because you do not ask. You ask and do not receive, because you ask with wrong motives, so that you may spend it on your pleasures." Praying with wrong motives or for selfish gain is a huge hindrance to prayer.

A fourth hindrance to prayer is lack of faith. James 1:5-7 (LSB) says, "But if any of you lacks wisdom, let him ask of God, who gives to all generously and without reproach, and it will be given to him. But he must ask in faith, doubting nothing, for the one who doubts is like the surf of the sea, driven and tossed by the wind. For that man ought not to expect that he will receive anything from the Lord." We must pray in faith, believing not only that God will do what He has said He will do but also that He is who He says He is. We must trust His power and promise to answer prayer. We must believe God will do what He has said He will do. Do you believe that?

A fifth hindrance to prayer is not praying in His name. This would be not praying according to His will or for His glory, which we have covered in our text.

Summary

We have looked at the method, the motive, and the miracle of prayer. In considering the method of prayer, which is praying in Jesus' name: Would you say that your prayers consist of this? Do you bow your will to His, or are you secretly hoping that He will bow His will to yours?

In considering the motive of prayer, that the Father would be glorified in the Son: Are you praying that God might be glorified or that you might be happy, or get something you're really wanting for your own selfish purposes?

In considering the miracle of prayer, that He will in fact do what we've prayed for; do you believe that God will answer your prayers? Does He answer your prayers? As believers in Jesus Christ, we should be seeing answers to prayer on a regular basis. What a miracle that God would hear and answer our prayers!

In the upper room, Christ has come to His final hours and He leaves His disciples with the promise that when He goes, they will have a new relationship with Him through prayer. What if they had gone on from there and never prayed? What would have happened to the early church?

Where would we be today if it weren't for those who have gone before us being men and women of prayer? You and I have the wonderful privilege of prayer, and yet we neglect it so often. What will be the outcome for our children and our grandchildren if we neglect the privilege of prayer? As one man has said:

> Prayer is the Christian's greatest resource and the one least used. It is his greatest obligation and the one most neglected. It is the most common form of devotion, yet the one least understood. Prayer is the gateway to God's presence, but few enter. Prayer is the channel of God's grace, but in most lives it is clogged. It is commonly supposed that anyone can pray, but only those who are accepted in Christ have full access to God. Many regard prayer as optional, but God requires prayer as the condition of His working and where there is not prayer, there is no power.[1]

God help us to be women of prayer!

---

[1] Edwin F Harvey, Lillian G Harvey, eds., *Kneeling We Triumph: Book One* (Hampton: Harvey and Tate, 1982), 16.

QUESTIONS TO CONSIDER

1. (a) In John 14:13-14, what profound statements does Jesus make regarding prayer? (b) According to these verses, what should be our motives as we pray?

2. Memorize John 14:13.

3. (a) From what you read in Matthew 6:5-13, contrast the way the hypocrites pray with the way believers are to pray. (b) How do the requests in the Lord's Prayer (found in verses 9-13) glorify the Father?

4. (a) Read and examine Daniel's prayer in Daniel 9:4-19. How does his prayer glorify the Father? (b) How does his prayer compare with many of the prayers we hear today?

5. (a) Read Luke 1:26-56. Did Mary pray "in His name" (see verse 38)? (b) How did her prayer glorify the Father? (c) What was the result of Mary's submission to God's will (see Luke 2:1-14)?

6. (a) What do you think Jesus means in John 14:13-14 when He directs His disciples to pray in His name? (b) In what ways are these verses sometimes taken out of context? (c) How could you use 1 Timothy 6:6-11 and James 4:1-4 to correct those who use John 14:13-14 to justify praying for selfish desires?

7. (a) Take some time this week to examine your prayer life. (b) How do you think your prayers glorify the Father? (c) Are your prayers mainly for selfish desires or do they concern Christ and His Kingdom?

8. Come prepared to share a prayer request that you know will glorify the Lord!

The Promise of the Spirit
John 14:15-18

MOST of us could share of a time in our lives when we felt all alone, or a time in our lives when we hurt so deeply that we thought no one could ever understand the pain we were going through. Most of us have gone through times when we desperately needed comfort. The question for each of us, then, is this: Where do I personally find comfort during these crucial times in my life? Do I turn to drugs, alcohol, food, or entertainment to drown my sorrows? We often turn to these kinds of solutions in the hope that they will provide us some comfort. Most believers turn to a friend, a spouse, or a family member to share their sorrows. And while doing so can be helpful at times, at other times we can find ourselves agreeing with the words of Job to his not-so-helpful friends: "Miserable comforters are you all" (Job 16:2).

The wonderful news is that for the believer in Jesus Christ there is comfort provided for us that the world knows nothing about. It is unexplainable to the unbeliever, but it is real, nonetheless. The comfort that you and I possess is the comfort of the Holy Spirit. The verses that we will cover in this chapter teach us of this comfort, a comfort crucial to our Christian lives, and I pray that they will penetrate your heart and make a lasting impact upon you. Let's read these words of encouragement together in John 14:15-18:

> "If you love Me, keep My commandments. And I will pray the Father, and He will give you another Helper, that He may abide with you forever—the Spirit of truth, whom the world cannot receive, because it neither sees Him nor knows Him; but you know Him, for He dwells with you and will be in you. I will not leave you orphans; I will come to you."

In this chapter, we will learn of *The Privileges of a Disciple Toward Our Lord* (v 15) and *The Promises of Our Lord to His Disciples* (vv 16-18). As we began chapter 14, we noted that Christ comforted his disciples with the promise of Heaven, the promise of His coming again, the promise of His person (that He is God), and the promise of answered prayer. By now, the disciples are probably thinking, "How great! What wonderful promises! And to think (as we saw in the last chapter) that He has just promised us that if we pray in His name, with the motive of the Father being glorified, then He will do it! Whatever we ask in His name, He will do it!" By now, they are likely becoming encouraged. Yet, in verse 15, Jesus follows His wonderful promise regarding prayer with a reminder to His disciples of two of the privileges of being disciples of Jesus Christ. Some of you might consider these to be responsibilities, but, my friend, when you consider that Christ has saved you, you see that they are indeed privileges! Let's see what they are.

The Privileges of a Disciple Toward Our Lord   *John 14:15*

"If you love Me, keep My commandments." (John 14:15)

It might at first appear that Christ has jumped from one topic to another, from the topic of prayer to the topic of keeping His commandments. But this is not a disjointed thought. There are several possibilities as to what the Lord is doing here. One possibility is that He is communicating to the disciples that they will have to show the genuineness of their faith by their dependence on Him through prayer, but they also will have to show the genuineness of their faith by their love and obedience to Christ. A second possibility is this: in the immediate context, Christ has just given the disciples several commandments (in 13:14, 34; 14:1, 11, 13-14) and He isn't finished giving them commandments in this Upper Room Discourse; He will go on to give them many more, as we will note in chapters yet to come. So, He's saying, "If you love me, you'll keep not only the commandment I am giving you now, but also all the commandments." A third possibility is this: we saw in verse 13 that our prayers are to have the glory of God as their focus; Christ is simply continuing on with His theme of giving Him glory and says, essentially, "Not only in your prayer life can you give Me glory, but also by loving

Me and obeying Me." A final possibility is this: it's possible that some of the disciples are thinking along the same lines that some of us tend to think, that we have a "blank check," so to speak, when it comes to prayer. So, Christ reminds them again that it is not only in His name and for His glory that they must pray, but that their prayer requests will be limited by their own love and obedience; in other words, they won't be asking for something that exceeds those boundaries. In 1 John 3:22 (LSB), John says, "And whatever we ask we receive from Him, because we keep His commandments and do the things that are pleasing in His sight." These are just some of my thoughts, and I trust that as you worked your way through the *Questions to Consider*, you came up with some of your own ideas.

Whatever the connection may be, Jesus now says *If you love Me, keep my commandments*. The word *love* is *agapao*, which indicates a direction of the will as well as finding one's joy in something. It is also in the third-class condition in the Greek, which means that it is communicating that one will keep on loving and keep on obeying. This is not a love that is fickle, but a love that is constant toward our Lord. Do you find your joy in God? Does it continue day after day? Is the direction of your life one of obedience to His commandments, to His will?

You might be wondering, "What are the commandments? Is this referring to the Ten Commandments that we're supposed to keep?" No, this is not referring to the Ten Commandments alone, though it certainly would include them. When Jesus uses the term *commandments* here, He is referring to the whole revelation of God's will, all the revealed truth in Scripture. (There are over 600 commandments in the Old Testament alone, which would have been the Scriptures the disciples had available to them at this time.) This is what Jesus is telling them here: "If you love me, you will find your joy in obeying Me, and it will be lasting." He will say this again in verses 21 and 23. And, in fact, when we come to the end of John's Gospel, we find our Lord asking Peter three times if Peter loves Him, to which Peter replies each time, "Yes, Lord, you know I do." Jesus reminds Peter there that if he loves Him, then it will show itself in keeping His commandments, and the specific commandment that Christ gives Peter at that point is to feed Christ's sheep. He knew that

Peter would find his joy in obeying God and that that joy would continue as he obeyed day after day. And we know from the book of Acts and the Epistles of 1 and 2 Peter that Peter did obey the Lord by feeding His spiritual sheep. In fact, it is most interesting that Peter picks up on these very words of Jesus and proclaims them to the elders in 1 Peter 5:2: "Feed the flock of God which is among you, taking the oversight thereof, not by constraint, but willingly; not for filthy lucre, but of a ready mind" (KJV).

Ladies, it is the same for us; our love for the Lord will also show itself in our obedience. John says in 1 John 5:2-3 (LSB), "By this we know that we love the children of God, when we love God and do His commandments. For this is the love of God, that we keep His commandments; and His commandments are not burdensome." Are God's commandments a burden to you? Are they irksome? John also says in 1 John 2:4 (LSB), "The one who says, 'I have come to know Him,' and does not keep His commandments, is a liar, and the truth is not in him." Our love for God will manifest itself in the keeping of His commandments. Show me an obedient Christian and I will show you one who loves the Lord. Show me a Christian who loves the Lord and I will show you an obedient Christian. As I have counseled women over the years, I have witnessed this to be true time and again. When women come to me for counseling, I usually have them fill out an information form which helps me to know why they are there and how they think I might be able to give them help. There's a place on that form that asks if they are a Christian, and they almost always check "yes." But then there is also a place to check the frequency of their Bible reading, prayer, and church attendance, and most counselees check "sporadic," at best. When I begin to probe, I am often grieved to discover that most do not have any kind of personal relationship with God or life of obedience to Him. With some, that grief goes further; when I point out what the Word says about these things, they respond with indifference. "How can this be?" I ask myself. Our Lord says that if we love Him, we will keep His commandments.

Notice also, before we go on, that Jesus puts emphasis on the fact that these are His commandments. They are neither yours, nor mine, but our gracious Lord's. So, we have seen that *the two privileges of a disciple toward his Lord are to love and to obey Him.* (And, my friend, these *are* privileges!) At this point, the disciples might be thinking, "But, how can we love You or even know what Your will is for us? You just told us that You're leaving us. How can we love and obey someone who isn't with us?" Well, the answers to those questions are found in verses 16-18, where Jesus gives the disciples two promises.

The Promises of Our Lord to His Disciples   John 14:16-18.

> "And I will pray the Father, and He will give you another Helper, that
> He may abide with you forever—" (John 14:16)

Before we get into the promises that Christ makes, note the context in which those promises are made. The promises are made to those that love Him and keep His commandments. *The first promise is that the Lord will pray to the Father.* Jesus says *and I will pray*, which indicates that this prayer will be in the future, probably after He ascended into Heaven. It is also worthy of mentioning that Christ will pray to the Father later on in the upper room, as we will see when we get to John 17.

The word for *prayer* here is used of asking that is based on close and intimate fellowship. It is also a term that implies the presentation of a wish or a desire from an equal to an equal. Jesus prays to the Father, one with whom He has close and intimate fellowship, one with whom He is equal. And it is an asking that seems to be in close association with what Christ has just mentioned to them in verses 13 and 14 regarding prayer. We know from God's Word that prayer is one of the roles of our Lord even now. Romans 8:34 (LSB) says, "who is the one who condemns? Christ Jesus is He who died, yes, rather who was raised, who is at the right hand of God, who also intercedes for us." Also, in Hebrews 7:25 (LSB), we read, "Therefore [Jesus] is able also to save forever those who draw near to God through Him, since He always lives to make intercession for them." Jesus prayed for us while He was on earth and He is praying for us at this very moment. That, my friend, is a humbling and amazing thought.

Notice what Jesus prays for. It is not for some selfish desire. It is a prayer that is certainly in the name of Jesus, one that will definitely bring glory to the Father. It is a prayer for the benefit of the Eleven and the benefit of you and me. The prayer is for *another Helper*, the Comforter, the Holy Spirit. *This is the second promise from the Lord—the promise of the Holy Spirit.* Again, we see our Lord loving His own to the end. Perhaps you're wondering who gives this Comforter? Jesus says *the Father* will give us the Comforter. Jesus will pray for this request, and the Father will grant it. The Father longs to give us good gifts, as James tells us in James 1:17 and our Lord mentions in His Sermon on the Mount in Matthew 7:11. The Helper, the Comforter, the dear Holy Spirit, is certainly a good and precious gift from our Father.

When Jesus speaks of the Father sending *another Helper*, He's indicating that the disciples already have a helper right now—Jesus Himself. But He will be leaving, and He does not want to leave the disciples without comfort, as He says in verse 18. He uses an interesting word here when He says *another*; this Greek word means another numerically but of the same kind. For example, if I say that I want to buy another dress, I could mean any dress. But if I use the Greek word *allos*, which Jesus uses here, and I say I want to buy another dress, it would mean one of the same kind; it would mean a dress of the exact same color, style, and everything. That is what Jesus is saying here. Jesus and the Holy Spirit are of the same kind. They are one, yet two. This would indicate that the Holy Spirit is a person, not just a power. We sing that truth when we sing, "Holy, Holy, Holy, merciful and mighty, God in *three Persons*, blessed Trinity!"[1] The word Helper, or Comforter, is *parakletos* and it is mentioned five times in the New Testament with each time referring to the Holy Spirit. Now, what does this word *Helper* mean? *Parakletos* comes from the word *parakaleo*, which means to call toward, or to speak cheerfully to, to encourage. *Parakletos* is one who has been called to help. It was used to speak of a legal advisor, pleader, or advocate. It is a comforter, one who stands alongside of one in need, in order to strengthen that one. The English word comes from two Latin words, *con* and *fortis*; one means to be in company with, and the other to strengthen or help to be brave. If you put these two words together, you have the Comforter, one who strengthens by companionship. The Holy Spirit gives us courage at times when we feel we have none left. He helps us do things we otherwise could not.

---

1 Reginald Heber, "Holy, Holy, Holy!", 1826.

Christ goes on to say that the Helper will be sent so *that He may abide with you forever*. The word *forever* indicates eternal security; it points to the eternal preservation of every Christian, which is a promise of God that Paul speaks of in Ephesians 1:13 (LSB), where he says, "In Him, you also, after listening to the word of truth, the gospel of your salvation—having also believed, you were sealed in Him with the Holy Spirit of promise."

Now, ladies, we need to crawl into the skin of the disciples and remember the context in which these words were spoken. We need to feel what the disciples are feeling at this point. Jesus has been with them for three and a half years. His bodily presence has been a comfort to them. But He is leaving, and they will no longer know the joy of His warm and intimate companionship. Jesus is leaving them, but now there is the promise of One Who is coming Who is just like Him. This would be both exciting and comforting to the disciples. One man has explained,

> How did the Lord Jesus comfort His disciples? He promised that the Holy Spirit from Heaven would so work in them a sense of the fullness of His life and of His personal presence that He would be even more intimately near and have more unbroken fellowship with them than they had ever experienced while He was upon earth.[2]

What a precious gift from the Father—and what excitement the disciples must have felt as they waited and prayed in another upper room, in Acts 1 and 2, for the fulfillment of this promise!

Before we move on, I want to briefly mention a side note here: It is interesting that all three persons of the Trinity are mentioned in this verse alone. The Son is praying, the Father is giving; and the Spirit is comforting. But the Holy Spirit is not only the Comforter; He is also the Spirit of Truth, as we see in verse 17.

---

2 Andrew Murray, *The Prayer Life* (Chicago: Fleming H. Revell Co., 1895), 15.

"the Spirit of truth, whom the world cannot receive, because it neither sees Him nor knows Him; but you know Him, for He dwells with you and will be in you." (John 14:17)

Jesus just described Himself as truth in verse 6, so it is fitting that He refers to the Spirit as *truth* also, since they are one and the same. Jesus will refer to this again in John 15:26 and in John 16:13. And in John's first epistle, he too states this same reality: "This is the One who came by water and blood, Jesus Christ; not with the water only, but with the water and with the blood. It is the Spirit who bears witness, because the Spirit is the truth" (1 John 5:6 LSB). Jesus says *the world cannot receive* this *Spirit of truth*. *The world* refers to those who are under the influence of the world and the things it holds dear, things like pride, ambition, and pleasure, things that are in opposition to God. We know from 1 John 5:19 that the whole world lies under the sway of the wicked one. And, because of that fact, it is obvious that the world cannot receive this Spirit of Truth. Paul reiterates this same truth in 1 Corinthians 2:14 (LSB): "But a natural man does not accept the depths of the Spirit of God, for they are foolishness to him, and he cannot understand them, because they are spiritually examined."

Notice that Jesus does not say that the world will not receive the Spirit of Truth but that the world *cannot* receive Him. Why can't they receive the Spirit? John gives us two reasons. First, they cannot receive Him because they don't *see Him*. *See* means to receive or behold. Paul tells us in 2 Corinthians 4:4 (LSB) why this is true when he says, "in whose case the god of this age has blinded the minds of the unbelieving so that they might not see the light of the gospel of the glory of Christ, who is the image of God." Satan has blinded the eyes of those in the world, and that is why they cannot see Him. Sometimes we can become concerned or frustrated with lost loved ones, and we think, "Why can't they see it?!" "Why don't they just turn their lives over to the Lord?!" They don't see it because they are blinded. We should pray Acts 26:18 (LSB) when praying for those who are blinded by Satan, that God would "open their eyes so that they may turn from darkness to light and from the authority of Satan to God, that they may receive forgiveness of sins and an inheritance among those who have been sanctified by faith in Me."

The second reason that the world cannot receive the Spirit of truth is because the world does not *know Him*. This means they don't know Him experientially. They don't have a knowledge of the Spirit. Listen to what Jude says, in Jude 1:18-19 (LSB), when he speaks of unbelievers: "that [the apostles] were saying to you, 'In the last time there will be mockers, following after their own ungodly lusts.' These are the ones who cause divisions, worldly-minded, not having the Spirit." Paul writes in 1 Corinthians 12:3 (LSB), "Therefore I make known to you that no one speaking by the Spirit of God says, 'Jesus is accursed,' and no one can say, 'Jesus is Lord,' except by the Holy Spirit." The world can't receive the Spirit because they don't see Him and they don't know Him. That is the bad news.

But the good news is that the Christian does know Him and they do see Him. Jesus says *you know Him, for He dwells with you and will be in you*. The word *dwell* is the same word that is translated as abide in verse 16. It means to remain. It means He is at our side. He is at home with us. In the Old Testament, the Spirit came upon some believers for special enablement or to reveal certain mysteries of God, but the Spirit did not indwell them, and He did not come upon them permanently. But after Pentecost, this would change; He would come to indwell every believer permanently. Notice that Christ is speaking of the future when He says of the Spirit that He *will be in you*. Why is that? Because, at this point the Holy Spirit has not yet been given. The disciples do not yet have the Spirit within them, but they will soon. Ladies, this is an amazing truth! The Spirit of God lives in us! The apostle Paul also speaks of this in 1 Corinthians 6:19 (LSB) when he says, "Or do you not know that your body is a sanctuary of the Holy Spirit who is in you, whom you have from God, and that you are not your own?" John also repeats this amazing truth in 1 John 3:24 (LSB); he says, "And the one who keeps His commandments abides in Him, and He in him. We know by this that He abides in us, by the Spirit whom He gave us." John says this is one of the ways that we know we are in the faith—by the Spirit who dwells in us. And it is interesting that John connects these two, the keeping of the commandments and the indwelling Spirit. John is listening intently to all that Jesus is saying here in the upper room, and many years later he will pick up his pen to write, reminding us of both the importance of keeping Christ's commandments and the promise of the indwelling Holy Spirit. Jesus now closes with some very comforting words to the Eleven.

> "I will not leave you orphans; I will come to you." (John 14:18)

Jesus first states something He will not do: *leave you as orphans*, as comfortless. And then He states something that He will do: *I will come to you*. *Orphan* means to be bereaved, comfortless, parentless, fatherless. Jesus was going to die the next day, and yet He was not going to leave His disciples comfortless or orphans. He was not going to abandon them; He was not going to leave them without a Comforter. To say that He will not leave them as orphans is especially fitting because Jesus has just referred to them as little children in John 13:33.

What does Jesus mean by the statement *I will come to you*? Some think that this means He will come to them after His resurrection and appear to them. Others think that it refers to the Lord's second coming, as seen in John 14:3. Both are true; the Lord did indeed appear after His resurrection to the disciples, and He will indeed come again. However, neither of these interpretations fit with the context, which is the promise of the Holy Spirit. Jesus is saying: *I* will not leave you comfortless; *I* will come to you. The Father will send another Comforter. Who is Jesus is referring to? He's referring to the Holy Spirit, the Comforter, who will indwell them. They are one and the same. This coming to them is connected to the giving of the Holy Spirit. What an incredible promise! Have you let this sink into your deepest soul? We do not have to be comfortless—Christ has come to us in the manifestation of the Holy Spirit within us!

Summary

We have two privileges as disciples of Jesus Christ, according to verse 15. The privileges of loving Him and obeying Him. Do you love God? If so, how does it manifest itself? Do you obey Him? Are you knowingly being disobedient in any area of your life this day? Perhaps, we should remind ourselves often of 1 John 2:3 (LSB), "And by this we know that we have come to know Him, if we keep His commandments."

We also have two promises from our Lord, according to verses 16-18. The first promise is that He will pray to the Father. Later on in our study of Jesus' Upper Room Discourse, we'll examine a prayer Jesus prays before He goes to the cross, a wonderful prayer which includes prayers for you and me. Have you thanked the Lord for His intercession for you? Think of it: He has prayed for you!

The second promise is that the Lord will send the Holy Spirit. This Holy Spirit will help us, will abide with us forever, will teach us truth, and will comfort us! Does He abide in you? Is He at home within you? Does He teach you as you read His Word? How has He helped you this week? How has He comforted you? Have you thanked God for His indwelling Holy Spirit? Ladies, the promise of the Spirit is a wonderful promise, especially in our troubled world. We have this promise of the Comforter, the indwelling Holy Spirit who lives in the heart of every believer to assist and to aid us in our darkest hour. We don't need to turn to what the world offers—believe me, it doesn't satisfy. Charles Haddon Spurgeon once said,

> And is not the Holy Ghost a loving comforter? Dost thou know, O saint, how much the Holy Spirit loves thee? ... He has loved thee long, he has loved thee well, he loved thee ever, and he still shall love thee; surely he is the person to comfort thee, because he loves. ... he is a faithful Comforter. Love sometimes proveth unfaithful. "Oh! sharper than a serpent's tooth" is an unfaithful friend! Oh! far more bitter than the gall of bitterness, to have a friend turn from me in my distress! Oh! woe of woes, to have one who loves me in my prosperity, forsake me in the dark day of my trouble. Sad indeed; but such is not God's Spirit. He ever loves, and loves even to the end—a faithful Comforter.[3]

Oh, my friends, may we never get over this precious promise, this precious gift from our heavenly Father, the gift of the Spirit!

---

[3] Charles H. Spurgeon, "The Comforter," *The Spurgeon Center*, https://www.spurgeon.org/resource-library/sermons/the-comforter/. Accessed 9/22/2023.

QUESTIONS TO CONSIDER

1. Read John 14 and put yourself in the shoes of the disciples. What are some of the thoughts and feelings that you think they might have been experiencing at this time?

2. Memorize John 14:16.

3. (a) What do you observe in John 14:16-18 regarding the Spirit? (b) How do these observations comfort you as a believer?

4. Consider the progression of verses 14-16. Why do you think Christ speaks about obedience and love (v 15) in between prayer (v 14) and the promise of the Spirit (v 16)?

5. (a) According to the following verses, what is the ministry of the Holy Spirit? John 14:26; 15:26-27; 16:7-15. (b) What comfort does this give you in your daily life?

6. According to the following verses, what are the evidences that one loves God? Matthew 10:37; 2 Corinthians 5:14-15; 1 John 2:3-5; 4:19-20; 5:2-3.

7. Read Acts 2-3 to see when the Lord's prayer in John 14:16 was answered. What exciting things happened when the disciples were given the gift of the Spirit?

8. (a) What acts of obedience have you done this week to show God that you love Him? (b) Is there an area of obedience that you need to work on? If so, what will you do about it? (These are personal questions.)

9. Recall a time when God the Holy Spirit comforted you. What did you learn? Thank God for the blessed Holy Spirit!

10. Is there an area in which you or a loved one need comfort? Using discretion, put your answer in the form of a prayer request.

Christ's Comforting Promises to Those He's Leaving

John 14:19-26

In the Belgian Congo, the weather was hot and damp. No breath of air stirred; leaves hung from the trees as though they were weighted. In the garden not far from the missionary home a small boy played under a tree. Suddenly, the father called to him, "Philip, obey me instantly—get down on your stomach." The boy reacted at once, and his father continued, "Now crawl fast, toward me." The boy again obeyed. After he had come about halfway, the father said, "Now stand up and run to me." The boy reached his father and turned to look back, and hanging from the branch under which he had been playing was a fifteen-foot snake.[1]

WOULDN'T we all love to have children who obey like that—who ask no questions but respond with humble obedience to whatever we ask of them? Our heavenly Father would also love to have children who obey like that—children who don't grumble and complain about what He asks them to do, who never question His commands, and who submit to His Word. Do you and I have a heart like young Philip? Are we always ready to obey God with no questions asked? Or do we say, "Really, God? Are you serious? You want me to do that? Would you mind telling me why first? Explain to me your plan, please, and then I'll obey." Or, "Lord, I'll get to that command the day after tomorrow. I want to watch my favorite show on television or catch up on social media—my 6,000 friends are waiting for me!"

My dear sister, did you realize that your love for God is measured by your obedience to Him? In fact, it really goes further than that. Did you know that the test of true discipleship is measured not only by your love for God but your obedience to Him as well? This is one of the truths the

---

1 J. Preston Eby, "From the Candlestick to the Throne, Book 2: The Seven Churches," *Kingdom Bible Studies*, 93. www.kingdombiblestudies.org/eBooks/Candlestick%20Book%202%20The%20Seven%20churches.pdf. Accessed 9/22/2023.

Lord drives home to His disciples in the upper room. Let's listen in on what He says in John 14:19-26.

> "A little while longer and the world will see Me no more, but you will see Me. Because I live, you will live also. At that day you will know that I am in My Father, and you in Me, and I in you. He who has My commandments and keeps them, it is he who loves Me. And he who loves Me will be loved by My Father, and I will love him and manifest Myself to him."
>
> Judas (not Iscariot) said to Him, "Lord, how is it that You will manifest Yourself to us, and not to the world?"
>
> Jesus answered and said to him, "If anyone loves Me, he will keep My word; and My Father will love him, and We will come to him and make Our home with him.
>
> "He who does not love Me does not keep My words; and the word which you hear is not Mine but the Father's who sent Me.
>
> "These things I have spoken to you while being present with you. But the Helper, the Holy Spirit, whom the Father will send in My name, He will teach you all things, and bring to your remembrance all things that I said to you."

We saw in the last chapter that there are two privileges a disciple has in relationship to His Lord, according to verse 15: to love and obey the Lord. We also saw that disciples have two wonderful promises from the Lord, found in verses 16-18: that He would pray to the Father for them, and that the Father would send the Comforter, the Holy Spirit, who will abide in them forever.

As we come to this chapter, we need to keep in mind that this is taking place the night before our Lord's death and that He is trying to comfort His troubled and despairing disciples. He is leaving them with words of comfort and words of instruction. These are the things that are on our Lord's heart. We'll see in these few short verses some wonderful promises the Lord leaves to His disciples and to us. There are four of them and each of them begin with the letter L, for your remembrance. Let's look at the first one in verse 19.

"A little while longer and the world will see Me no more, but you will see Me. Because I live, you will live also." (John 14:19)

The phrase *A little while longer and the world will see Me no more* is a phrase that Jesus has used often; you'll find it in John 7:33; 12:35; 13:33; and 16:16-19. Jesus is reminding His disciples once again that the crucifixion is near at hand. The world will not see Jesus physically anymore because He will be going to Heaven.

However, there will come a day when the unbelieving world will see Him in the physical realm, according to Revelation 1:7 (LSB): "Behold, He is coming with the clouds, and every eye will see Him, even those who pierced Him; and all the tribes of the earth will mourn over Him. Yes, amen." John also writes of this fact again in Revelation 20:12 (LSB): "Then I saw the dead, the great and the small, standing before the throne, and books were opened; and another book was opened, which is the book of life. And the dead were judged from the things which were written in the books, according to their deeds." The world will certainly see Jesus then! Paul even says in Philippians 2:10-11 (LSB), "so that at the name of Jesus every knee will bow, of those who are in Heaven and on earth and under the earth, and that every tongue will confess that Jesus Christ is Lord, to the glory of God the Father." The only time the world will see Jesus will be when it is too late, and He will judge the living and the dead and cast the wicked into everlasting punishment.

So, Jesus says the world won't see Me, *but you will see Me*. The word *but* is a strong contrast. In contrast to the world, who will not see me, you will see me! The disciples will see Him physically during the 40 days following His resurrection and prior to His ascension, but that is not what Jesus is speaking of here. By the meaning of the word *see*, which means to behold with spiritual eyes, we understand that Jesus is talking about the disciples seeing Him spiritually. It is the same for you and me. We do not see Jesus physically now, but we do see Him spiritually. So, what does Jesus mean by saying that the disciples will see Him spiritually? He is talking about the manifestation of the Spirit, who will come to dwell within them and give them eyes to see spiritually, something He just spoke to them about in verses 16 and 17. Because the world does not possess the Spirit, it does not have eyes to see Jesus. As Paul says in Romans 8:9 (LSB), "However, you are not in the flesh but in the Spirit, if indeed the Spirit of God dwells in you. But if anyone does not have the Spirit of Christ, he does not belong to Him."

Jesus goes on to give them a wonderful promise: *because I live you will live also*. What is Christ promising to His disciples? *He is promising them Life Eternal. This is the first promise that Christ mentions in this text.* Paul speaks of this very thing in 1 Corinthians 15:20-22 (LSB), where he states, "But now Christ has been raised from the dead, the first fruits of those who have fallen asleep. For since by a man came death, by a man also came the resurrection of the dead. For as in Adam all die, so also in Christ all will be made alive." And, later on in the same chapter, Paul says, "Behold, I tell you a mystery: we will not all sleep, but we will all be changed, in a moment, in the twinkling of an eye, at the last trumpet. For the trumpet will sound, and the dead will be raised incorruptible, and we will be changed. For this corruptible must put on the incorruptible, and this mortal must put on immortality" (1 Corinthians 15:51-53 LSB). 1 Corinthians isn't the only place Paul mentions this, though; he also mentions this wonderful promise in Philippians 3:20-21 (LSB): "For our citizenship is in Heaven, from which also we eagerly wait for a Savior, the Lord Jesus Christ, who will transform the body of our humble state into conformity with the body of His glory, by His working through which He is able to even subject all things to Himself." Christ is promising the disciples that because of His resurrection, they too will be resurrected. They have eternal life! Jesus says in John 11:25 (LSB), "I am the resurrection and the life; he who believes in Me will live even if he dies." Ladies, this promise isn't only for the eleven disciples in the upper room but also for all who know Him. This promise is not just an immediate hope, but also a future hope—the blessed guarantee of eternal life, of immortality. We could close our chapter now and go away rejoicing at these things alone, but we have three more promises to rejoice about! Christ leaves His disciples with yet another promise, in verse 20.

> "At that day you will know that I am in My Father, and you in Me, and I in you." (John 14:20)

What day is Jesus talking about? Some scholars think that when Jesus says *that day*, He is referring to the resurrection of Christ, but that interpretation doesn't seem to fit in the context of the promise of the Spirit. It is more likely a reference to the Day of Pentecost, the day that the Holy Spirit will come. In Luke 24:49 (LSB), Jesus says, "And behold, I am sending the promise of My Father upon you, but you are to stay in the city until you are clothed with power from on high." Indeed, when we read the book of Acts, we see the power that came and indwelt the disciples and the marvelous things which happened as a result. Thousands were converted to Christianity; numerous miracles took place. The disciples knew this power was not from themselves but from that One who had come to dwell within them. *This is the second promise Christ leaves with them, that He will Live in them!* So, what does this mysterious statement mean? It means that we are not only indwelt by the Spirit and Christ, but that they are together in a supernatural union. We are one with God in Christ. We are in a blessed union which can never be severed. At that day, the day of Pentecost, the disciples will begin to understand this great mystery, this great union that Christ is talking about.

This union is only a promise for New Testament saints and those who follow after them. Old Testament saints knew nothing of this mysterious union. Remember what David said in his prayer in Psalm 51:11? "Do not take Your Holy Spirit from me." In the Old Testament, the Holy Spirit came and went from individuals, but He did not indwell God's children. This is a new promise. When we consider this union we have with God through the Holy Spirit, we realize just how ludicrous it is for us to sin! When we sin, we drag all three, God the Father, God the Son, and God the Holy Spirit, into that sin with us. Can you imagine what that does to the heart of God? Remember what Paul says in 1 Corinthians 6:19-20 (LSB)? "Or do you not know that your body is a sanctuary of the Holy Spirit who is in you, whom you have from God, and that you are not your own? For you were bought with a price: therefore glorify God in your body." No wonder we so often grieve or quench the Holy Spirit! Perhaps, this is one of the reasons Christ speaks to the issue of obedience in the next few verses. He not only speaks to the issue of obedience, but He also gives another promise.

> "He who has My commandments and keeps them, it is he who loves Me. And he who loves Me will be loved by My Father, and I will love him and manifest Myself to him." (John 14:21)

This verse is really an elaboration of verse 15, where Jesus said, "If you love Me, keep My commandments." Here, Jesus mentions the one who *has My commandments and keeps them*. It's important for us to keep in mind that having His commandments and keeping His commandments are two different things. Having Christ's commandments means to have them in one's inner being; keeping Christ's commandments means observing them in one's daily life. Isn't that really the promise of the New Covenant, according to Ezekiel 36:26-27 (LSB)? "Moreover, I will give you a new heart and put a new spirit within you; and I will remove the heart of stone from your flesh and give you a heart of flesh. I will put My Spirit within you and cause you to walk in My statutes, and you will be careful to do My judgments."

The one who has and keeps Christ's commands, Jesus says, *is he who loves Me*. Obedience is a proof of one's love for God. The word for *love* here is the same word we've seen before, *agapao*, which indicates a direction of the will and finding one's joy in something. (All the words for love in this chapter are *agapao*.) So, if we have and keep Christ's commandments, we prove our love for him.

But Jesus goes further and says something quite astonishing! He says *and he who loves Me will be loved by My Father, and I will love him and manifest Myself to him*. Here we find our third promise: that we are Loved by God! Jeremiah speaks of this love in Jeremiah 31:3 (LSB): "Yahweh appeared to him from afar, saying, 'I have loved you with an everlasting love; Therefore I have drawn you with lovingkindness.'" The apostle Paul speaks of this as well, in Romans 8:35-39,

> Who shall separate us from the love of Christ? Shall tribulation, or distress, or persecution, or famine, or nakedness, or peril, or sword? As it is written: "For Your sake we are killed all day long; we are accounted as sheep for the slaughter."
> Yet in all these things we are more than conquerors through Him

> who loved us. For I am persuaded that neither death nor life, nor angels nor principalities nor powers, nor things present nor things to come, nor height nor depth, nor any other created thing, shall be able to separate us from the love of God which is in Christ Jesus our Lord.

Even John, the author of this Gospel, says in his first epistle, in 1 John 4:10 (LSB), "In this is love, not that we have loved God, but that He loved us and sent His Son to be the propitiation for our sins."

And, if it isn't enough to be loved by Almighty God, Jesus adds *and I will manifest myself to him*. What does Jesus mean here? Well, the word *manifest* means to exhibit in person or disclose by words; to appear, to declare plainly. The unseen and risen Christ will be a real and spiritual presence to the believer who loves and obeys God. How is this done? Through the coming of the Holy Spirit, as promised. He's saying, "I will, in the future, manifest myself to you." You might hear someone claim that they are a Christian but also add that they don't sense the presence of the Lord or He doesn't seem real to them. Usually, what they mean is that they're seeking some experiential thrill or feeling. They want that "loving feeling" without meeting the conditions for it. But notice here that there are conditions behind Christ manifesting Himself: keeping His commandments and loving Him. If you don't sense His presence, His manifestation, in your life, then I would encourage you to examine your life to see if you are living in obedience to Him. Remember, according to Romans 8:16, our spirit bears witness with His Spirit that we are the children of God! Well, this statement by our Lord causes another one of the disciples to ask a question:

> Judas (not Iscariot) said to Him, "Lord, how is it that You will manifest Yourself to us, and not to the world?" (John 14:22)

Perhaps as you read this verse, you were wondering who this *Judas* is. It is not Judas Iscariot because John specifically says *not Iscariot*. That Judas has already gone out, at this point, to betray our Lord; Judas Iscariot did not come back after he left. The Judas John is referring to here seems to be Judas Lebbaeus, whose surname was Thaddeus. He was the brother of James and the author of the Epistle of Jude, and is mentioned in Matthew 10:3 and Acts 1:13. He appears to be a man of few words; apart from his epistle, these words in John are Judas' only recorded words in Scripture. His epistle is quite short, but it is strong regarding false teachers! (Perhaps he was afraid of being identified with Judas the betrayer because they had the same name, and so made clear by the tone of his letter that he was not of the same mind as Judas Iscariot.)

Here, in the upper room, this Judas asks a question. He's not the first disciple to ask a question; we've already seen Peter ask a question in chapter 13 and Thomas ask one near the beginning of chapter 14. Philip asked for a vision of the Father to satisfy them, in 14:8, and now Judas wants to know *how is it that you are going to manifest Yourself to us, and not to the world?* The disciples are spiritual children, and just like our earthly children have questions at times, so these spiritual children have questions. It appears that Judas is still ignorant of what Jesus has just said. He's just said in verses 17 and 19 that the world cannot see Him but that the disciples could; He's just said that they would know on that day. Judas' question shows the ignorance of man and his inability to learn anything apart from God's grace. Judas is thinking like all Jews thought, that Messiah would come and set up an earthly Kingdom. He's probably thinking that Jesus will come back physically, so he simply cannot understand why the world won't see be able to see Jesus. Jesus has just said that the world wouldn't understand. He's just said in verse 20 that they wouldn't understand until that day, the day of Pentecost. But Jesus answers Judas' question anyway. Jesus remains very patient and doesn't treat Judas in a derogatory manner; He simply answers Judas' question in verse 23 with a statement similar to what He just said in verse 21. Jesus' answer about manifesting Himself to His disciples goes back to this: love for God is shown by obedience to God.

> Jesus answered and said to him, "If anyone loves Me, he will keep My word; and My Father will love him, and We will come to him and make Our home with him." (John 14:23)

Jesus has now said this three times, so it must be very important, and we, along with the disciples, would do well to heed what is being said here. It is interesting that Jesus uses the word *anyone* here, emphasizing the responsibility for each disciple to ask personally whether he loves Jesus. This would indicate that each of them and each one of us needs to examine our own hearts. Do I love Jesus? If I do, I will keep His words. I will obey Him. The Greek tense here indicates that the phrase means to keep on loving Me. Jesus is saying, "It is only if a man loves Me and keeps My words, then the Father will love him." What a promise for those who love God and keep His commandments! And, according to Romans 8:38-39, once we have that union, nothing is able to separate us from that love of God, which is in Christ Jesus our Lord.

Jesus then says *We will come to him and make Our home with him*. Now what does that mean? It means that they, the Father, the Son, and the Spirit, will make their habitation within us. This indicates a permanent dwelling, a resting place. It indicates a very close and intimate relationship. They, the Father, Son, and Holy Spirit will take up their residence in the hearts of believers as a dwelling place, as a temple fit for their abode. What a humbling thought! What a motivation to keep our inward and outward selves pure! Listen to how Paul puts it in 1 Corinthians 3:16: "Do you not know that you are the temple of God and that the Spirit of God dwells in you?" And in 2 Corinthians 6:16: "And what agreement has the temple of God with idols? For you are the temple of the living God. As God has said: 'I will dwell in them and walk among them. I will be their God, and they shall be My people.'"

Now, as we look at verse 24, we see that Jesus is stating negatively what He has just stated positively in verse 23. He's also answering Judas' question as to why the world won't be able to see Him.

> "He who does not love Me does not keep My words; and the word which you hear is not Mine but the Father's who sent Me." (John 14:24)

This statement only makes logical sense. Do not expect any manifestation of Christ if you don't bother to keep His sayings. There must be complete obedience to the Father. If you don't love God, if you are of the world, then you won't endeavor to *keep* His sayings. If you don't cherish the Word of God, you have no part with Him. The world doesn't see Him because they don't love Him or keep His words. In case the disciples are a little frightened by these strong words, Jesus says *and the word which you hear is not Mine but the Father's who sent Me*. This would have been an important statement, because the Jews did believe in God; the term *Father* would have held great weight to them. It was God in the flesh that was difficult for them to grasp. Jesus is reassuring them that He is only speaking the things that the Father has desired Him to speak. In John 8:28; 12:49; and 14:10, Jesus makes similar statements. He's only spoken what the Father has asked Him to speak. I'd like to bring out a principle here, if I may.

My friends, when you and I speak the words of God it has greater affect than when we speak our own words. Man's words are foolishness; God's words are powerful and piercing. When I am endeavoring to help someone spiritually, I often have them read out loud the words Christ speaks, and it is far more powerful than any counsel I might give. Jesus is speaking the words of God! And in verses 25 and 26, Jesus leaves His disciples with one more promise.

> "These things I have spoken to you while being present with you." (John 14:25)

What *things* is Christ talking about? The things He has said while He has been with them in the upper room. It also could refer to what He has said the last three years He has been with them. *I have spoken* these words, *being present with you*, He says,

> "But the Helper, the Holy Spirit, whom the Father will send in My name, He will teach you all things, and bring to your remembrance all things that I said to you." (John 14:26)

But is a reminder and a contrast, indicating that He is present now but will soon be leaving. But He isn't leaving without sending them a Comforter. Jesus says *But the Helper, the Holy Spirit, whom the Father will send in My name, He will teach you all things, and bring to your remembrance all things that I said to you*. Here the Spirit is called *the Helper*. He has already been called the Spirit of Truth in verse 17, and now He is called the Helper, or the Comforter. The *Spirit* is referred to as *Holy* because He is sinless, just as the Father and the Son are sinless. So, Jesus says, after

I leave, then the Holy Spirit, the Comforter, the Helper, will come. *The Father will send* Him (Jesus is confident in this answer to prayer, verse 16) *in My name*. We had the words *in My name* when we looked at verses 13 and 14. We saw there that when an individual prays in Jesus' name, it means that the individual is praying on behalf of Christ, or for His sake; Christ is the beneficiary. It means to seek what He seeks, what He desires. Used here, the phrase means the same thing. The Father will send the Holy Spirit in Christ's name, on behalf of Christ, on His account, to perfect His work. The Holy Spirit will seek and desire the same things that Christ will desire. It is Christ whom the Spirit will desire to bring glory to, not Himself (see John 15:26 and 16:13-15). Unfortunately, today, many groups are glorifying the Holy Spirit, and yet these verses are clear that the Spirit's ministry is to glorify Christ. The Spirit points to Christ and not to Himself; we are to major on Christ as well.

The work of the Holy Spirit in this verse is twofold. First, *He will teach you all things*. Why will the disciples need a teacher? Because Jesus will no longer be with them to teach them. The words *all things* are relative words, not indicating everything. That would be ludicrous! If it did mean literally everything, then it could refer to everything from how to cook to how to sew to how to plant a garden. It would make the disciples omniscient! But the Holy Spirit does not teach those things. The *all things* here refers to what the disciples need for spiritual maturity, the things they need to grow in the grace and knowledge of the Lord. The Holy Spirit is our teacher as well. He often teaches us a truth or helps us to understand the Word of God; apart from Him being our teacher, our understanding of the Word of God would be very shallow. We could all testify to times in our lives when the Holy Spirit has been our teacher.

The second aspect of the Holy Spirit's work, Jesus says, is to *bring to your remembrance all things that I said to you*. The disciples will remember every word that Christ said to them. Again, it's not everything; Jesus clearly states that it is whatever *I said to you*. It's not remembering how to bake a cake without the recipe, or remembering how the earth rotates, or any of those kinds of things. The all things Jesus speaks of here is in reference to what Christ has already said to the disciples. If you've read the Gospels, you know that the disciples did not understand everything the Lord tried to teach them. What a promise to them—they will be taught by the Spirit Himself! *Ladies, this is the fourth promise to the disciples and to us: that we will be led by the Spirit.* How soon they will forget what is said, and so they will need supernatural power to recall all that Christ has said. Doesn't He do that in our lives as well? How many times do you get a nudging from the Holy Spirit: "Remember, Jesus said do unto others as you would have them do unto you." "Remember, Jesus said if you don't forgive men their trespasses, neither will your Father forgive your trespasses." "Remember, do all things without murmuring and disputing." "Remember that the words of a talebearer are as wounds, and they go down into the innermost parts." There are other ways that the Holy Spirit calls things to our remembrance. I can't tell you how many times I've been studying and writing chapters and the Holy Spirit has reminded me of a verse or a passage of Scripture that will help to clarify or illustrate what I'm teaching. I am so thankful, because I know that my mind simply can't remember all I need to remember. I am very thankful for the help of the Holy Spirit, who consistently brings things to my remembrance.

Summary

In these verses, we have four precious promises that Christ leaves to the disciples and to us:

1. *The Promise of Life Eternal* (v 19): Do you have eternal life? How do you know?

2. *The Promise that He will Live in Us* (v 20): Does the Spirit live in you? Again, how do you know?

3. *The Promise that He Loves Us* (vv 21-24): Do you dwell on this wonderful truth that you are loved by God?

4. *The Promise that We Will be Led by the Spirit* (vv 25-26): When is the last time the Holy Spirit led you, convicted you, or taught you?

Four wonderful, comforting promises to the disciples and to us! But with these promises comes responsibility. Our responsibility is to love Christ and to obey Him, as Christ mentioned three times in these verses. Why did the young boy, Philip, whom I mentioned in the introduction to this chapter, obey his earthly father? Because of his love for him and his desire to obey and please him. He also must have trusted his father so explicitly that he knew his father had his best interests at heart. What would have happened to Philip if he had not obeyed his earthly Father? The story would have had a very sad ending, would it not? We probably would have read about a trip to the hospital or perhaps even a funeral. Why do you and I obey our heavenly Father? Because of our love for Him and our desire to obey Him and please Him. Do you and I trust Him explicitly, knowing that He has our best interests at heart?

What will happen if you and I don't obey our heavenly Father? That story will also have a sad ending, as John puts it in 1 John 2:4 (LSB): "The one who says, 'I have come to know Him,' and does not keep His commandments, is a liar, and the truth is not in him." That, my friends, is a sad ending. Life eternal without Christ in everlasting punishment. My prayer for all of us is that we are loving and obeying our Lord each and every day, and, as we do, that we are sensing His love for us, His leading of us, His life in us, and are looking forward to life eternal with Him!

QUESTIONS TO CONSIDER

1. (a) Read John 14 and list all the statements that begin with the word "if." (For example, in verse 23, "If anyone loves Me, he will keep My word.") (b) What do you learn from these if-then statements?

2. Memorize John 14:23.

3. (a) What do you think is the main theme of John 14:19-26? (b) What are the promises in these verses? (c) How would the words Jesus speaks in John 14:19-26 be a comfort to the disciples? (d) How are they a comfort to you?

4. (a) In the following passages, how do we see the Holy Spirit working? Luke 2:25-35; Luke 4:1-13; Acts 2:4; Acts 16:6; Ephesians 1:13-14. (b) How is the Holy Spirit working in your life?

5. (a) What do John 7:33; 12:35; 13:33; 14:19; and 16:16-19 all have in common? (b) What does Jesus mean by what He says in these passages?

6. What do the following verses say about our union with Jesus Christ? Romans 8:1; 1 Corinthians 1:30; 2 Corinthians 5:17; Galatians 2:20; Colossians 1:27; 1 John 4:12.

7. (a) What things did the Holy Spirit bring to the disciples' remembrance, according to John 2:13-22; John 12:12-16; and Acts 11:15-18? (b) Recall a time when the Holy Spirit reminded you of a truth from the Word of God. (c) What were the results?

8. What are some evidences in your own life that Christ is in you?

9. What is your prayer request after studying this chapter?

Five Peace-Stealers
John 14:27-31

THERE is a song from Handel's Messiah that is taken from Isaiah 9:6 and is often sung around Christmastime. The lyrics go like this: "For unto us a child is born, unto us a Son is given, and the government shall be upon His shoulder and His name shall be called, Wonderful Counselor, the Mighty God, the Everlasting Father, and the Prince of Peace." The world sings about the Prince of Peace, but do they know this Prince of Peace they sing about? Does the world have the peace that only comes from the Prince of Peace?

Throughout history mankind has searched for peace. They're still searching for peace today. But have they found it? No. In fact, after World War II the United Nations was created for the purpose of promoting world peace. But did you know that since that year, 1945, there hasn't been a single day of peace? Lasting peace is only a dream to our world. The New York Times quipped: "Peace is a fable." In fact, wars and crime remain on the increase all throughout the world.

For Christians, however, those who know the Prince of Peace, peace is not a fable—it's a fact. In the verses before us in this chapter, the Lord, the Prince of Peace, gives the disciples and us another wonderful promise: the promise of peace. But as we well know, there are a multitude of things that can steal the peace in our lives, if we're not careful. There are areas that we must keep in check, lest we become like the world—without peace. In this chapter, we will learn of five peace-stealers the disciples were facing. But as we consider these threats to our peace, we will also consider five cures for each of these peace-stealers. Let's read verses 27-31 of John 14 and discover the five things that can steal our peace, if we let them.

> "Peace I leave with you, My peace I give to you; not as the world gives do I give to you. Let not your heart be troubled, neither let it be afraid. You have heard Me say to you, 'I am going away and coming back to you.' If you loved Me, you would rejoice because I said, 'I am going to the Father,' for My Father is greater than I.
>
> "And now I have told you before it comes, that when it does come to pass, you may believe. I will no longer talk much with you, for the ruler of this world is coming, and he has nothing in Me. But that the world may know that I love the Father, and as the Father gave Me commandment, so I do. Arise, let us go from here."

In our last chapter, we learned of how Christ assured His disciples that He would not leave them as orphans; instead, He left them with four wonderful promises: the promise of life eternal, the promise that He would live in them, the promise that He loves them, and the promise that they will be led by the Spirit as He will teach them and bring the things to their remembrance that Christ has taught them. There is a natural transition here from what Christ has just spoken of in verse 26, the Holy Spirit, to the peace He speaks of in verse 27. Peace is one of by-products of the Spirit, as Paul tells us in Galatians 5:22-23 (LSB): "But the fruit of the Spirit is love, joy, peace, patience, kindness, goodness, faithfulness, gentleness, self-control. Against such things there is no law." Let's listen in as Jesus begins to share with His disciples the things that are on His heart. Let's see what things can steal the peace that God promises.

> "Peace I leave with you, My peace I give to you; not as the world gives do I give to you. Let not your heart be troubled, neither let it be afraid." (John 14:27)

Jesus once again gives His disciples another promise as He reminds them of His departure. This time His promise is the promise of peace; He says *Peace I leave with you*. What is *peace*? Peace is rest, in contrast to strife. Peace is not a feeling one has, but is a condition of one's soul. The Hebrew word for peace is *shalom*, which relates to everything that is good. It is a positive word, relating to the highest kind of goodness. In fact, it is a peace that doesn't make sense in the midst of circumstances. As John

MacArthur once said, peace is a "divine tranquilizer."[1] It's interesting to consider how the word peace has been translated in a number of tribal languages: "to sit down in one's heart," "to have a song in your body," "quiet goodness," "quiet heart." These are great and appropriate parallels because peace guards the soul against anxiety and strife and grants to it solace and harmony. This is a spiritual peace that only Christ can give and which comes only from possessing a right relationship with God. In fact, Jesus says *My peace I give to you*. Christ's peace is different from the world's idea of peace. It is an unbroken peace with God, which allows us to be always at rest in spite of people or circumstances.

Ladies, that kind of peace is available to you and me. Jesus will remind His disciples of this once again after His resurrection and before His ascension, in John 20:19-21:

> Then, the same day at evening, being the first day of the week, when the doors were shut where the disciples were assembled, for fear of the Jews, Jesus came and stood in the midst, and said to them, "Peace be with you." When He had said this, He showed them His hands and His side. Then the disciples were glad when they saw the Lord.
>
> So Jesus said to them again, "Peace to you! As the Father has sent Me, I also send you."

The disciples evidently needed to be reminded again of the peace the Lord gives, just like we need to be reminded of it. I can be doing so well in trusting the Lord and enjoying His marvelous peace and then—whamo!—something very unexpected comes up and I need to remind myself that God is still in control and that I need to be at peace. So, Jesus leaves His disciples with the promise of peace, but when He says *not as the world gives do I give to you*, He is reminding them His peace is not the kind of peace that the world gives. What kind of peace does the world offer? The so-called peace the world offers is found in money, fame, pleasure, success, drugs, alcohol, sex, and other such things. But ladies, the world is unable to give the kind of peace that Christ gives. His peace is lasting, and is not dependent on circumstances, people, or possessions.

---

[1] John MacArthur, "The Gift of Peace," *Grace to You*, https://www.gty.org/library/articles/P21/the-gift-of-peace. Accessed 9/22/2023.

A famous actor once said in a television interview that he had everything but peace and that he hoped to find it when he died. As believers, we don't have to live in turmoil like that actor; we can enjoy peace now while we are still living! The world will never know peace; Isaiah 48:22 (LSB) tells us: "'There is no peace for the wicked,' says Yahweh.'" The world will not find peace because peace isn't a worldly issue; it's a spiritual issue.

After His promise of peace, Jesus gives His disciples a command, one He already has given them in verse 1: *Let not your heart be troubled, neither let it be afraid*. The Greek tense here gives it the more literal sense of "let not your heart keep being troubled, let not it keep being afraid." Sometimes, it's hard for us to understand that Jesus had to say this to them again, after all the promises He gave them in chapter 14, but He did. May I lovingly remind us that we also know many promises in the Word and yet we become troubled as well? The word *troubled* means to be agitated. The word *afraid* means to be fearful, and it is a word that refers to the palpitating of the heart. It involves being cowardly, timid, or fearful. The disciples, Jesus is saying, were to stop being afraid and troubled. *So, we see that the first peace-stealer is a fearful or troubled heart.* The disciples were fearful and troubled about many things. Judas had gone out to betray their Lord; Peter was going to deny Him soon; Jesus was leaving them; they still didn't understand many of the truths Jesus was trying to convey to them.

Ladies, there are many things that come into our lives that have the potential to steal our peace. There are things that tempt our hearts to become fearful. What does our future hold for our children and for us? How am I going to die? Will my husband die before me and leave me a widow? Is my husband going to lose his job? Is my lost loved one ever going to be saved? *Do you want to know the cure for a fearful and troubled heart? Pray!* Listen to what Paul says in Philippians 4:6-7, "Be anxious for nothing, but in everything by *prayer* and *petition* with *thanksgiving* let your *requests* be made known to God. And the peace of God, which surpasses all comprehension, will guard your hearts and your minds in Christ Jesus." (LSB emphases mine). Paul tells us four times in these verses that when we are troubled we are to pray. In the Sermon on the Mount, Jesus commands us not to be anxious, and the cure He gives there is to seek first the Kingdom of God and His righteousness, and He assures us that, if we do in fact seek first His Kingdom, all the things we're concerned about will be added unto us (Matthew 6:25-34). Jesus is stressing the same idea Paul is stressing. Be prayerful; concern yourself with the things of the Kingdom. We are to stop being anxious, troubled, and afraid, no matter what. Next, in verse 28 Christ mentions the second thing that will rob the disciples of their peace.

> "You have heard Me say to you, 'I am going away and coming back to you.' If you loved Me, you would rejoice because I said, 'I am going to the Father,' for My Father is greater than I." (John 14:28)

Christ has already mentioned to His disciples the fact that He is leaving them; He mentioned this back in John 13:33 and 14:2-3. He has been preparing them that He is leaving them, but He has also told them that He will come again unto them. How will He do this? By the dear indwelling Holy Spirit whom He has just spoken of in the previous verses. *The second peace-stealer Christ mentions is change in relationships.* Christ was leaving them and their relationship with Him would no longer be the same. No longer would they be able to physically touch Christ or see Him or hear Him speak audibly to them. This frightened them. Changes in relationships can also rob us of peace. I recall many times the Lord has changed relationships with family members or dear friends, and it has always been hard. But, even amidst these changes we can have peace. *The cure for this peace stealer, change in relationships, is to believe in a Sovereign God who works everything out to His perfect will in our lives.* Paul puts it well in Romans 8:28 (LSB), "And we know that for those who love God all things work together for good, for those who are called according to His purpose." There is no reason for being unsettled when changes come in relationships. You and I have the same dear Holy Spirit promised to us as was promised to the disciples. Christ dwells in us by way of His Spirit! Remember that God is the blessed controller of every event of our lives; remember the comfort of the dear Holy Spirit.

Jesus goes on to make a very startling statement; He says *if you loved Me, you would rejoice because I said, "I am going to the Father."* The tense of this Greek verb indicates that the disciples did not love Jesus at this present time as they should. Remember that the word for love is *agapao*, which indicates a direction of the will and finding one's joy in something. The disciples were not loving Jesus as they should; if they were, they would be rejoicing and glad for Him. They were not finding their joy in Him; they were too occupied with their own grief. Instead of grieving, they should be rejoicing at the Divine plan, a plan which entailed the Lord returning to Heaven to His Father. They should be rejoicing that soon the Holy Spirit will come and take up residency in them as they minister on behalf of Christ. True love does not seek its own way but looks out for the interests of others. The disciples' love for Christ was selfish at this point because they did not want Him to leave. *The third peace-stealer is lack of love for God.* Jesus is telling them, "If you were loving Me as you ought to be loving Me, you would be rejoicing at what I'm telling you!" When we do not love the Lord as we should, with complete devotion of our lives, it takes away our peace. When we are selfish with our love, our selfishness robs us of peace, and we are left with unrest in our souls. *The cure for not loving God as we should is doing the first works.* Now, that answer might surprise you. But, John the apostle, who wrote this Gospel, also wrote the Book of the Revelation. And, in the beginning of that book, John records what Jesus has to say to the seven churches in Asia. The first church He addresses is Ephesus:

> To the angel of the church of Ephesus write, "These things says He who holds the seven stars in His right hand, who walks in the midst of the seven golden lampstands: I know your works, your labor, your patience, and that you cannot bear those who are evil. And you have tested those who say they are apostles and are not, and have found them liars; and you have persevered and have patience, and have labored for My name's sake and have not become weary. Nevertheless I have this against you, that you have left your first love. Remember therefore from where you have fallen; repent and do the first works, or else I will come to you quickly and remove your lampstand from its place—unless you repent" (Revelation 2:1-5).

The disciples had the same problem the church at Ephesus had; they did not love God as they should. Jesus tells the Ephesian believers to repent and to remember from where they have fallen and to do the first works.

These first works would entail what their lives were like when they first embraced Christ as Lord. In other words, Jesus is saying, "Return there, to the same zeal, love, passion, and prayer you started with!"

Jesus goes on to say *if you loved Me you would rejoice because I am going to the Father*. The disciples did not love the Lord as they should, and that lack of love was robbing them of their peace. Jesus' statement here explains why funerals of believers should be a time of rejoicing and not of sorrow. Why? Because, like our Lord, our loved one is going to the Father. We should be rejoicing that they are now in glory! We need to remember that our tears are for us, and our loved ones are in a much better place. We ought to find comfort as we remember what Jesus said in verse 3, that He Himself receives us at the time of our death.

Jesus says that He is going *to His Father*, and we know from statements He makes later in this discourse that this means He will be restored again to full glory. Jesus will pray in John 17:5, "And now, O Father, glorify Me together with Yourself, with the glory which I had with You before the world was." But here, Jesus adds a statement which Jehovah Witnesses and Mormons love: *for my Father is greater than I*. What does Jesus mean by this statement? We know that He and the Father are one, according to John 10:30, so how can the Father be greater than the Son? Paul gives us this answer in Philippians 2:5-11. He says,

> Let this mind be in you which was also in Christ Jesus, who, being in the form of God, did not consider it robbery to be equal with God, but made Himself of no reputation, taking the form of a bondservant, and coming in the likeness of men. And being found in appearance as a man, He humbled Himself and became obedient to the point of death, even the death of the cross. Therefore God also has highly exalted Him and given Him the name which is above every name, that at the name of Jesus every knee should bow, of those in heaven, and of those on earth, and of those under the earth, and that every tongue should confess that Jesus Christ is Lord, to the glory of God the Father.

How was the Father greater than Jesus? As Paul said, Christ did not consider His equality with God as something selfishly to be grasped.

Instead, Christ humbled Himself and became a man. He emptied Himself of His riches, His glory, and His authority. He took upon Himself the form of a servant. He stooped from sovereignty to slavery. That's how His Father was greater than He was. In the days of His incarnation, Jesus had been below the Father in terms of outward glory and official position. And He will pray in John 17:5 for that glory to be restored. Jesus goes on in our text to say something, in verse 29, which He has already said once in the upper room, in 13:19.

> "And now I have told you before it comes, that when it does come to pass, you may believe." (John 14:29)

Jesus is once again considering the disciples as more important than Himself. He is letting them know all of this before it happens. What Christ is saying is, "Before My death, resurrection, and ascension, I am telling you all of this so that after those things have happened, you might believe." The word *believe* here does not refer to belief unto salvation; rather, it refers to their faith being strengthened when they see all that Christ has said come to pass. Jesus' arrest and death would undoubtedly shake their faith to its foundation, and Jesus wished to prepare them for the strain that His leaving them would place upon them, so that they might believe Him. I don't know about you, but there are certain things that Christ has said in His Word that serve to strengthen my faith, especially as I see them unfold before my eyes. His comforting words here are especially important given that His time with them is drawing to a close. Look at verse 30:

> "I will no longer talk much with you, for the ruler of this world is coming, and he has nothing in Me." (John 14:30)

Jesus says *I will no longer talk much with you*, and indeed He doesn't; the remaining chapters in this discourse can be spoken in about ten minutes. Ten minutes isn't much time, is it? And the reason, Jesus says, that He will not be able to talk much longer with His disciples is because *the ruler of this world is coming*. The Prince of Peace is leaving them, and the prince of this world is coming. Who is this prince of this world, this *ruler of this world*? It is Satan. Paul describes Satan in Ephesians 2:2 as the prince of the power of the air. Satan is also mentioned in Scripture by a number of other names: the devil (Matthew 4:1), a dragon (Revelation 12:3), the evil one (Matthew 5:37), the angel of the bottomless pit (Revelation 9:11), the god of this age (2 Corinthians 4:4), Apollyon (Revelation 9:11), Abaddon (Revelation 9:11), Belial (2 Corinthians 6:15), and Beelzebub (Matthew 10:25).

What does Jesus mean when He says that Satan *is coming*? Was Satan himself coming? We get an answer to what Christ is saying when we look back at John 13:27: "Now after the piece of bread, Satan entered him. Then Jesus said to him, 'What you do, do quickly.'" Remember, at this time Satan had entered into the heart of Judas, and Judas was planning in the next few hours to come and betray the Lord with a kiss. Jesus, being all-knowing, was aware of the footsteps of Judas, the Roman soldiers, and the members of the Sanhedrin; He knew how all of them were being led by the prince of the power of the air. Christ knew they were on their way (see Luke 22:47-53). *The fourth peace-stealer is the enemy, the devil.* I am certain that the disciples were at least a little fearful when Jesus said that He would no longer talk much with them because the ruler of this world was coming. They knew it would change everything. Listen, ladies, we should not be ignorant of Satan and his devices. Dear Christian, Satan would like nothing more than to rob you of your peace. And he will do anything to steal that peace, even send a Judas in your life. I have had this happen in my life more than once, and it is a difficult to remain peaceful when someone betrays you, someone whom you thought was one of your closest friends. But it is possible. *What is the cure for this peace-stealer, the devil? The cure for this is to be alert, to resist him, and to remain steadfast in the faith.* Consider Peter's words in 1 Peter 5:8-9 (LSB): "Be of sober spirit, be watchful. Your adversary, the devil, prowls around like a roaring lion, seeking someone to devour. But resist him, firm in the faith, knowing that the same experiences of suffering are being accomplished among your brethren who are in the world." Ladies, we must be sober, be vigilant, be on the alert, because our adversary the devil, like a roaring lion, is walking about seeking for those he can devour. And here is the key: resist him, stand fast against him, remain steadfast in your faith. Run away from his temptations, as Joseph did when he fled when the enemy tempted him with Potiphar's wife (Genesis 39). Do not give in to his tactics! Jesus wants His disciples to know that He has nothing to do with Satan, so He adds *he has nothing in Me*. He has no authority over Me! Jesus had no fear of Satan because Satan had no claim on Him. He will conquer death and He will conquer the enemy, Satan. Even though from day one Satan tried to destroy Jesus, Satan had nothing in Him. There is no link of any kind that exists between Jesus and Satan. So then, you might be wondering, why is Jesus about to yield to Satan and his plan to have our Lord murdered? Well, Jesus answers that question in verse 31.

> "But that the world may know that I love the Father, and as the Father gave Me commandment, so I do. Arise, let us go from here." (John 14:31)

In contrast to Satan, with whom Jesus has no part, the world will *know*, or recognize, that Jesus loves the Father. Jesus had nothing to do with Satan, with evil. Instead, He was going to the cross so that the world would know that He *loved the Father*. His love for His Father was manifested by His obedience in going to the cross; that was the Father's plan from the beginning. This act of love would get the attention of the world. How was Christ's love for His Father manifested? The same way yours and mine is. Notice what Jesus says: *as the Father gave Me commandment, so I do*. In all things Jesus obeyed the Father, even in the face of calamities, persecutions, temptations, and death. Remember what He prayed in Matthew 26:39 in the garden? "My Father, if it is possible, let this cup pass from Me; yet not as I will, but as You will" (LSB). Jesus obeyed His Father so that the world might know that He loved His Father. Obeying the Lord is an evidence of our love for Him, and this is the same truth that Jesus has been trying to teach His disciples throughout His time with them (see 14:21-24).

Christ ends by saying *arise, let us go from here*. This seems like a curious thing for Jesus to say at this point. Did He and the disciples actually leave the upper room at this point? Some scholars think that they did, and that what occurs in chapters 15-17 unfolds as the disciples were on their way to the Garden. But let's look at John 18:1-4:

> When Jesus had spoken these words, He went out with His disciples over the Brook Kidron, where there was a garden, which He and His disciples entered. And Judas, who betrayed Him, also knew the place; for Jesus often met there with His disciples. Then Judas, having received a detachment of troops, and officers from the chief priests and Pharisees, came there with lanterns, torches, and weapons. Jesus therefore, knowing all things that would come upon Him, went forward and said to them, "Whom are you seeking?"

This occurred after the time in the upper room, so what is most probable is that Jesus' directive about arising and going simply indicates that they got up from the couches where they had been dining and that they lingered in an outer room until Jesus finished speaking the next three chapters. They had already been together for several hours and, as I mentioned, the next few chapters could be spoken in about 10 minutes. It is doubtful that the next three chapters were spoken while they were in motion, and John doesn't indicate that they stopped along the way at all. Most all of you can identify with this: You have company over for dinner or you're at someone's house for dinner, and it is time to go; you get up from the meal to leave, but the conversation continues in another room or even at the door for a long time. It was about midnight at this point in John's account, and the scene we're witnessing is of great interest and tenderness. Jesus is saying to them, "Arise, let's go. I am going to meet my death." *The fifth peace-stealer we see is the fear of the unknown.* The disciples have no idea what is ahead for them and for their Lord. It is an unrestful time. What will happen to their Lord in His coming hours? What will happen to them? When will Peter deny Him? When will Judas betray Him? When is the prince of this world coming? What will he do? We, too, can be robbed of peace if we dwell on the fear of the unknown. What if I lose my husband, or my child? What if I get cancer? All the "what ifs" we women too often dwell on can rob of us our peace. *What is the cure for the fear of the unknown? Isaiah 26:3 has the cure: keep your mind fixed upon God.* "You will keep him in perfect peace, whose mind is stayed on You, because he trusts in You." The key is get your mind off the "what ifs," the unknowns, and focus on the solution, which is to trust in God. Keep your mind fixed upon Him. If we would spend more time trusting God, we wouldn't be so worried about all the "what ifs." We would understand that all the "what ifs" are in the loving arms of a Sovereign God.

Summary

What are the five peace-stealers?

1. *A fearful or troubled heart.* Jesus said, "Let not your heart be troubled." What is the cure? Pray and seek God's Kingdom.

2. *Change in relationships.* Jesus said, "I am going away." What is the cure? Remember the sovereignty of God and the comfort of the Holy Spirit.

3. *Lack of love for God.* Jesus said, "If you loved me you would rejoice." What is the cure? Repent of your lack of love for God and do the things you did when you first trusted Christ.

4. *Satan.* Jesus said, "The ruler of this world is coming." What is the cure? Be alert to His devices, resist Him, and remain steadfast in the faith.

5. *Fear of the unknown.* "Arise let us go from here." What is the cure? Trust God for your future.

Are you experiencing God's peace? Is there something that is robbing you of your peace? Do you have a fearful and troubled heart over a situation you can't control? My dear sister, pray and seek heavenly things. Or maybe it is a change you're experiencing in a relationship. A son or daughter has left home for college or is getting married. A friend is moving away. Your husband has divorced you. A parent has died. Remember that God is sovereign and cling to the comfort of His dear Holy Spirit. Is it a lack of love for the Lord that has stolen your peace; has your heart become cold and calloused? Repent, dear one, and do what you did when you first loved Christ. Perhaps it is Satan who has taken your peace. Ladies, be sober and alert to what he uses in your life, resist him, and remain steadfast in your faith. Maybe it is the fear of tomorrow, the fear of the unknown, that is stealing your peace. Trust in God, dear one. For the Christian, there is no excuse for lack of peace. Jesus said, "Peace I leave with you, My peace I give unto you." Nothing that you and I are facing today should rob us of the peace that is promised to us, the peace that surpasses all understanding.

Many years ago, I had a friend who died of ovarian cancer. In her last days, she asked for a certain song to be played over and over again; its lyrics brought her peace. I want to end this chapter with an invitation for you to locate the song "Rest" by Steve Green and allow the words to permeate your heart and mind. Dear friend, think of the things that rob you of your peace and determine to be at peace, no matter what!

QUESTIONS TO CONSIDER

1. (a) Read John 14 and list your favorite promises. (b) How are these promises a personal comfort to you? (c) Spend some time thanking God for each promise. (d) How could you use these promises to help someone who is going through troubling times?

2. Memorize John 14:27.

3. Jesus says in John 10:30, "I and My Father are one." Since that is true, what does Jesus mean in John 14:28, when He says, "For My Father is greater than I"? Prove your answer from the Scriptures.

4. (a) What do the following verses say about peace? Psalms 29:11; 72:7; 85:10; Isaiah 9:6-7; 26:3; 32:17; John 16:33; Romans 5:1; 8:6. (b) What comfort do these verses provide?

5. (a) According to Philippians 4:6-7, what is God's antidote for anxiety? (b) How does God's peace affect a believer's heart and mind?

6. (a) What is the requirement for acquiring peace, according to John 16:33 and 1 Peter 5:14? (b) What does the God of peace desire to accomplish within you, according to 1 Thessalonians 5:23 and Hebrews 13:20-21?

7. (a) Write down all the things that could or that are stealing your peace. (b) What is the remedy for peace in each one of these things?

8. After prayerfully considering question number seven, please write down your need in the form of a prayer request.

The Vine and the Branches
(Are You Producing Fruit?)
John 15:1-6

JOHN Bunyan once said, "It is said that in some countries trees will grow, but will bear no fruit, because there is no winter there."[1]

Fruit-bearing. What exactly is it? And what is the process the Lord uses in our lives to make sure that you and I are bearing such fruit for His Kingdom? This chapter will provide tremendous help for all of us who desire to bear fruit for our Lord. As we listen in on our Lord's words regarding fruit-bearing, remember that the scene in which these words are spoken is just after the Lord has given His disciples the promise of peace. He's just said to them, "Arise, let us go from here." They're still in the upper room, and they've risen from the couches where they were eating, and they're probably lingering in an outer room near the upper room. It is about midnight now, and Jesus says in John 15:1-6:

> "I am the true vine, and My Father is the vinedresser. Every branch in Me that does not bear fruit He takes away; and every branch that bears fruit He prunes, that it may bear more fruit. You are already clean because of the word which I have spoken to you. Abide in Me, and I in you. As the branch cannot bear fruit of itself, unless it abides in the vine, neither can you, unless you abide in Me.
>
> "I am the vine, you are the branches. He who abides in Me, and I in him, bears much fruit; for without Me you can do nothing. If anyone does not abide in Me, he is cast out as a branch and is withered; and they gather them and throw them into the fire, and they are burned."

In our last chapter, we discovered five peace-stealers that Christ mentions to His disciples as well as the five cures for those peace-stealers. 1. A fearful or troubled heart: "Let not your heart be troubled." What is the

---
[1] George Offor, ed., *The Works of John Bunyan: Vol. II*, "Seasonable Counsel," (Glasgow: Blackie and Son, 1862), 694.

cure for a troubled heart? Pray and seek God's Kingdom. 2. A change in relationships: "I am going away." What is the cure? Remember the sovereignty of God and the comfort of the Holy Spirit. 3. A lack of love for God: "If you loved me you would rejoice." What is the cure? Repent of your lack of love for God and do the things you did when you first trusted Christ. 4. Satan: "The ruler of this world is coming." What is the cure? Be alert to his devices and resist him. 5. Fear of the unknown: "Arise, let us go from here." What is the cure? Trust God for your future.

We left off at the end of John 14 with Christ informing His disciples that He would not be talking much longer with them, because the prince of the world is coming. The transition into the parable before us seems very clear. It's as if Jesus is saying, "Men, if you want to avoid the tactics of the enemy, the one who is the prince of this world, then you'll need to abide in Me, because without Me you're not going to be able to do anything!" As we consider this abiding, this chapter will draw our attention to: *The Persons Involved* (vv 1-2); *The Pruning Tool* (v 3); *The Point of the Parable* (v 4); *The Purpose of Abiding* (v 5); and *The Punishment of the Pretenders* (v 6). Let's consider this parable of the vine and the branches and look first at the persons involved, in verses 1 and 2.

The Persons Involved *John 15:1-2*

"I am the true vine, and My Father is the vinedresser." (John 15:1)

Christ begins by telling His disciples that He is *the True Vine*. You might recall some of the other metaphors Christ has used in the Gospel of John to describe Himself: the Bread of Life, in John 6:35; the Light of the World, in John 8:12; the Door, in John 10:7; the Shepherd, in John 10:11; the Resurrection and the Life, in John 11:25; and the Way, the Truth, and the Life, in John 14:6. Here, in John 15, He refers to Himself as the Vine, and not just the Vine, but the True Vine. He has used this word true in the Gospel of John when describing Himself as the True Light, in John 1:9, and as the True Bread, in John 6:32. When Jesus says He is *the True Vine*, what does He mean? To describe Himself as *true* means that He is genuine, He is real. It is possible that Jesus has in mind here the analogy of the vine in the Old Testament as it relates to Israel. You saw some of these when you completed the *Questions to Consider* that accompany this chapter (Psalm 80:8-16; Isaiah 5:1-7; Jeremiah 2:21; Ezekiel 15; Hosea 10:1). All of these Old Testament passages refer to Israel's unfaithfulness. In fact, in every instance when Israel is described as the vine, it is while she is also under the judgment of God. God intended for the nation of Israel to bring forth fruit, but she did not. In fact, in Hosea 10:1, Israel is referred to as an empty vine. In Isaiah 5:4, Isaiah said that God looked for Israel to bring forth good grapes, but she brought forth only wild grapes. In biblical times, the vine was the symbol of the nation of Israel and was even found on coins during the Maccabean period. During the time of Christ, Herod's Temple had engraved on it a vine overlaid with gold that some have estimated was worth $12 million. Israel was the vine of the Old Testament—but Christ is the Vine of the New Testament. Jesus describing Himself as the True Vine paints a vivid contrast to Israel as the unfaithful vine. So, the image of a vine would be something the disciples could identify with. Grape vines grew all over the land of Israel; in fact, they still do to this day. They grow on terraces and around the doors of houses, and I just imagine that one could even be seen at this very moment from a window in the upper room where Jesus was with the eleven disciples. Christ may even have been pointing at one as He spoke these words. (As we learned in our last chapter, "Arise, let us go from here," did not necessarily mean that they had already left the upper room.)

Just what does a *vine* do? A vine yields proper water and nourishment to all its branches, whether they be large or small. All the nourishment for each branch and tendril passes through the main stalk, the vine, that is rooted in the ground. So when Jesus is saying that He is the Vine, He is saying that He is the source of all real strength and grace for His disciples; He is their nourishment. So keep that reality in mind as we study this parable. When Jesus says, "I am the True Vine," He's saying, "I am the true source of all of your nourishment."

But someone else is the Vinedresser. Jesus says *My Father is the vinedresser*. What is a vinedresser? A vinedresser is a land worker, a farmer, a husbandman. He is responsible for the care of a vineyard, and he nurtures, trims, and defends the vine. He protects the vine, watches over it, and is faithful in that work. He has a deep interest in its growth and welfare. Because of that, He also is responsible to prune any branches that do not bear fruit. And it is that fruit which the Lord speaks of next, in verse 2. That fruit comes from the third person involved in this parable: the branches. And the Lord mentions two kinds of branches: those that bear fruit and those that do not.

> "Every branch in Me that does not bear fruit He takes away; and every branch that bears fruit He prunes, that it may bear more fruit." (John 15:2)

First of all, notice that both kinds of branches are in Him—that is, in Christ—one kind is bearing fruit and one is not. The first one *does not bear fruit*. So what does the Father, the Vinedresser, do to those that are not bearing fruit? Those branches *He takes away*. Now, this phrase has been understood by some to be a purging away of dead branches in precisely the same sense that branches are said to be cast forth and burned in verse 6. But that interpretation presents a lot of problems, because the verse here says these branches are in Christ, and we know that those who are in Christ are eternally secure. The Greek words for *in Me* mean to be in a fixed permanent position and the word for *Me* means mine. We must also remember that Christ is addressing true believers; Judas has already gone out from among them at this point. Jesus doesn't say these branches never bore fruit, but they are not bearing fruit now for some unspecified reason. The tense reads like this: "every branch in Me not bearing fruit He takes away." In the physical realm there are three things which cause branches to quit bearing fruit. Those three things are disease, old age, and running to leaf, which means they produce only leaves due to a lack of adequate minerals and nutrients. Disease in the physical realm would represent sin in the spiritual realm. Old age is a reality in both the physical and spiritual realms, but we should never let old age prevent us from being fruit-bearers. A lack of minerals and nutrients in the physical realm would represent a lack of spiritual food—the nourishment of the Word of God—in the spiritual realm. Peter tells us in 1 Peter that we are to be like newborn babies when it comes to our appetite for the Word of God. Just as a newborn babe needs the physical nourishment of milk for its physical growth, so we will only grow spiritually by the spiritual nourishment of the Word (1 Peter 2:2).

Ladies, there are also things in our own lives that cause us to become unfruitful. While we don't have space here to look at all of the Scriptures that pertain to this, Peter addresses the importance of having certain things present in our lives, lest we become unfruitful. Consider 2 Peter 1:5-8 (LSB): "Now for this very reason also, applying all diligence, in your faith supply moral excellence, and in your moral excellence, knowledge, and in your knowledge, self-control, and in your self-control, perseverance, and in your perseverance, godliness, and in your godliness, brotherly kindness, and in your brotherly kindness, love. For if these things are yours and are increasing, they render you neither useless nor unfruitful in the full knowledge of our Lord Jesus Christ." The clear implication of Peter's words is that if these things are missing from our lives, you and I can become barren and unfruitful. We need to be examining our lives to make sure that we are indeed bearing fruit.

So, if Jesus is saying that these branches in verse 2 are genuine believers—which they are—what does Jesus mean that the vinedresser takes them away? The words *takes away* are translated from the Greek word *airo*, which means to lift up or pick up. We get our English word airplane from this word *airo*. Every branch in Christ that does not bear fruit, He lifts up, so as to keep it from trailing on the ground. This would indicate that the Vinedresser, the Father, lifts the branches up so that they are exposed to the sun and the fruit is able to develop properly. In the physical sense, vine branches must hang free to be given a chance to properly develop; by lifting those branches up into the sunlight, the vinedresser facilitates this, while also carefully removing from the vine any insects, moss, or parasites which might be hindering its growth. In the spiritual sense, this lifting up would mean that God lifts up the believer, carefully inspecting our lives for reasons that we are not bearing fruit, and removing those things that might be hindering our fruit-bearing. Those hindrances might include a friendship, a material possession, or an idol in your life.

The word for *branch* is interesting itself; it refers to offshoots of the vine, the tender and easily broken parts, including all the smallest tendrils that shoot out from the parent stalk. This makes sense in the spiritual sense as well, because some weaker Christians or new Christians are not bearing fruit as they should for one reason or another, and so the Father tenderly lifts them up and cares for them so that they go on developing properly and producing fruit.

Now, before we go on to consider the second part of this verse, I want to make it clear that the Scriptures do teach that a Christian will bear fruit (consider Matthew 7:15-20; Matthew 13:18-30; John 15:16; Galatians 5:22-23). Some will bear more fruit than others, certainly, but for a believer to live their entire life not bearing fruit is totally contrary to the teaching of Scripture. What we have pictured here in this verse is those believers who, for one reason or another, have stopped bearing fruit for a period of time and the Father gently lifting them up to encourage them to be fruitful. Now, let me also say here that it would be a dangerous thing to continue on in such a barren state, failing to produce appropriate fruit. A Christian who continues to be stagnant in his or her walk, who stops producing fruit, is setting themselves up for serious judgment from the Lord, possibly even death, according to 1 John 5:16-17. Jesus makes abundantly clear in the parable of the soils, in Matthew 13, that the only one who is saved is the one who produces fruit.

In the second part of this verse, Jesus mentions the second type of branch: *every branch that bears fruit*. What does the vinedresser do to this kind of branch? *He prunes* it, *that it may bear more fruit*. This pruning would serve to clean up or purify the branch. God purifies or prunes all true Christians so that they may become more useful. Ladies, God doesn't want you to just get by in your Christian walk and bear a little fruit; He wants you to bring forth *more fruit*. And He wants you to continue to bear fruit even into your old age, as Psalm 92:13-14 says, "Those who are planted in the house of the LORD shall flourish in the courts of our God. They shall still bear fruit in old age; they shall be fresh and flourishing."

It was such a joy for me personally to observe my Dad, who lived to be 96, bearing fruit in his old age. He continued teaching the Bible till he was 93, always talked about the Lord, read the Word, prayed, and looked for opportunities to share the gospel! That's fruit in old age! In fact, look over at what Jesus says in John 15:16, "You did not choose Me, but I chose you and appointed you that you should go and bear fruit, and that your fruit should remain, that whatever you ask the Father in My name He may give you." It is God's will for us to bear fruit. That is why He saved us!

Now, how does the vinedresser go about this pruning of the branches? Respected Bible commentator, Albert Barnes, helps us here as he describes the pruning process:

> He takes away that which hinders their usefulness; teaches them, quickens them, revives them, makes them more pure in motive and in life. This He does by the regular influences of His Spirit in sanctifying them, purifying their motives, and teaching them the beauty of holiness. He does it by taking away what opposes their usefulness, however much they may be attached to it, or however painful to part with it; as a vine-dresser will often feel himself compelled to lop off a branch that is large, apparently thrifty, and handsome, but which bears no fruit, and which shades or injures those which do. So God often takes away the property of His people, their children, or other idols. He removes the objects which bind their affections, and which render them inactive. He takes away the things around man, as He did the valued gourds of Jonah, so that he may feel his dependence and live more to the honor of God and bring forth more proof of humble and active piety.[2]

If the Vinedresser has ever pruned you, then you know what Barnes is saying. It is a needed, but often painful, process. Perhaps you have an idol in your heart or a friendship that is pulling you away from devotion to God. Trials are often the means by which this pruning takes place in our lives, so that we become more fruitful. And even though that pruning is painful at times, we are often able to look back and thank God for it, because now our lives are lived more for His glory because of it. Jesus put it well in John 12:24 (LSB), when He said, "Truly, truly, I say to you, unless a grain of wheat falls into the earth and dies, it remains alone; but if it dies, it bears much fruit." But what is the instrument by which our Father, the Vinedresser, does this pruning? What exactly is the pruning tool? Jesus answers that in verse 3.

---

2 Albert Barnes, *Barnes' Notes*, 337.

The Pruning Tool   *John 15:3*

> "You are already clean because of the word which I have spoken to you." (John 15:3)

What does Jesus mean when He says *you are already clean*? This is an emphatic statement, so it means already you are clean. The word *clean* refers to purity in a spiritual sense, being clean from the pollution and guilt of sin. How is this done? Jesus says it is *because of the word which I have spoken to you*. The divine pruning instrument is God's Word; this blessed knife cuts deep into our souls. The word for *word* here is the Greek word *logos*, which indicates the whole teaching of Christ. The writer to the Hebrews says, "For the word of God is living and active and sharper than any two-edged sword, and piercing as far as the division of soul and spirit, of both joints and marrow, and able to judge the thoughts and intentions of the heart" (Hebrews 4:12 LSB). Also, the Psalmist says, in Psalm 119:9, that the Word is how young men are kept clean: "How can a young man keep his way pure? By keeping it according to Your word" (LSB). The Word of God condemns sin, inspires holiness, and promotes growth. I like what Spurgeon says:

> It is *the Word* that prunes the Christian, it is the truth that purges him, the Scripture, made living and powerful by the Holy Spirit, which effectually cleanses the Christian.... Affliction is the handle of the knife. Affliction is the grindstone that sharpens the Word. Affliction is the dresser that removes our soft garments, and lays bare the diseased flesh, so that the surgeon's lancet may get at it. Affliction merely makes us ready to feel the Word, but the true pruner is the Word in the hand of the Great Husbandman.[3]

There is nothing like the truth of God's Word to prune the believer and make her more fruitful.

The Lord goes on in the next verse to remind His disciples of the importance of abiding in Him—and this is the point of the parable.

---

[3] Charles H. Spurgeon, "A Sharp Knife for the Vine-Branches," *Spurgeon Gems,* http://www.spurgeongems.org/vols13-15/chs774.pdf. Accessed 9/22/2023.

By the way, when you read a parable in Scripture, you shouldn't analyze it to death, as some try to do. There is usually one main truth that the Spirit is conveying. In this parable, the main point is that we ought to abide in Christ.

The Point of the Parable — John 15:4

> "Abide in Me, and I in you. As the branch cannot bear fruit of itself, unless it abides in the vine, neither can you, unless you abide in Me." (John 15:4)

The condition of a fruitful life is abiding in Christ. What does it mean to *abide in* Christ? It means to remain or to dwell. Now, you might be wondering how this abiding is done, and there are several ways this abiding is done. First, a believer who is abiding in Christ is continually in contact with Him in prayer, as Paul says we are to pray without ceasing. Second, a believer who is abiding in Christ is thinking on Him throughout the day, consciously remaining in His presence as a regular practice. Third, a believer who is abiding in Christ is meditating regularly on the Word, reading and studying what God says and allowing it to permeate her thinking.

When you think about it, you and I have many relationships with others and we spend a great deal of time cultivating those relationships. But how much time do you and I spend cultivating the most important relationship we have, that of our heavenly Father? We must actively maintain a vital spiritual connection with Christ. Oswald Chambers says: "*Get a move on*; begin to abide *now*. In the initial stages it is a continual effort until it becomes so much the law of life that you abide in Him unconsciously. Determine to abide in Jesus wherever you are placed."[4]

Not only must we abide in Him, but Jesus also says *and I in you*. He has already told the disciples of this great mystery, this great promise, in John

---

4 Taken from *My Utmost for His Highest*, classic edition, ©1927 in the UK by Oswald Chambers Publications Association, Ltd., on behalf of Oswald and Gertrude (Biddy) Chambers and ©1935 by Dodd, Mead & Company, Inc. Copyright renewed in the USA 1963 by Oswald Chambers Publications Association, Ltd. All rights reserved., 166.

14:20. (Just a side note: Did you notice that all three of the Godhead play a part in this parable of the vine and the branches? Christ is the Vine; the Father is the Vinedresser; and when Christ says *I in you*, He is referring to the indwelling Holy Spirit.) He also adds *as the branch cannot bear fruit of itself, unless it abides in the vine, neither can you, unless you abide in Me*. A *branch cannot bear fruit* lying around by itself; it has to be connected to the vine. I have taken leaves and branches off of plants, and I will tell you that, if left alone, they will die. Those branches have to be connected to a main vine to survive. Christ is saying that we cannot produce spiritual fruit without a vital connection to Him. If you are not abiding in Christ, the Vine, then I can guarantee that you are barren and unfruitful.

What is the purpose of this abiding? Jesus gives the answer in verse 5: that we might bear fruit.

The Purpose of Abiding *John 15:5*

> "I am the vine, you are the branches. He who abides in Me, and I in him, bears much fruit; for without Me you can do nothing." (John 15:5)

Jesus repeats again what He has already said, that He is *the vine*. And then He reminds His disciples that they are *the branches*. Sometimes, I am afraid we like to think that we are the Vine and He is the branch, but we are not the Vine, despite what our narcissistic world tells us.

Next, Christ gives us a wonderful promise. If we are abiding in Him, and He is in us, then we *bear much fruit*. And notice that it is *much* fruit, which is an abundance of fruit. I don't know about you, but I desire to bring forth much fruit for the Lord. So the question we might ask is, "What is fruit?" If you looked up the verses on the *Questions to Consider* that accompany this chapter, then you saw the many kinds of fruit that we should be producing. Sometimes we think of fruit in a believer's life as only the fruit of the Spirit mentioned in Galatians 5, but Scripture shows us many other types of fruit that we should be bearing: the fruit of our lips, the fruit of our thoughts, the fruit of our actions, the fruit of repentance, just to name a few.

Now, my friend, you cannot produce this fruit on your own, and if you've ever tried, you know it doesn't work. Jesus puts it this way: *for without me you can do nothing*. Without Him we can do *nothing*! Not one thing. The words *without me* mean separate from me. Separate from Christ, you can do nothing. We, as the branches, are absolutely dependent on Jesus, the Vine. Sadly, modern-day Christianity would like to reword this phrase to say, "Without us, He can do nothing!" We have come to the delusion that Christ can't carry out His work without us and that we are something special, but the truth of the matter is this: without Him, it is we who can do nothing. Have you ever tried to serve the Lord in your own flesh? It doesn't work, does it? When I try to minister in my own strength, it is fruitless. But when I am depending on the strength of the Lord and know I can do nothing of myself, the Lord seems to use those times in tremendous ways, and I step back and think, "Who was that? It wasn't me!" You and I are just vessels He chooses to use for His service—and, ladies, it is a humble honor to be able to serve the Lord!

Well, we end on a sobering note, found in verse 6. Here, we find the punishment of the pretenders.

The Punishment of the Pretenders — John 15:6

> "If anyone does not abide in Me, he is cast out as a branch and is withered; and they gather them and throw them into the fire, and they are burned." (John 15:6)

The key to understanding what Jesus is saying here is in the word *not*. Jesus says here: *If a man does not abide in Me*. In other words, this person never has been genuinely connected to the Vine. If a man is not truly united to Christ by faith, then he is not abiding in Christ and never has. These individuals are those who profess Christianity but do not possess any true connection with Christ. And, sadly, our churches are full of them. If a man does not truly abide in Christ, then *he is cast forth as a branch and is withered*. Note: he is not a branch but is cast forth *as* a branch. The word *withered* means to shrivel or pine away. Souls who are not truly connected with the Vine are like that, aren't they? We often meet "professing Christians" and wonder where the life, the joy, the peace, and the fruit are in their lives? They seem liked dried-up prunes! And after a while, you wonder, "Are they truly connected?" They're not. Genuine saving faith does not lie dormant, devoid of any spiritual life. Where there is no fruit, there is no life. Let me repeat that: Where there is no fruit, there is no life.

Jesus ends with these sobering words regarding those who do not abide in Him: *and they gather them and throw them into the fire, and they are burned*. It is interesting that up until now Christ has been using the pronouns *you* and *me*, and now he says *them*, referring to a different class of people, a class of people who are of the mindset of Judas. Perhaps the disciples will remember this vivid parable after the soon betrayal of Judas. As Jesus said in Matthew 26:24b (LSB) regarding Judas, "It would have been good for that man if he had not been born."

You might be wondering what Christ is referring to here when He says that *they are thrown into the fire*. What is Christ talking about here? Let's consider Jesus' words in Matthew 13:24-30 and 36-43.

> Another parable He put forth to them, saying: "The kingdom of heaven is like a man who sowed good seed in his field; but while men slept, his enemy came and sowed tares among the wheat and went his way. But when the grain had sprouted and produced a crop, then the tares also appeared. So the servants of the owner came and said to him, 'Sir, did you not sow good seed in your field? How then does it have tares?' He said to them, 'An enemy has done this.' The servants said to him, 'Do you want us then to go and gather them up?' But he said, 'No, lest while you gather up the tares you also uproot the wheat with them. Let both grow together until the harvest, and at the time of harvest I will say to the reapers, "First gather together the tares and bind them in bundles to burn them, but gather the wheat into my barn."'" (Matthew 13:24-30)
>
> Then Jesus sent the multitude away and went into the house. And His disciples came to Him, saying, "Explain to us the parable of the tares of the field."
>
> He answered and said to them: "He who sows the good seed is the Son of Man. The field is the world, the good seeds are the sons of the

kingdom, but the tares are the sons of the wicked one. The enemy who sowed them is the devil, the harvest is the end of the age, and the reapers are the angels. Therefore as the tares are gathered and burned in the fire, so it will be at the end of this age. The Son of Man will send out His angels, and they will gather out of His kingdom all things that offend, and those who practice lawlessness, and will cast them into the furnace of fire. There will be wailing and gnashing of teeth. Then the righteous will shine forth as the sun in the kingdom of their Father. He who has ears to hear, let him hear!" (Matthew 13:36-43)

It appears from these passages that the angels will do the gathering, and it will be the hypocrites who are gathered up for fuel to be burned in everlasting punishment. These are the pretenders, the tares, the ones who profess to be connected to the Vine but who are not actually connected to the Vine, and they will be burned forever. These are certainly very sobering words to end on, but words which should cause us to examine ourselves. We are either vitally connected to the Vine and bringing forth fruit, or we have spuriously attached ourselves and in the end will be discovered to be hypocrites.

Summary

In this parable of the vine and the branches, we have learned of the persons involved, and they are the Vine, the Vinedresser, and the branches (vv 1-2). We have learned of the pruning tool, which is Word of God (v 3). We have come to understand the point of the parable, which is for us to abide in Christ (v 4). We have seen that the purpose of abiding is for us to bear fruit (v 5). And we have been sobered by the punishment of the pretenders, which will be eternal fire (v 6).

As we bring this chapter to a close, let's evaluate our personal lives by asking ourselves some questions that I trust you will answer honestly. Are you abiding in Christ? Do you have an ongoing, vital connection to Christ through His Word and prayer? Is He alone your nourishment for your soul? Do you deem His words to be of more value than your necessary food?

Are you bearing fruit for your Lord? Would others look at your life and say, "There's a woman who is abiding in Christ and bringing forth much fruit"? If you're not bearing fruit, why not? Is the Lord trying to prune you so that you can bring forth much fruit for His glory? Are you allowing the pruning process? If you have never produced fruit, have you asked yourself why?

Are you genuinely connected to the Vine? I can think of no better way to begin this day than to make sure you are truly connected to the Vine. I beg you to not put it off, but be reconciled to God! For those of you who are connected to the Vine and are bearing fruit, are you endeavoring to bring forth more and more fruit?

When your works are judged by fire, as Paul in 1 Corinthians 3 says they will, will those works be wood, hay, and stubble, which will not withstand the fire, or will they be gold, silver, and precious stones, lasting for all eternity? When you stand before the Lord on that day, and your works are put to this test of fire, will they be burned up like ash, or will they be beautiful rewards? Will the ashes start at your feet and continue rising above your body as you enter into eternity with a handful of rewards? Or will your works stand the test of fire, and as you go into eternity, will you cast your beautiful crowns at the foot of the Savior? Ladies, this is forever, for eternity. I don't know about you, but I desire to hear from my blessed Savior, "Well done, good and faithful slave. You were faithful with a few things, I will put you in charge of many things; enter into the joy of your master" (Matthew 25:21b LSB).

QUESTIONS TO CONSIDER

1. (a) Read John 15, making note of the characteristics that should be evident in the life of a believer. (b) How do you see believers manifesting these things?

2. Memorize John 15:5.

3. Read John 15:1-6 in order to answer the following questions. (a) Who is the Vine? (b) What is the purpose of the Vine? (c) What happens to those who abide in the Vine? (d) What happens to those who do not abide in the Vine? (e) What does Jesus mean in verse 2, when He says, "Every branch in Me that does not bear fruit He takes away?" Prove your answer from the Bible.

4. Read the following passages to understand the connection between the vine and Israel and also to answer the following questions. Psalm 80:8-16; Isaiah 5:1-7; Jeremiah 2:21; Ezekiel 15; and Hosea 10:1. (a) What was God's desire for the nation of Israel? (b) What happened instead? (c) How does this help you understand why Christ refers to Himself as the True Vine in John 15? (d) What do you notice that is similar in all of these passages?

5. (a) According to the following verses, what is the fruit we should be producing as Christians? Proverbs 11:30; 18:21; 31:31; Isaiah 3:10; Jeremiah 17:10; Matthew 3:8; Romans 6:22; Galatians 5:22-23; Ephesians 5:9-10; Philippians 4:17; Hebrews 12:11; 13:15; James 3:18. (b) Which of these fruits are you producing? Which of these fruits do you need to begin producing? (Personal questions)

6. (a) What is God's will for the believer, according to Matthew 25:14-30; John 15:16; and Ephesians 2:10? (b) Do you think it is possible for a believer not to bear fruit? Why or why not? Prove your answer from the Word of God.

7. What evidence is there in your life that you are abiding in the Vine?

8. (a) Share a time in your life when you knew the Vinedresser (the Father) pruned you. (b) What did you learn? (c) What were the results?

9. (a) What counsel would you give to someone who claims attachment to Christ (the Vine), and yet bears no fruit? (b) Are you willing to share your concern with them? (See Ezekiel 33:8)

10. What changes need to be made in your life so that you might bear more fruit for our Lord? Please write your need in the form of a prayer request.

The Blessings of Abiding in Christ
John 15:7-11

THERE are times in our lives as believers that we are plagued with thoughts like, "The Christian life is too hard. The struggles are too great. There are too many trials, too many persecutions, and too much suffering." Have you ever found yourself thinking those kinds of thoughts? If we're honest with ourselves, I'm sure each of us have. I know that I have had those thoughts from time to time, only to then bring myself back to the truth that Christ said these things would indeed happen. In fact, I should not be surprised by them, and I should embrace them with joy. Meditating on these truths brings needed comfort.

But it's worth asking the question, "Is the Christian life nothing but sorrow and woe?" There are some people who will try to convince you of that, but it certainly is not true. There are blessings for the believer that are almost impossible to number! We could spend an entire day rehearsing the blessings of God in our lives and still could not exhaust them all. Proverbs 28:20 encourages us with this reality: "A faithful man will abound with blessings." In this chapter, we are indeed going to focus on the blessings of being a believer. We'll take a look at four of those blessings, to be exact. I trust they will be an encouragement to your heart. Let's read John 15:7-11 to discover these blessings.

> "If you abide in Me, and My words abide in you, you will ask what you desire, and it shall be done for you. By this My Father is glorified, that you bear much fruit; so you will be My disciples.
>
> "As the Father loved Me, I also have loved you; abide in My love. If you keep My commandments, you will abide in My love, just as I have kept My Father's commandments and abide in His love.
>
> "These things I have spoken to you, that My joy may remain in you, and that your joy may be full."

Our outline for this chapter will focus our attention on four blessings of abiding in Christ, and they will all start with the letter F: *The Blessing of Faithful Answered Prayer* (v 7); *The Blessing of Fruit-Bearing* (v 8); *The Blessing of the Father's Love* (vv 9-10); and *The Blessing of Fullness of Joy* (v 11).

We began our last chapter by looking in John 15:1-6 at the parable of the vine and the branches. We saw the persons involved, which were the Vine, the Vinedresser, and the branches. We learned that the pruning tool is the Word of God. We discovered that the point of the parable is that we are to abide in Christ. We saw that the purpose of abiding is to bear fruit. And we ended on a sober note, that the punishment of the pretenders is eternal fire.

It's likely that the words just spoken by Christ in verse 6 were grievous to the eleven disciples (John 15:6, "If anyone does not abide in Me, he is cast out as a branch and is withered; and they gather them and throw them into the fire, and they are burned."). They might have been thinking of Judas, whom Jesus said would betray Him, and of Jesus' words to Peter about how he would deny Jesus. Perhaps, the disciples were not really relishing the idea that they too might be among those who are not abiding in Christ. So Christ turns now from the subject of those who are not abiding in Him, to those who are abiding and the blessings that come with that abiding, blessings which are theirs to enjoy.

The Blessing of Faithful Answered Prayer   *John 15:7*

> "If you abide in Me, and My words abide in you, you will ask what you desire, and it shall be done for you." (John 15:7)

There are some in our day and age who have taken verse seven and have said, "Great! I can have anything I want from God!" Boy, are they wrong! There are two conditions here in this verse for answered prayer and, of course, many other conditions in other parts of Scripture for having our prayers answered. Let's look at condition number one of answered prayer, according to this text. First, we must abide in Christ. Jesus says *if you abide in Me*. To *abide* in Him means we remain or dwell in Him. It is to maintain a spirit of absolute, entire dependency on Him. One writer puts it this way: "To abide in Christ means to keep up a habit of constant close communication with Him—to be always leaning on Him, resting on Him, pouring out our hearts to Him, and using Him as our Fountain of life and strength, as our chief Companion and best Friend."[1] One of the marks of a true believer is that he or she abides in Christ. That is the first condition of having your prayers answered.

The second condition of answered prayer that Jesus mentions here is that *My words abide in you.* What does it mean that His words abide in us? His *words* would refer to all that He has communicated to His people, especially His commands; it would indicate the operative and all-powerful word or command of God. So God's words must abide, dwell, remain in us. This means that the Scriptures must regulate our lives. Hasn't Christ already referred to this in John 14:23 and 15:3? The words of Christ must control our lives. This would imply that we know the word, study the word, and apply the word to the way we think and live our lives. Paul tells the church at Colossae, in Colossians 3:16a (LSB), "Let the word of Christ dwell in you richly." The church at Colossae would have had a special challenge in letting the word of Christ dwell in them because most New Testament saints did not have a written copy of the Word. They would have to have been hiding God's Word in their heart by memorization in order for it to abide in them richly! (For help in how you can do the same, see *A Call to Scripture Memory.*[2]) One man has put it this way: "To have His words abiding in us is to keep His sayings and precepts continually before our memories and minds, and to make them the guide of our actions and the rule of our daily contact and behavior."[3]

So with those two conditions in mind—us abiding in Christ and His Word abiding in us—Jesus then says *you will ask what you desire, and it shall be done for you.* The Greek rendering indicates that we must ask, not may ask. This presents a problem, in my opinion, because many believers never even stop to ask. I am always amazed when speaking to women and they share with me a burden they may have, I usually ask them if they

---

1 J. C. Ryle, *Expository Thoughts on the Gospels.*

2 Susan Heck, *A Call to Scripture Memory* (Irvine: Three Sixteen Publishing), 316publishing.com.

3 J. C. Ryle, *Expository Thoughts on the Gospels.*

have prayed about it. Many times, they have not! James clearly says in James 4:2b, "You do not have because you do not ask" (LSB). Sometimes in my own life, I have thought to myself, "You know, I really should pray about this," and then I do. And you know what happens? An amazing thing happens! God answers my prayer! But many times, I just have not asked! *The first blessing of this abiding in Christ is faithful answered prayer.* Jesus says that if we ask, it will be done.

Now, ladies, this verse has been taken out of context by many to mean the most ridiculous things! Some people will say that God has basically given us a blank check here. Therefore, I can ask anything I want at all, and He will give it to me. I can ask for a million dollars and I will have it. I can ask for a new husband and I will have one! I can ask God for a new Lexus, a new house, a new whatever, and I will have it! It's always amazing to me how we neglect the context of what Christ is saying. Look very carefully at this verse. The key here to our prayers being answered is abiding in Christ. If we are abiding in Christ and His words are abiding in us, we won't be asking for things that are not for His glory, will we? Why? Because we will be altogether consumed with the will of the Father—like Jesus praying before He went to the cross, "Not my will, Father, but Yours." He delighted to do the will of His Father, even though it would be painful. Jesus has already mentioned in John 14:13 that whatever we ask in His name He will do, that the Father may be glorified in the Son. We must be asking in His name and for the glory of God. If having a million dollars will somehow glorify God (maybe you want to give it to a needy missionary or someone with a financial need) and you are abiding in Him and His words are abiding in you, then maybe you will get it.

The Greek *it shall be done for you* literally reads as "it shall come to pass." James even mentions in James 5:16b, "The effective prayer of a righteous man can accomplish much" (LSB). A righteous man's prayers accomplish quite a bit. But notice that James explicitly states what the character of the one who is praying should be; this person is a righteous man, a righteous woman, one who is living rightly before God. This would obviously be one who is abiding in Christ and has Christ's words abiding in him or her. Do your prayers avail much? Is there someone you know who prays like that? If so, I imagine that you could testify that they abide in Christ and that His words abide in them.

It was said of John Knox that Queen Mary said she feared his prayers more than an army of 20,000 men. Why? Because they accomplished much! There really is no reason that all of us should not have answers to our prayers daily. If God isn't answering our prayers, then perhaps we need to ask ourselves, "Am I abiding in Christ"? "Are His words abiding in me?" "Am I seeking to obey Him in all I know to do?" One of the reasons we probably see so few prayers answered is because we see very little close communication with the Lord and so little strict obedience to the Word. The person who sees answers to prayers is a person who is abiding in Christ and who is allowing His words to abide in him. Psalm 37:4 (LSB) says, "Delight yourself in Yahweh; and He will give you the desires of your heart."

Now, before we go on, it's possible that some of you are wondering about Paul's prayer in 2 Corinthians 12 where he asked the Lord three times to remove his thorn in the flesh. Was Paul not abiding in Christ? Were Christ's words not abiding in him? What happened? Wasn't the apostle Paul a man of great faith? Again, we must go back to John 14:13 and the fact that our praying must be in the name of Jesus and for His glory. One of the things Christ told Paul was that, "My strength is made perfect in weakness." There was a reason that the Lord did not answer Paul's petition and that reason was so that the power of Christ would rest upon Paul and in his weakness Christ would be shown to be his strength. God had a plan much bigger and better for the apostle Paul than the comfort of having his thorn removed. In my own life, I've also noticed that God often does not answer my prayers because He is more interested in my humility and holiness than in my happiness.

We also would do well to remember the man who was born blind, whom we read about in John 9. John records the following in John 9:2-3 (LSB): "And His disciples asked Him, saying, 'Rabbi, who sinned, this man or his parents, that he would be born blind?' Jesus answered, 'Neither this man nor his parents sinned, but this was so that the works of God might be manifested in him.'" All this was for the glory of God. Sometimes, there is a bigger picture that we cannot see. Sometimes, there is a bigger spiritual blessing in the Lord not granting to us what we've asked of Him.

In verse 8 of John 15, Jesus is still focusing on what glorifies the Father, and what He says we will look at in the next section.

The Blessing of Fruit-Bearing John 15:8

> "By this My Father is glorified, that you bear much fruit; so you will be My disciples." (John 15:8)

Notice, first of all, that Jesus says that the *Father is glorified* when we *bear much fruit*. To *glorify* the Father means that we recognize, or praise, or honor Him. How can the disciples give God glory? How can you and I give glory to God? We can glorify God by bearing *much fruit*. Notice that it is not a little fruit, but *much* fruit. No one should take comfort in the fact that they are a Christian if they do not have within them a deep desire to bear much fruit. In fact, the Greek tense here is indicating that we keep on bearing fruit, as an ongoing reality of our lives. Bearing fruit is what a disciple does throughout their whole life on earth! This is how we can honor our Lord. You have to wonder if the disciples thought on these words of Christ after He ascended into Heaven, because when you read the book of Acts you certainly see that the disciples bore much fruit for the Kingdom. *So, the second blessing of abiding in Christ is fruit-bearing.* It is a privilege.

It is in this bearing of much fruit, Jesus says, that *you will* prove to *be My disciples*. A *disciple*, we know, is simply a follower of Christ, a pupil, a learner. It is one who learns by putting what one learns into practice. There are a lot of things that we could be learners or pupils of. We might be disciples of music, cooking, running, gardening, fishing, or hiking, and all of those are good things. But to be called a disciple of Jesus Christ, to follow after and learn from Him—what a blessing! Did you know that our good works, our fruits, glorify God even in the eyes of the unbeliever? They see fruit we bear and they know that we are different. Consider what Peter says in his first epistle, in 1 Peter 2:12 (LSB), "by keeping your conduct excellent among the Gentiles, so that in the thing which they slander you as evildoers, they may because of your good works, as they observe them, glorify God in the day of visitation."

Now, before we go on, I want to get practical, but also a little personal, about fruit-bearing for us as women. What is some of the fruit that we, specifically as women, should be producing? What should the believer and the unbeliever be seeing in our lives as Christian women? When they look at any one of us, they should see a woman whose life is holy; a woman whose husband trusts her, who is submissive to her husband and loves him tenderly, who does him good and not evil all the days of her life; a woman who works hard as a keeper of her home, who is diligent in her work, not laying around on the couch watching TV and checking social media every five minutes. The world should see a woman who gives generously to the needy and looks for ways to do so; a woman who is wise with her speech and not a gossip; a woman who is kind; a woman who has a tender affection for her children and whose children call her blessed; a woman who fears the Lord and lives in holiness. Ladies, if the unbelieving world doesn't see these things in our lives, then it blasphemes the word of God, as Paul says in Titus 2:5.

Well, in view of the fact that He is soon leaving them, Jesus again reminds His disciples of His love for them, in verse 9.

The Blessing of the Father's Love — John 15:9-10

> "As the Father loved Me, I also have loved you; abide in My love." (John 15:9)

How did the Father love the Son? In Jesus' prayer in John 17:24 he says this to the Father: "Father, I desire that they also whom You gave Me may be with Me where I am, that they may behold My glory which You have given Me; for You loved Me before the foundation of the world." The Father's love for the Son has no beginning and no end. That's how much the Father loved the Son. Ladies, I don't know about you, but there are people in my life, that I have had a deep love for at one time but no longer have that same love for them now. But that does not describe the Father's love for the Son. It is eternal; it is unchanging. It existed before the foundation of the world. Jesus says that's how much He loves us! Imagine! *As the Father loved Me, I also have loved you*. Both of these words for *love* come from the Greek term *agapao*, which indicates a direction of the will and finding one's joy in something. *The third blessing of abiding in Christ is the Father's love.* Jesus tells His disciples that He loves them as the Father loves Him. The Father's love for His Son is the basis of the Son's love for His disciples. Remember how the Upper Room Discourse started, in John 13:1? What did John say? "Having loved His own who were in the world, He loved them to the end." I think we should endeavor to be mindful more often of our Lord's love. I know that I often dwell more on the Lord's judgment or wrath than on His love. But the Scriptures are full of verses that deal with the love of God. Perhaps we would do well to mention just a few. One that quickly comes to mind is Deuteronomy 7:7-8, which speaks of God's relationship with Israel: "Yahweh did not set His affection on you nor choose you because you were more in number than any of the peoples, for you were the fewest of all peoples, but because Yahweh loved you and kept the oath which He swore to your fathers, Yahweh brought you out with a strong hand and redeemed you from the house of slavery, from the hand of Pharaoh king of Egypt" (LSB). Or, how about Jeremiah 31:3? "Yahweh appeared to him from afar, saying, 'I have loved you with an everlasting love; therefore I have drawn you with lovingkindness'" (Jeremiah 31:3 LSB).

At the end of verse 9, Jesus follows up this incredible statement about His love with a command for His disciples to *abide in My love.* What does that mean? It means to remain in His love once and for all. May it endure to the end. It's as though He is saying, "Continue in the shelter of my love for you." And the word for love here is *agape*, which, again, is a love that is not shown by doing what the person loved desires but what the one who loves deems as needed by the one loved. For example, John 3:16 tells us that God loved man so much that He gave them what they needed and what was necessary for them, which was eternal life. For man to show *agape* love to God or to continue in that love, he must first appropriate God's *agape* love, because only God has such genuine, unselfish love. Our love for God is, of course, shown by our obedience, which is what the Lord now addresses in verse 10.

> "If you keep My commandments, you will abide in My love, just as I have kept My Father's commandments and abide in His love." (John 15:10)

Notice the condition that Jesus mentions here. *If you keep My commandments,* then *you will abide in My love.* The keeping of God's *commandments* is not an arbitrary condition that is imposed on us; rather, it is a result of our love for the Father. The greatest way to keep His commandments is to abide in His love, and the greatest way to abide in His love is to keep His commandments. The two go hand in hand. When we don't keep God's commandments, when we know that we are being disobedient to the Lord, it is a miserable place to be and we don't sense His abiding love, we don't sense His presence. But when we are obedient, we abide in His love; we remain there once for all! Note that the Lord does not require anything of them that He has not done Himself, as evidenced by the words *just as I have kept My Father's commandments and abide in His love.* It is said of Christ in Psalm 40:7-8 (LSB), "Then I said, 'Behold, I come; in the scroll of the book it is written of me. I desire to do Your will, O my God; Your law is within my inner being.'" Did you notice that Christ delighted to do the Father's will? It was not drudgery to Him. Even John tells us, in 1 John 5:3, that keeping His commandments is not burdensome. They're not irksome; they are a delight. Christ kept the Father's commandments perfectly, and that is to be the goal of all of us, as Jesus says in the Sermon on the Mount, in Matthew 5:48 (LSB): "Therefore you are to be perfect, as your heavenly Father is perfect."

Well, are all these words to be nothing but a bunch of sorrow and drudgery to the Eleven? I think not! Listen to what Jesus says in verse 11 to the Eleven.

The Blessing of Fullness of Joy John 15:11

> "These things I have spoken to you, that My joy may remain in you, and that your joy may be full." (John 15:11)

The connection between verses 10 and 11 is very interesting, because love and obedience are the secrets of true joy. "Joy," wrote C. S. Lewis, "is the serious business of heaven."[4] Elisabeth Elliot said she loved that

---

4 C. S. Lewis, quoted in Elisabeth Elliot Gren, "Joy to the World," *The Elisabeth Elliot Newsletter,* November/December 1996, cdn.elisabethelliot.org/newsletters/EENews_1996_11_12.pdf. Accessed 9/22/2023.

quote by C. S. Lewis because, she said, "I am sure it must be true, for heaven is peopled with those who want no other business but to love God and to manifest that love perfectly and continuously, by a glad obedience. Jesus said, 'If you obey my commands, you will remain in my love, just as I have obeyed my Father's commands and remain in his love. I have told you this so that my joy may be in you and that your joy may be complete.'"[5] (See John 15:10-11.) What are *these things* that Jesus is referring to? The things He has been saying in this discourse. What things has He been saying to them that should have brought them joy? The fact that they have a place in Heaven (14:2); the promise of being where He is (14:3); the promise of greater works that they would do (14:12); the new privilege in prayer (14:13-14); the gift of the Spirit (14:16); the privilege of being loved of the Father and the Son (14:21); the promise of the Holy Spirit being their teacher and bringing things to their remembrance (14:26); the promise of peace (14:27); the promise of bearing fruit (15:1-5); the promise of answered prayer (15:7); the promise of His love (15:9,10); the promise of abiding with Him as we keep His commandments (15:10). Now, I may have left some out, but you get the picture—these things bring joy! And if these things don't bring us joy, then I don't know what will! The biggest reason, of course, that any Christian should be joyful is their salvation. Jesus made this clear, in Luke 10:20, to the 70 disciples He had sent out, as they come back with that great report that the demons were subject to them. Jesus said to them, "Nevertheless do not rejoice in this, that the spirits are subject to you, but rejoice that your names are recorded in heaven" (Luke 10:20 LSB).

Why has Christ spoken these words to the disciples and to us? He gives two reasons why He has spoken this to them. The first reason, He says, is so *that My joy will remain in you*. The word *joy* refers to exuberant joy, good cheer, or gladness of heart. Joy should be the characteristic of all true disciples of Jesus Christ. And note, my friend, that it is His joy that should remain and abide in us. Our joy comes from Him alone. The disciples were losing their joy because they didn't understand what was happening and they knew the Lord was leaving them. They didn't

---

[5] Elisabeth Elliot Gren, "Joy to the World."

understand that He would continue with them through the Spirit and the Word. We must also hold to these truths. It is very concerning to see people who profess the name of Christ who are always living in gloom and doom. In fact, it almost seems a contradiction of terms, doesn't it? Gloomy Christian? But, unfortunately, we see too many sad faces and sour looks. We should be the happiest of all people because God's joy remains in us. The Psalmist put it well in Psalm 16:11 (LSB), "You will make known to me the path of life; in Your presence is fullness of joy; in Your right hand there are pleasures forever."

The second reason the Lord has spoken these things to them, He says, is so *that your joy may be full*. So, our joy isn't simply to remain, but it is to be *full*. This means it is to be filled up and perfect or complete. I don't think it is a coincidence that the promise of joy comes after the admonition to keep His commandments. It goes without saying, but I will say it anyway, that joy comes from obedience. When I am obedient to the Lord, it does bring joy; when I am disobedient, it brings sorrow, depression, and shame. *This is the fourth and final blessing of abiding in Christ: fullness of joy.*

Summary

We see four blessings of abiding in Christ in the text we've examined in this chapter. Those blessings are:

1. *The Blessing of Faithful Answered Prayer* (v 7): Does God answer your prayers? Has He answered your prayers today? This week? What are the prayers He has answered?

2. *The Blessing of Fruit-Bearing* (v 8): Are you bearing much fruit? What kind of fruit is in your life? Do others see that fruit? Is there anything you need to prune from your life so that you can bear more fruit for the Father?

3. *The Blessing of the Father's Love* (vv 9-10): Do you sense the love of the Father in your life? If so, how do you sense it? If you do not,

consider whether you are abiding in His commandments.

4. *The Blessing of Fullness of Joy* (v 11): Does your life exhibit fullness of joy? If not, have you asked yourself why? It may be due to sin in your life, as David articulated so well in Psalm 51 when he asked the Lord to restore the joy of his salvation after he had repented of his sin with Bathsheba. David had lost his joy for a time, due to unconfessed sin in his life. It may also be that you are allowing the cares of life to steal your joy; perhaps it's a difficult person or a difficult situation. But, as God's daughter, my friend, you should have fullness of joy!

My dear sisters, if you will look at each one of these blessings, you will find that they each are present as we abide in Christ, as we obey Him. And, they each are absent when we are disobedient, are they not? As someone once said to me, so now I say to you, "It really all boils down to one thing, Susan. Trust and obey. There is no other way to be happy in Jesus, but to trust and obey."

QUESTIONS TO CONSIDER

1. Read John 15 and list all the promises for the believer that you can find in that chapter.

2. Memorize John 15:11.

3. (a) According to John 15:7, what must take place before we experience answered prayer? (b) Does God answer your prayers? (c) Which of your prayers has He answered this week?

4. (a) What is God's will for you, according to John 15:8? (b) Should a believer be concerned about bearing fruit? Prove your answer from the Word. (c) What fruit does God expect from women in particular? See Proverbs 31 and Titus 2:1-5.

5. In John 15:9, Jesus refers to the Father loving Him. What does John 17:24 say about the Father's love for the Son?

6. Jesus says in John 15:10 that He kept the Father's commandments. (a) In the following verses, how is Jesus seen obeying His Father, and what were the attitudes that accompanied His obedience? Psalm 40:7-8; Isaiah 42:1-4; Matthew 3:13-17; John 4:34; John 8:29; John 12:49-50; John 17:4; Hebrews 10:5-10. (b) How do these verses encourage you to keep the commandments of Christ with a righteous attitude? (c) Would others say you keep His commandments? (Perhaps, ask a parent, husband, child, or close friend.)

7. (a) According to the following verses, what are the sources of joy? Psalm 16:11; 21:1; 32:11 35:27; 43:4; John 15:11; Romans 5:11; Galatians 5:22; James 1:2-4; 1 Peter 1:8-9; 4:13; 1 John 1:4. (b) How do these sources differ from the sources that the world tells us will bring joy? (c) According to Psalm 51, what could cause a believer to lose her joy, and what is the solution? (d) Do others characterize you as a woman of joy?

8. Write down at least 10 blessings of abiding in Christ and come prepared to share them with joy!

9. Write down a praise to God for one of the blessings you listed in answer to question 8.

What a Friend We Have in Jesus!
John 15:12-17

SEVERAL years ago, someone said to me something I have not forgotten to this day: "Susan, if you have one true friend in your lifetime, you are indeed blessed." With that truth in mind, we might ask ourselves, "What *is* a friend?" Humanly speaking, Michael Josephson offers a simple poem describing the many aspects of friendship. The A-Z of Friendship:

> **A**ccepts you as you are,
> **B**elieves in you,
> **C**alls you just to say, "Hi,"
> **D**oesn't give up on you.
> **E**nvisions the whole of you (even the unfinished parts),
> **F**orgives your mistakes,
> **G**ives unconditionally,
> **H**elps you,
> **I**nvites you over,
> **J**ust "be" with you,
> **K**eeps you close at heart,
> **L**oves you for who you are,
> **M**akes a difference in your life,
> **N**ever judges,
> **O**ffers support,
> **P**icks you up,
> **Q**uiets your fears,
> **R**aises your spirits,
> **S**ays nice things about you,
> **T**ells you the truth when you need to hear it,
> **U**nderstands you,
> **V**alues you,
> **W**alks beside you,

Xplains things you don't understand,
Yells when you won't listen, and
Zaps you back to reality.[1]

Copyright 2020 Michael Josephson. Reprinted with permission.

Those are pretty good qualities for a friend, are they not? But, what are the qualities of those who are friends of our Lord? Well, I don't have 26 qualities for you, but in the passage we are going to look at in this chapter, our Lord does give us six defining qualities of those who are truly His friends. What does it take to be a friend of Jesus? Let's see what Jesus says in John 15:12-17.

> "This is My commandment, that you love one another as I have loved you. Greater love has no one than this, than to lay down one's life for his friends. You are My friends if you do whatever I command you. No longer do I call you servants, for a servant does not know what his master is doing; but I have called you friends, for all things that I heard from My Father I have made known to you. You did not choose Me, but I chose you and appointed you that you should go and bear fruit, and that your fruit should remain, that whatever you ask the Father in My name He may give you. These things I command you, that you love one another."

In these verses, we'll see six qualities that characterize those who are friends of the Lord, and they'll form an acrostic: **FRIEND** (they will not be presented in that order, though). In our previous chapter, we learned that there are four blessings of abiding in Christ: the blessing of faithful answered prayer; the blessing of fruit-bearing; the blessing of the Father's love, and the blessing of fullness of joy. Now, as we come to the next passage in John 15, Jesus speaks of a new and intimate relationship that only those who are His disciples, those who abide in Him, can claim. That relationship is that of being His friend. He says,

> "This is My commandment, that you love one another as I have loved you." (John 15:12)

---

[1] Michael Josephson, *True Friendship*, https://whatwillmatter.com/2013/07/poster-quote-true-friendship-a-z-by-michael-josephson/. Accessed 9/25/2023.

What is His *commandment* that He deems essential to those who would call Him Master? The commandment is that we *love one another*. And the tense in which this commandment is delivered indicates that we are to keep on loving one another. Our love for one another should be continuous, and it should be for the duration of our life. Jesus has already said, back in John 15:10a, "If you keep My commandments, you will abide in My love," and now He mentions a specific commandment and that is to love one another. But this isn't the first time the Lord has said this to them during this Upper Room Discourse. Perhaps we should recall His words in John 13:34-35 that we have already studied, "A new commandment I give to you, that you love one another; as I have loved you, that you also love one another. By this all will know that you are My disciples, if you have love for one another." We saw then that this commandment originated in Leviticus 19:18 where God commanded the Israelites to love their neighbors as themselves, for He is the Lord. In and of itself, this is not a new commandment, but the new aspect of the commandment is that they are to love each other, Jesus says, *as I have loved you*. This would include the ways He loved them while He was on earth, and we examined some of those when we studied John 13, so we won't repeat them here. But, remember what Paul says in Ephesians 5:2 (LSB), "and walk in love, just as Christ also loved us and gave Himself up for us, an offering and a sacrifice to God as a fragrant aroma." Our love for one another must be a love that will pour itself out in sacrifice. The only possible way that you and I can love one another like that is by abiding in Christ, as Jesus has just mentioned in the previous verses. J. C. Ryle has a strong word for us on this subject. He says,

> He that supposes he is right in the sight of God, because his doctrinal views are correct, while he is unloving in his temper, and sharp, cross, snappish, and ill-natured in the use of his tongue, exhibits wretched ignorance of the first principles of Christ's Gospel. The crossness, spitefulness, jealousy, maliciousness, and general disagreeableness of many high professors of "sound doctrine" are a positive scandal to Christianity. Where there is little love there can be little grace.[2]

---

2 J. C. Ryle, *Expository Thoughts on the Gospels*.

You know, you can have your doctrine perfectly correct, but if you do not love others, then this presents a serious problem biblically. In the next verse, the Lord goes on to raise the level of our love for one another, by saying,

> "Greater love has no one than this, than to lay down one's life for his friends." (John 15:13)

Jesus is literally saying that there is no greater love than to lay down your life for, or on behalf of, or in place of, your friends. Notice that the laying down of one's life is for the benefit of the friend, not the one laying down his or her life. The word for *friend* means dear, and it is a term which means to love with affection; it denotes an intimate and affectionate relationship. Up until this point, the word friend has only been used once in John's Gospel. In John 11:11-16, we read,

> These things He said, and after that He said to them, "Our friend Lazarus sleeps, but I go that I may wake him up." Then His disciples said, "Lord, if he sleeps he will get well." However, Jesus spoke of his death, but they thought that He was speaking about taking rest in sleep.
> Then Jesus said to them plainly, "Lazarus is dead. And I am glad for your sakes that I was not there, that you may believe. Nevertheless let us go to him."
> Then Thomas, who is called the Twin, said to his fellow disciples, "Let us also go, that we may die with him."

This is the account in which Jesus goes on to raise Lazarus from the dead. In verse 11, Jesus refers to Lazarus as their friend, and Thomas comments that they should all go and die with him. The disciples wanted to lay down their lives too. The laying down of one's life is the test of a true friend.

Now what does Jesus mean when He says that we should lay down our lives for our friends? The word for *life* in the Greek means soul. This means we should be willing to lay down our souls for one another. The laying down of one's life is the greatest measure of human love. In fact, Plato said, "Only those who love wish to die for others." I thought, perhaps, this human illustration I once heard might best explain what Jesus means:

> A crippled girl, living in the slums, underwent an operation that might enable her to walk again. When the operation was over, she needed a blood transfusion; her 14-year-old brother, a tough boy of the streets, volunteered. He was taken to the hospital, to the bedside of his crippled sister. He stared in tight-lipped silence while the vein in his arm was opened so that the blood might flow into the body of his unconscious sister. When it was over, the doctor put his hand on the boy's shoulder and told him that he was very brave. The boy did not comprehend; he had not understood the nature of a transfusion. After a moment, he looked and said "Doc, how long will it be before I croak?" As far as the boy was concerned he had been dying; slowly and willingly, he had stoically watched the blood flow-drop by drop, expecting his sister's life to mean his own death. There indeed is the highest in human love. If this human love is to be seen in its highest degree, it will be through the words of Christ, who said, "Greater love has no one than this, than to lay down one's life for his friends."[3]

Unfortunately, most people don't love others in this way. In fact, many won't even give up their time, energy, or finances for another, much less their very lives. Can you imagine if the Christian world would really love each other like this? What an impact we could have on a lost and dying world! They might actually listen to the message of the gospel of Jesus Christ!

We have some great examples of this sacrificial love in the Word of God. Besides Jesus, probably one of the best examples of this in Scripture is the apostle Paul. Consider Acts 20:22-24, where Paul says this: "And now, behold, bound by the Spirit, I am on my way to Jerusalem, not knowing what will happen to me there, except that the Holy Spirit solemnly testifies to me in every city, saying that chains and afflictions await me. But I do not make my life of any account nor dear to myself, so that I may finish my course and the ministry which I received from the Lord

---

3 Donald Grey Barnhouse, *Let Me Illustrate* (Grand Rapids: Baker Book House, 1967), 211.

Jesus, to testify solemnly of the gospel of the grace of God" (LSB). Even in Romans 9:1-3, Paul mentions that he would be willing to go to hell if it meant his Jewish brethren would be saved: "I am telling the truth in Christ, I am not lying, my conscience testifies with me in the Holy Spirit, that I have great sorrow and unceasing grief in my heart. For I could wish that I myself were accursed, separated from Christ for the sake of my brothers, my kinsmen according to the flesh" (LSB). He also mentions his willingness to lay down his life for the church at Philippi, in Philippians 2:17 (LSB): "But even if I am being poured out as a drink offering upon the sacrifice and service of your faith, I rejoice and share my joy with you all." And, in addition to the example set by the apostle Paul, we also have Priscilla and Aquila, who are mentioned in Romans 16:3-4 by Paul as a couple willing to risk their lives for others: "Greet Prisca and Aquila, my fellow workers in Christ Jesus, who for my life risked their own necks, to whom not only do I give thanks, but also all the churches of the Gentiles" (LSB). *So the first defining quality of those who are friends of God is the **D** on your acrostic: **D**eath to self because of the love of God.* Of course, the Supreme example of the One who died to Himself and lived for others is our Lord. Consider John 10:11; Romans 5:6-8; Ephesians 5:1-2; and 1 John 3:16. In fact, the day after Jesus spoke these words in the upper room, He laid down his life for all His friends. In the next verse, verse 14, Jesus gives the disciples a second defining quality of being His friend. He says,

> "You are My friends if you do whatever I command you." (John 15:14)

We are His friends, Jesus says, *if you do whatever I command you. If we do*, or keep on obeying, His *commands*. The idea here is of a continuous action, day after day, month after month, and year after year. It is not when I feel like it or if I feel like it. That should not be the heartbeat of a true disciple of Jesus Christ. That would be like giving your child a command to clean up his room, and he says, "Mom, I'll do it tomorrow," or "Mom, I just don't feel like it right now." That is not obedience. And notice that Jesus says it is *whatever I command you*. The Christian life is not a smorgasbord where I can pick and choose what I want to obey. The Christian life is characterized by a heart that beats like Mary's, who said, "may it be done to me according to your word" (Luke 1:38b

LSB). We also have the examples of Abraham and Moses, whose lives were characterized by obedience, and that is why they were called God's friends. To be called the friend of God is a holy privilege, and we should not take it lightly. *The second quality of those who are called God's friends is the **F** on your acrostic: **F**ollows the commandments of God.* Christ goes on in verse 15 to expound more on this friendship we have and gives the third defining quality of His friends.

> "No longer do I call you servants, for a servant does not know what his master is doing; but I have called you friends, for all things that I heard from My Father I have made known to you." (John 15:15)

Jesus now speaks of a new intimacy with the disciples. They are no longer going to be called servants, but friends. Jesus had referred to them as being servants, and called them to take on that role, after washing their feet. Consider His words in John 13:13-16: "You call me Teacher and Lord, and you say well, for so I am. If I then, your Lord and Teacher, have washed your feet, you also ought to wash one another's feet. For I have given you an example, that you should do as I have done to you. Most assuredly, I say to you, a servant is not greater than his master; nor is he who is sent greater than he who sent him." They were to be *servants*, which indicates that they were to be in a permanent relation of servitude to another, their will altogether consumed in the will of the Christ. In biblical times, a servant did not normally have a close relationship with his or her master, even though being a servant was not a title of shame, as we might think of it in our day. In the Old Testament, Moses, Joshua, and David were called servants of God. In the New Testament, Paul and James were called servants of God and both counted that an honor. In biblical times a servant simply did what his master said, without question. And that's what Jesus means when He says *for a servant does not know what his master is doing*. The master isn't required to tell his servant anything or to give his servant reasons for why he commands certain things. But now, Jesus says *no longer do I call you servants ... but I have called you friends*. Now they have a different relationship with Him. But even though He now calls them friends, this does not mean they are equals with Him; He is still their Savior, their Lord, and their Master. The disciples would still receive orders from their Master, yet they would be treated as friends by Him. They would still carry out His desires and the work He had called them to do. To be called the friends of God was a glorious privilege for them, and it is for you and me too, dear friends.

Now, what would be implied by this new term friend? Jesus tells them what is implied when He says *for all things that I heard from My Father I have made known to you*. The word *friend* would imply a confidante. In the human realm, we may have a lot of friends, but there are only a few that we share our secrets with. When we have an intimate friend, a confidante, we share our heart with them. Jesus has been opening His heart up to these men. Jesus has told them such things as why He was sent to earth by the Father, why He was going to lay down his life, why He had to leave this earth, what He would do at his return, and how a man could get to Heaven. All these things He shared with them were the things He heard from His Father. Ladies, this is a mark of a true friend; friends have open and honest communication and bare their souls to each other. Jesus has been sharing His most intimate thoughts in His final hours. He has been sharing with them the things He had heard from His own Father. *So the **I** on our acrostic of those who are friends of God is: **I**ntimacy with God.* There is a wonderful promise in Psalm 25:14 (LSB) which says, "The secret of Yahweh is for those who fear Him, and He will make them know His covenant."

Now, in the human realm, when we think of choosing our friends, we usually choose our friends because we like their personality, or because of their dedication to the Lord, or because of their warmth or their humor, or because of their looks, or for a number of reasons. But that's not how God chooses His friends; it has nothing to do with any human quality we might possess. (By the way, Proverbs 12:26 says that a righteous man should choose his friends carefully.) Notice what Jesus says in verse 16 about those who are His friends:

> "You did not choose Me, but I chose you and appointed you that you should go and bear fruit, and that your fruit should remain, that whatever you ask the Father in My name He may give you." (John 15:16)

Jesus makes it very clear there, that those who are His friends did not choose Him, but He chose them. *So the N on our acrostic of those who are friends of God is: Nominated by God.* (Now, you might be thinking, "Aren't you stretching this a bit, Susan?" Actually, I'm not, because the thesaurus does list the word nominated as a synonym for chosen!) The phrase *you did not choose Me* is a strong emphatic in the Greek language. *You* did not choose *Me! Choose* means to select, to choose for oneself, not necessarily implying the rejection of what is not chosen, but giving favor to the chosen subject. It involves preference and choice from among many. What exactly is Christ saying here to the Eleven when He says *but I chose you*? You might think back to Luke 6:12-16, where we see the choosing of the Twelve to be His disciples:

> Now it came to pass in those days that He went out to the mountain to pray, and continued all night in prayer to God. And when it was day, He called His disciples to Himself; and from them He chose twelve whom He also named apostles: Simon, whom He also named Peter, and Andrew his brother; James and John; Philip and Bartholomew; Matthew and Thomas; James the son of Alphaeus, and Simon called the Zealot; Judas the son of James, and Judas Iscariot who also became a traitor.

This is the choosing of the Twelve for the purpose of being His disciples. The choosing that John is referring to here is most likely for salvation. Consider Ephesians 1:4 (LSB), where Paul says, "just as He chose us in Him before the foundation of the world, that we would be holy and blameless before Him in love." Also, Acts 13:48 (LSB) states, "And when the Gentiles heard this, they began rejoicing and glorifying the word of the Lord, and as many as had been appointed to eternal life believed." We did not choose Him, but He chose us. It's like John tells us in 1 John 4:19, that the only reason we loved Him is because He loved us first! Now, I realize that some would like to say that we choose Him and therefore make our salvation totally up to us! But it is clear from the Word of God that He chose us. In fact, the reference here is more than likely a reference to salvation over the reference to choosing them as disciples because at this point Judas is now gone, and we know Judas isn't in Heaven. He was chosen as a disciple but not as a child of God!

Now, there was a reason that Jesus chose them. He had a mission in mind for them, a fruit-bearing mission. Jesus puts it like this: *that you should go and bear fruit, and that your fruit should remain*. Jesus appointed them for a special service, and that special service was that they would bring forth fruit, and that it would remain. This, again, is another proof that the choosing here was for salvation, because unbelievers cannot bear the fruit of salvation. Jesus has already made that clear with the parable of the vine and the branches. Fruit-bearing has been the theme of what He has been speaking about since the beginning of chapter 15. In fact, we can look through the New Testament and see that, indeed, the disciples did bear much fruit, and their fruit is still remaining, is it not? No doubt, their fruit has affected every one of us. We are able to pick up the Word of God and read things they wrote for us through the power of the Holy Spirit. We also can learn from their examples, which challenge us to live more Christlike lives, and that is certainly is fruitful! And, ladies, there is a reason that the Lord chose us also, and it wasn't to sit around and bask in the fact that we are Christians. He chose us for the same reason He chose the first disciples—to go and bring forth fruit and that our fruit should remain. *So the **R** on our acrostic of those who are truly God's friends is: **R**emaining fruit for God.* Paul says in Ephesians 2:10 (LSB), "For we are His workmanship, created in Christ Jesus for good works, which God prepared beforehand so that we would walk in them." Every one of us has a mission from God: that we should be producing fruit and that fruit should *remain* or endure. The fruit we should be producing should last, and it should have eternal value. In our last chapter, from Proverbs 31 and Titus 2, we learned of some specific fruit we as women should be producing. Our fruit should not be like that of false teachers that Jude mentions in verse 12 of his epistle, "late autumn trees without fruit, twice dead, pulled up by the roots." What a graphic picture!

Jesus then goes on to repeat something He already said in verse 7: *that whatever you ask the Father in My name He may give you*. Now, in the context, this is probably referring to the requests that the disciples would have regarding their service to God, that is, their fruit-bearing. Jesus has already given them the promise of answered prayer in John 14:13-14, and so it would seem in the context here that this is in reference to their intercession for things that pertain to them bearing fruit. Ladies, it is so important, so vital, that we spend time in intercessory pray for those we are investing our lives in, especially our husbands, children, and grandchildren. As single women, we have the joy of praying for our families, whether they are our physical family or spiritual family. We need to ask God to help us as we bear fruit in our investment in their lives. I know I am always asking the Lord to use me to help others. I want the time I spend with others to have eternal value, eternal fruit. If you are not seeing changes in the lives of those that you are investing in, then you might ask yourself, just how much time do I spend in prayer for them? This is a wonderful promise for us as well as for the disciples.

As we endeavor to bear fruit for the Lord, and as we pray, He will hear and answer our petitions. *So the **E** on our acrostic for those who are friends of God is: A friend of God **E**xperiences answered prayer by God.* What a wonderful promise for the friends of Christ! We experience answered prayer! Those with whom Christ has entrusted His most intimate truths can now continue that intimacy with Him by sharing our thoughts and petitions with Him. And so, Jesus ends, in verse 17, with a reminder of what we began with in verse 12: a command to love one another.

"These things I command you, that you love one another." (John 15:17)

Why does Jesus repeat this? I am not really sure, except that I do know the disciples needed to be reminded again of this great commandment, just as you and I do. On this very night, according to Luke 22:24, there was strife among them, specifically about who was the greatest among them. So Christ reminds them of the need to *love one another*. They will need, more than ever, to bond together in Christ's love after He has gone. They must have one heart and one mind if they are to bear fruit and have it remaining. You and I cannot bear fruit where there is strife. James puts it well in James 4:1-3 (LSB): "What is the source of quarrels and conflicts among you? Is not the source your pleasures that wage war in your members? You lust and do not have, so you murder. You are envious and cannot obtain, so you fight and quarrel. You do not have because you do not ask. You ask and do not receive, because you ask with wrong motives, so that you may spend it on your pleasures." There is nothing more hindering to the Lord's work than Christians not getting along.

It stunts the efforts of producing fruit and spiritual growth in the church. There is no way that we who are unlovely at times can love our brother who is also unlovely at times, unless we constantly reflect on the love of Christ and abide in Him, our Dearest Friend.

Summary

Are you a friend of Jesus? How do you know? According to our text, there are six defining qualities of those who are Jesus' friends. A **FRIEND** of Jesus:

- ◊ *Follows the commandments of God* (v 14): "You are My friends if you do whatever I command you." Do you follow the commandments of God? All of them?

- ◊ *Remaining fruit for God* (v 16): "You did not choose Me, but I chose you and appointed you that you should go and bear fruit, and that your fruit should remain." Are you fruitful for the Lord and His Kingdom? What fruit are you producing? Are you producing more fruit today than last year at this time?

- ◊ *Intimacy with God* (v 15): "No longer do I call you servants, for a servant does not know what his master is doing; but I have called you friends." Do you have an intimate relationship with the Lord through His Word and prayer? And, I might ask, do you enjoy it? True friends enjoy one another.

- ◊ *Experiences answered prayer by God* (v 16): "You did not choose Me, but I chose you and appointed you that you should go and bear fruit, and that your fruit should remain, that whatever you ask the Father in My name He may give you." Does God answer prayer in your life on a regular basis, especially prayers that pertain to those you invest your life in?

- ◊ *Nominated by God* (v 16): "You did not choose Me, but I chose you." Have you been chosen by God? How do you know? Does your life have valid proof today that you belong to the Lord?

◊ ***Death to self because of the love of God*** (vv 12-13): "This is My commandment, that you love one another as I have loved you. Greater love has no one than this, than to lay down one's life for his friends." Do you love the brethren as God has loved you, and does it manifest itself in a willingness to lay down your life? Who have you laid down your life for lately?

If you could answer yes to the above questions then I think you can with confidence say, "Yes, I am a friend of God! I am a friend of Jesus!" What a joy and privilege this friendship is!

In closing, I would like for us to focus on this wonderful friendship we have with the Savior, our Lord! And to do so, I'd like for us to reflect on the lyrics of the song *What a Friend We Have in Jesus*. This song was written by Joseph Scriven, a man who had it all—wealth, education, a devoted family, and a pleasant life in Ireland. Then, unexpected, tragedy entered his life. On the night before his scheduled wedding, his fiancée drowned. In his deep sorrow, Joseph realized that he could find the solace and support he needed only in his dearest friend, Jesus. Soon after this tragedy, Mr. Scriven drastically changed his lifestyle, devoting all of his extra time to being a friend and help to others, so much so that he became known as the "Good Samaritan of Port Hope." When his mother became ill, he wrote a letter to her, enclosing in it the words of this poem, reminding her of her never-failing heavenly Friend. As we end this chapter and you consider the lyrics to Joseph Scriven's poem, I encourage you to remind yourself of the privilege it is to have such a friend like Jesus.

> What a friend we have in Jesus,
> all our sins and griefs to bear!
> What a privilege to carry
> everything to God in prayer!
> O what peace we often forfeit,
> O what needless pain we bear,
> all because we do not carry
> everything to God in prayer.

Have we trials and temptations?
Is there trouble anywhere?
We should never be discouraged;
take it to the Lord in prayer.
Can we find a friend so faithful
who will all our sorrows share?
Jesus knows our every weakness;
take it to the Lord in prayer.

Are we weak and heavy laden,
cumbered with a load of care?
Precious Savior, still our refuge;
take it to the Lord in prayer.
Do thy friends despise, forsake thee?
Take it to the Lord in prayer!
In his arms he'll take and shield thee;
thou wilt find a solace there.[4]

---

[4] Joseph M. Scriven, "What a Friend We Have in Jesus," 1865.

QUESTIONS TO CONSIDER

1. (a) Read John 15 and list all the commandments you find in it. (b) How are you obeying these commandments? (c) Read John 15:12-17. Why does Christ repeat verse 12 in verse 17?

2. Memorize John 15:13-14.

3. Read Matthew 22:34-40. (a) What is the greatest commandment? (b) What is the second greatest commandment? (c) What did Jesus mean when He said "on these two commandments hang all the Law and the Prophets"? (d) How does this Matthew passage relate to what Jesus says in John 15:12-14?

4. John 15:14 says, "You are my friends, if you do whatever I command you." (a) In 2 Chronicles 20:7; Isaiah 41:8; and James 2:23, who is called the friend of God? (b) According to James 2:21-24, why was Abraham called the "friend of God"? (c) Read Genesis 18:16-33 and Genesis 22, and list any other reasons that would cause God to call Abraham His friend. (d) How do these relate to the qualities that Jesus lists for His friends in John 15:12-17?

5. (a) What were the reasons Christ chose the disciples, according to John 15:16? (b) According to Ephesians 1:4, when did Christ choose *all* who would become His disciples? (c) Why did He choose us, according to Deuteronomy 7:7-8 and 1 John 4:10? (d) Did we have anything to do with choosing God? Prove your answer from the Word of God.

6. (a) Do you think you would lay down your life for your friends? (b) What qualities in your friends would inspire or motivate you to die for them? (c) Christ laid down His life for you, His friend. What qualities are present in you that would cause Him to die for you?

7. How do you know you are a friend of Jesus, according to John 15:12-17?

8. Write a prayer request after prayerfully considering the following questions: Are you loving others as Christ loved you? Are you obeying God? Are you bringing forth fruit? Are you experiencing answered prayer?

The World's Twofold Response to Christians: Hatred and Persecution
John 15:17-21

SEVERAL years ago I was having a group of ladies over for a meal in my home. One of the ladies was a new believer in Jesus Christ, and so, during the meal, I asked her, "What has been the most surprising thing you have discovered since you became a Christian?" Her answer was interesting, yet timely, since I was studying this portion of Scripture in the Gospel of John. She said, "It is hard!" The rest of us around the table readily agreed with her. Being a Christian *is* hard. Jesus Himself said the way to eternal life is narrow, and it is hard, and few there will be who will find it.

What are some of the things that are difficult about being a follower of the Lord Jesus Christ? Some of the things that come to my mind are: warring with our old man; warring with the enemy, the devil; boldness in proclaiming the gospel; disciplining ourselves unto godliness; and confronting others. These are just a few of the things which are difficult about being a Christ-follower. But, there is one very tough aspect of being a believer and that is the hatred and persecution we receive from friends, family, and the world. When you first heard the gospel of Jesus Christ, were you told to expect hatred and persecution if you gave your life to the Lordship of Christ? It is a rare happening, indeed, to hear a person share the gospel of Jesus Christ in this way: "Listen, I need to tell you one more thing besides what I've already told you—that God is holy, man is a sinner, God sent His son Jesus Christ into the world to save sinners, and you need to acknowledge Him as Lord and Master over your life in order to be saved from His holy punishment of your sin. I need to tell you one more thing: that you will be hated and persecuted if you come to Christ." I would venture to say that most of us probably were not told that specific detail of the Christian life. If the message had been presented to us in that way, it's possible that some of us might have rejected it, with the intention of never thinking about

Christianity again. We forget that Jesus tells us to consider the cost of being His disciples (Luke 14:26-33). My dear sister, according to Jesus, hatred and persecution are part of the gospel message. Jesus was open with His disciples about the fact that there would be persecution that would result because they had committed to leave all and follow Him. He didn't leave them in the dark regarding the fact that there would be a cost for becoming a disciple of Jesus Christ.

In the passage we'll study in this chapter, we will see five reasons why the world hates us. Thankfully, Christ did not just speak difficult things to His disciples; He has already spoken to them of peace, eternal life, the blessed Holy Spirit, loving one another, a place in Heaven, answered prayer, and the friendship they have with Him. In fact, in our last chapter, we looked closely at six qualities of those who are the friends of Christ. We put them in the form of an acrostic, **FRIEND**: **F**ollows the commandments of God (v 14); **R**emaining fruit for God (v 16); **I**ntimacy with God (v 15); **E**xperiences answered prayer by God (v 16); **N**ominated by God (v 16); and **D**eath to self because of the love of God (vv 12-13).

While Jesus has just shared the benefits of being His friend, He now speaks to His disciples regarding the cost of being His friend, a cost that will not be financial but emotional. In the human realm, a true friend isn't only there for the good times but is also there for the difficult times. As Proverbs 17:17 (LSB) states, "A friend loves at all times, and a brother is born for adversity." And the same holds true for our relationship with Christ. Let's listen in as Jesus explains this hard truth to His disciples in John 15:17-21:

> "These things I command you, that you love one another.
>
> "If the world hates you, you know that it hated Me before it hated you. If you were of the world, the world would love its own. Yet because you are not of the world, but I chose you out of the world, therefore the world hates you. Remember the word that I said to you, 'A servant is not greater than his master.' If they persecuted Me, they will also persecute you. If they kept My word, they will keep yours also. But all these things they will do to you for My name's sake, because they do not know Him who sent Me."

Before Christ gives the five reasons why the disciples will receive persecution and hatred from the world, He gives them the command to love one another.

> "These things I command you, that you love one another." (John 15:17)

We saw this at the end of our last chapter: Christians are to *love one another*. We learned then that we must even be willing to lay down our lives for each other, the way that Christ laid down His life for us. This repeated command to love one another is essential to the eleven disciples, and to us, as we face hatred and persecution from the world. Christian love is placed in contrast to what they will get from the world, which is hatred! Disciples of Christ will be known for their love, but the world will be known for its hatred. And so He warns them in verse 18,

> "If the world hates you, you know that it hated Me before it hated you." (John 15:18)

The words *if the world hates you* form a first class conditional statement, and that form gives the statement the meaning that the world certainly does hate the disciples. Now, what would *the world* include? Jesus is not talking here about the earth that we live on. The definition for *world* in this context refers to the mass of unbelievers who are indifferent or hostile to God and His people; it is the evil system of sin as influenced by Satan and acted out by men. The word *hate* means to detest and especially to persecute. It is also has the idea of a fixed hatred. Jesus is warning the disciples that the world will hate them, just as the world hates Him too. And the reality is that the world hates us, too, ladies—or, it should hate us, just as it hated the disciples. The hatred comes because we do not conform to their patterns. We do not have their goals or ambitions or desires. We are an affront to their sin! This would not be a new concept to the disciples because they had been with Jesus for three years and had seen the ongoing persecution He received as well as the attempts that were made to kill Him. The Jews He came to save rejected Him and hated Him and, ultimately, would crucify Him.

As Jesus is speaking these words, His disciples are lacking understanding as to what is awaiting their Lord—His crucifixion is near at hand. And, little do they know what is awaiting them, either, as each would go to eventually be martyred for their faith. John, who is sitting right next to the Lord in the upper room, will pick up his pen many years later, just before his own death, and write, in 1 John 3:13, "Do not marvel, my brethren, if the world hates you." Peter also, who is listening to these words of Jesus, will years from this night write to a group of persecuted Christians, in 1 Peter 4:14, "If you are reproached for the name of Christ, blessed are you, for the Spirit of glory and of God rests upon you. On their part He is blasphemed, but on your part He is glorified." The good news is that this doesn't necessarily mean that all unbelievers will hate us, but many will; as wise old Solomon says in Proverbs 16:7 (LSB), "When a man's ways are pleasing to Yahweh, He makes even his enemies to be at peace with him." But, for the most part, ladies, the world does not like us at all. Just yesterday at church, I was talking to a woman who shared about a friend who refused to sign a petition which would seek to do away with Bibles and Christian counselors in her state, and the person who was trying to persuade her to sign it actually pushed her groceries out of her arms and called her a name I will not repeat!

Now, in the next few verses, Jesus is going to explain five reasons why the world hates His followers. But before we look at those, I thought it would be profitable to consider some other reasons the world hated believers in biblical times. There were a number of slanderous reports which were started by the Jews and reported to the governing authorities: (1) Christians were reported to be insurrectionists, because they would not claim Caesar as Lord. Even though they were the best citizens and paid their taxes, they were branded as disloyal to Caesar. (2) Christians were said to be cannibals. This came from a misunderstanding of our Lord's words in Luke 22:19-20 (LSB): "And when He had taken some bread and given thanks, He broke it and gave it to them, saying, 'This is My body which is given for you. Do this in remembrance of Me.' And in the same way He took the cup after they had eaten, saying, 'This cup which is poured out for you is the new covenant in My blood.'" The rumor was that when Christians gathered to eat, they were actually practicing cannibalism. (3) Christians were also said to practice immorality. This accusation arose from the weekly meals Christians had together, which they called *Agape* Meals or Love Feasts. They were accused of having these meals so they could engage in orgies and sexual indulgences. (4) Christians were accused of breaking up families. Often, when a husband or a wife would become a Christian and his or her spouse did not, it would cause marital tension or split families. Of course, this accusation was, sadly, not a rumor but true.

Looking back to our text, we see that Jesus says take heart, the world will hate you, but *there is a reason for their hatred of you, and the first reason listed here is this: The world hated Christ first.* Jesus says *if the world hates you, you know that it hated Me before it hated you.* In fact, the Greek word for *before* literally means first. Jesus is comforting His troubled disciples with the fact that He was hated first; He had already been touched with the feeling of hurt because of those who hated Him. It is a comfort to me to know that the Lord and others have gone through some of the difficulties I face. When you are hated, my friend, because of your faith, meditate on the fact that your Lord was hated also and He understands your hurt.

At the time Jesus was speaking these words, the disciples did not yet fully realize the measure of the world's hatred toward Jesus, but in a few short hours, they will have a fuller glimpse as He hangs on Golgotha's tree and in the days and years to follow as they themselves suffer persecution for the gospel. The *hate* here is also in the perfect tense, which means that the hatred endures. The world hated Jesus then, and the world still hates Jesus today; the world hated the disciples then, and the world still hates Jesus' disciples today. Jesus continues on in verse 19 to give us a second reason for the world's hatred.

> "If you were of the world, the world would love its own. Yet because you are not of the world, but I chose you out of the world, therefore the world hates you." (John 15:19)

The second reason we are not loved by the world is that: Believers are not of the world. If you were of the world, if you belonged to the world, then the world would love you, *would love its own.* The world would have an affection for you, if you belonged to it. The *if* here implies that the disciples are not of the world. Ladies, be careful, if you find the world loving you. If they love you, then you have a problem, and perhaps a bigger one than you realize. John writes about this in his first epistle, in 1 John 2:15 (LSB) he says, "Do not love the world nor the things in the world. If anyone loves the world, the love of the Father is not in him." If the disciples loved the world and the things of the world, like earthly pleasure, wealth, fame, sensual pleasures, and the like, then the world would not oppose them. It is obvious from this verse that the disciples were *not of this world*. In fact, Jesus will mention this in His High Priestly prayer, in John 17:16: "They are not of the world, just as I am not of the world."

Now, when Jesus says that *the world would love its own*, He uses a word for *love* that is not *agape*, God's love that only God's people can reproduce. Rather, the word used here is *phileo*, which is a word that means to love someone because of having common interests or because they are your friend. That's about the only kind of love the world has to offer, isn't it? It does not compare to God's kind of love, *agape*, which indicates a direction of the will and finding one's joy in something. God's love is a love that would die for others.

When Jesus says *if you were of the world, the world would love its own*, the words *its own* mean literally its own thing. The world certainly has a tone and character that is different from those who belong to Christ. The world has an opposition to God in thought and action. They are doing their own thing and loving their own thing, not having any thoughts of God. Jesus goes on to say *yet because you are not of the world, but I chose you out of the world*, the world hates you. He has already told them that He chose them, in John 15:16. Christ chose the disciples for salvation and He chose them for a specific work, as we saw in our last chapter. Christ has also chosen each one of us who are redeemed not only for salvation but for a specific work. Because the disciples are not of the world, Jesus says, *therefore the world hates you*. Jesus is warning them tenderly about this hatred they will receive, and later on His concern for them will be expressed in His prayer in John 17:14-16, when He prays to the Father, "I have given them Your word; and the world has hated them because they are not of the world, just as I am not of the world.

I do not pray that You should take them out of the world, but that You should keep them from the evil one. They are not of the world, just as I am not of the world." Jesus knew that Satan and his evil world would hate the disciples with the same hatred they had for Him, and so He prays for them, "Oh, God, keep them from the evil one!" I am glad He prayed that, aren't you? At this point, the disciples might have been thinking, "Maybe this Christianity business isn't such a good deal after all!" And so Christ says:

> "Remember the word that I said to you, 'A servant is not greater than his master.' If they persecuted Me, they will also persecute you. If they kept My word, they will keep yours also." (John 15:20)

Jesus is saying to them that they need to *remember* what He's already told them, *the word that I said unto you*, that *a servant is not greater than his master*. Now, when did Jesus say this? He said this back in John 13:16, "Most assuredly, I say to you, a servant is not greater than his master; nor is he who is sent greater than he who sent him." Those words were spoken immediately after Jesus had washed the disciples' feet. He was telling them that a servant is not greater than his Lord, his Master. He was telling them that they should humbly serve one another, just as He had done for them. He was telling them that they should not think of themselves as being above menial and mundane tasks, they aren't greater than Him when it comes to service, and they aren't greater than Him when it comes to persecution and hatred. So, here in this verse, Jesus is essentially asking, "You don't think that if your Master is persecuted that you're going to get away without persecution, do you?" If the Master is persecuted, the servant will also be persecuted. In fact, in Matthew 10:22-24, Jesus gave the Twelve their marching orders before sending them out, and one of the things He mentioned to them is what He's saying here: "And you will be hated by all for My name's sake. But he who endures to the end will be saved. When they persecute you in this city, flee to another. For assuredly, I say to you, you will not have gone through the cities of Israel before the Son of Man comes. A disciple is not above his teacher, nor a servant above his master." Evidently, Peter didn't get it then because we have this account, in Matthew 16:21-28.

> From that time Jesus began to show to His disciples that He must go to Jerusalem, and suffer many things from the elders and chief priests and scribes, and be killed, and be raised the third day.
>
> Then Peter took Him aside and began to rebuke Him, saying, "Far be it from You, Lord; this shall not happen to You!"
>
> But He turned and said to Peter, "Get behind Me, Satan! You are an offense to Me, for you are not mindful of the things of God, but the things of men."
>
> Then Jesus said to His disciples, "If anyone desires to come after Me, let him deny himself, and take up his cross, and follow Me. For whoever desires to save his life will lose it, but whoever loses his life for My sake will find it. For what profit is it to a man if he gains the whole world, and loses his own soul? Or what will a man give in exchange for his soul? For the Son of Man will come in the glory of His Father with His angels, and then He will reward each according to his works. Assuredly, I say to you, there are some standing here who shall not taste death till they see the Son of Man coming in His kingdom."

Some of us think that we should be treated differently than Christ and His disciples were. We think that persecution stuff was for the early church but certainly not for American Christians. If you want to identify with Christ, my friend, then part of that identification is suffering. Remember what Paul said to Timothy in 2 Timothy 2:11-12? "It is a trustworthy saying: for if we died with Him, we will also live with Him; if we endure, we will also reign with Him; if we will deny Him, He also will deny us" (LSB). In fact, Peter finally does get it, and when he writes in 1 Peter 2:21 (LSB), he says, "For to this you have been called, since Christ also suffered for you, leaving you an example that you should follow in His steps." In his early years as a Christian, Peter did not understand the joy of persecution, but later on in his life, as spiritual maturity took hold of him, he learned the joy of suffering for Christ; he came to understand that it was one of the means to his sanctification. I know, the older I get in the Lord, the less I am concerned about pleasing others and actually expect people to hate me. We have the Lord, my friend, and He is enough! *The third reason then that we are hated is because: Believers are not greater than the Lord; if they persecuted our Lord, then they will also persecute His followers.*

Now, before we go on, let's define the word *persecute*, as it is an interesting word. It means to chase like a wild beast, to harass, to treat in an evil manner. Jesus is telling His disciples that they would be persecuted, but, interestingly enough, they did not receive that persecution while Jesus was with them. Very little in Scripture indicates that the disciples were subject to persecution while Jesus was with them. But they were persecuted eventually, and we will deal more with that in a future chapter. The world will persecute you and me if we are following Christ, because they hate the very standard that we represent. Sinful people will not tolerate a righteous standard. My husband and I have served in ministry long enough to experience hatred and persecution, and sometimes, sadly enough, it comes from so-called believers as well as from the world. A righteous standard is convicting, and people certainly don't like the restraint you represent. 2 Timothy 3:12 is a good reminder to all of us: "Indeed, all who desire to live godly in Christ Jesus will be persecuted" (LSB). If we are not suffering persecution, it's possible that we are merely professing Christians only, and not truly genuine in our faith. Jesus Himself said in Luke 6:26 (LSB), "Woe to you when all men speak well of you, for their fathers were doing the same things to the false prophets."

Now, the form of persecution that you and I go through may not be like that of the early Christians, at least not yet. Many of them were smeared with pitch and burned alive to light Nero's garden parties. Some were crucified. Still today, in countries around the world, there are believers who are tortured and killed for their faith. For the most part, these things have not yet happened in the United States. But, nonetheless, the world still hates us. You may receive persecution in the form of ridicule for not joining in a sinful activity with your family or friends. You may receive persecution for standing up for truth and not compromising. You may have lost good friends or strained family ties because of your faith and commitment to Jesus Christ. You may be treated with disdain by so-called believers within your own church who have a loose standard of living. Unfortunately, some Christians mistakenly think that the more Christlike they become (kind, gentle, and humble), the more they will overcome the enmity of unbelievers. But, ladies, the fact of the matter is this: the more Christlike we become, the more we will be antagonized and shunned.

I want to stop here, before we go on, so that we can consider what our attitude should be when we are persecuted. And it's not to go hide in a corner, be depressed, or take drugs! In Matthew 5:10-12, Jesus tells us what our attitude should be: rejoicing. Listen to what He says: "Blessed are those who have been persecuted for the sake of righteousness, for theirs is the kingdom of heaven. Blessed are you when people insult you and persecute you, and falsely say all kinds of evil against you because of Me. Rejoice and be glad, for your reward in heaven is great; for in the same way they persecuted the prophets who were before you" (LSB). This attitude of rejoicing when one is being persecuted is difficult for most of us. But Jesus doesn't simply tell us to rejoice; He also tells us of the reward for suffering persecution—and He says our reward in Heaven is great! In Matthew 19:29, He says that when we leave all to follow Him, even leaving our own families, if need be, we receive a hundredfold in this life and eternal life as well: "And everyone who has left houses or brothers or sisters or father or mother or children or farms for My name's sake, will receive one hundred times as much, and will inherit eternal life" (LSB).

Maybe you're thinking, "Wow! If all I ever get for standing up for Jesus is persecution, maybe this isn't such a good deal." Well, Jesus does go on to say that not all will hate us and persecute us. There is some important encouragement here: *If they kept My word, they will keep yours also.* There will be some that will accept what we say and will come to Christ. Jesus' statement here is an indication that His words should be our words. His words are presented by us as His representatives. And some *will keep*, will believe, that *word*. Not all will reject the message and the messenger— praise be to God! In fact, in the High Priestly Prayer, in John 17, Jesus prays in verse 20 for those who will receive this message: "I do not pray for these alone, but also for those who will believe in Me through their word."

In verse 21, we end with the final two reasons why believers are hated by the world.

> "But all these things they will do to you for My name's sake, because they do not know Him who sent Me." (John 15:21)

What *things* is Jesus talking about and who will do these things? *They*, the world, will hate Jesus' followers, persecute them, and not have any affection for them. All those things they will do to them. Why? Jesus says *for My name's sake*, or on account of Christ. What does this mean? Simply this: Loyalty to the name of Christ will bring hatred and persecution, and the disciples will soon discover this to be true. *So the fourth reason believers will be hated is: Because of the name of Christ.* Christ has already told them in the upper room to pray in His name (John 14:13-14) and now He tells them they will suffer because of His name. My friend, suffering is a gift from God. Listen to what Paul says in Philippians 1:29 (LSB): "For to you it has been granted for Christ's sake, not only to believe in Him, but also to suffer for His sake." And when we read the book of Acts, we see that many of the disciples received this gift of suffering by being beaten and imprisoned for the sake of Christ and the gospel.

We come to our final reason that Christians are hated by the world and this is the main reason we are not loved by the world. Jesus says *because they do not know Him who sent Me. The fifth reason we are hated by the world is this: The world does not know Christ.* The world does not know God; therefore, they hate us. They do not have a personal relationship with Him because they are in ignorance of the fact that God had sent the Son into the world to save sinners. The world did not know that He was the Messiah. They thought He was crazy. They thought He had a demon. So, in ignorance the world hated and persecuted what it did not know, Jesus, and in ignorance they will hate and persecute the disciples, and in ignorance they will persecute and hate you and me. (The following verses are further indication of this truth: Acts 3:17; 13:27, 1 Cor. 2:7-8; 1 John 3:1.) The world is ignorant of who God is and that, my friend, is the main reason for the hatred and suffering and persecution that comes from them. They don't have a clue as to what you are about, because they do not know the One whom your life is about, the Lord Jesus Christ.

Summary

As we reflect on this chapter, we should really be encouraged and not discouraged. We should take courage in the fact that *the world hated Christ first* (v 18): "If the world hates you, you know that it hated Me before it hated you." In verses 25 of this same chapter of John, Jesus will even say that they hate Him without a cause, for no reason at all! And sometimes that's how it is in our own life—people hate us for no reason! As you go through times of persecution, remember that Christ went through it first and, therefore, He has been touched with the feelings of your infirmities. Dear sister, come to the throne of His grace that you might find the mercy you need in the time of your need.

Be encouraged that you are hated because *believers are not of the world* (v 19): "If you were of the world, the world would love its own. Yet because you are not of the world, but I chose you out of the world, therefore the world hates you." I don't know about you, but this encourages me. I have no desire to be identified with a system of evil. We should be grateful for the privilege of being salt and light in the midst of despair and darkness.

We also should be encouraged by the fact that *believers are not greater than the Lord* (v 20): "Remember the word that I said to you, 'A servant is not greater than his master.' If they persecuted Me, they will also persecute you. If they kept My word, they will keep yours also." What a joy to identify with our Lord in His sufferings. Remember what Paul said in Philippians 3:10: "that I may know Him and the power of His resurrection and the *fellowship of His sufferings*, being conformed to His death," (LSB, emphasis mine). We are not greater than our Lord, and it is a privilege, my friend, to suffer for His sake.

We should be encouraged because we suffer *because of the name of Christ* (v 21a): "But all these things they will do to you for My name's sake, because they do not know Him who sent Me." Suffering is an identification that we are God's child. It is a sign that we bear the name "Christian." Just think: as you suffer because of His name, you also have been chosen, selected, among many to live with Him eternally.

The overriding reason the world hates you is that *the world does not know Christ* (v 21b): "But all these things they will do to you for My name's sake, because they do not know Him who sent Me." Do you have a heart of compassion for the world, dear one? Instead of wishing evil upon them for the evil they do to you, see them as lost and dying without Christ.

See them in a Christless eternity. Pray for their souls. Pray that they will know the name of Christ and embrace Him as Lord.

Perhaps all this sounds foreign to some of you, and you're thinking, "I have not been hated or persecuted for my faith." I would challenge you to ask yourself why this is so. The Word of God is clear: if we live in godliness, we will suffer (2 Timothy 3:12). With that in mind, I want to leave you with a challenge from Amy Carmichael, who endured much suffering and persecution for the Lord's sake. She spent 53 years in South India as a missionary, without a furlough. She founded Donavur Fellowship, a refuge for children who were in moral danger. And ladies, working there was no easy matter. In fact, consider just 2 of the 25 questions that were asked of those who desired to come and work there: 1. Do you truly desire to live a crucified life? (This may mean doing very humble things joyfully for His Name's sake.) 2. Does the thought of hardness draw you or repel you? Here is the challenge from this precious saint of God that I would like to leave you with as we bring this chapter to a close.

> Hast thou no scar?
> No hidden scar on foot, or side, or hand?
> I hear thee sung as mighty in the land,
> I hear them hail thy bright ascendant star,
> Hast thou no scar?
> Hast thou no wound?
> Yet I was wounded by the archers, spent,
> Leaned Me against a tree to die; and rent
> by ravening beasts that compassed Me, I swooned:
> Hast thou no wound?
> No wound, no scar?
> Yet, as the Master shall the servant be,
> and pierced are the feet that follow Me;
> But thine are whole: can he have followed far
> Who has no wound nor scar?[1]

---

1 Amy Carmichael, *Toward Jerusalem* (Fort Washington: Christian Literature Crusade, 1936), 85.

QUESTIONS TO CONSIDER

1. Read John 15 and list all the warnings Jesus gives to the disciples.

2. Memorize John 15:18.

3. (a) Jesus told His disciples that the world hated Him before it hated them. According to the following verses, what kind of hatred did Jesus endure, and what was His response? John 1:10-11; 5:16-18; 6:66; 7:1, 30-32; 8:40, 59; 10:31-39; 11:57.

4. (a) Jesus prepares the disciples by telling them that they will be persecuted (John 15:20). Read the following verses and write down what kinds of persecution some of the New Testament saints endured. Also, if it is recorded, note the attitudes which accompanied their sufferings. Acts 5:40-42; Acts 7:54-60; Acts 8:1-4; Acts 12:1-4; Acts 16:16-34; 1 Corinthians 4:11-14; 2 Corinthians 4:8-11; 2 Corinthians 11:23-28; Galatians 6:17. (b) How do these compare to your sufferings and your attitudes while going through suffering?

5. (a) Read Matthew 5:13-16 and 2 Timothy 3:12, and list some possible reasons why some Christians may not be receiving the persecution that Jesus promised would happen. (b) How do believers become "salt that is worthless" or "lamps that have been placed under a bushel"?

6. (a) How does the world today manifest hatred towards Christians? (b) Has the world become more Christianized, or have Christians become more worldly? Explain your answer.

7. How have you prepared those whom you disciple, your children, and those you teach, that persecution and hatred will indeed happen to them?

8. (a) Share a time when you were hated or persecuted because you were a Christian. (b) Were you able to rejoice? (c) What did you learn about Christ, about the world, and about yourself during that time?

9. Are you currently being persecuted because of your faith? If so, how can we pray for you? If not, how might we pray to prepare you for when those times of persecution come? ("Yes, and all who desire to live godly in Christ Jesus will suffer persecution" 2 Timothy 3:12)

The Three Witnesses
John 15:22-27

AFTER I became a believer in Jesus Christ, one of my frustrations for a long time was the fact that I didn't know how to effectively share my faith with others. I knew what I believed, I knew it had changed my life, and I desperately wanted others to have a personal relationship with Jesus Christ, but I didn't know how to effectively share the gospel with them. I thought, "Well, they will hopefully *see* that I am a good Christian, and then they will ask me about the hope that is within me." And so, I eased my conscience with those thoughts.

But as I grew in Christ, I realized that such a scenario rarely happens. I began to see from Scripture that I was commanded to go and proclaim the good news. I had a responsibility, and I had neglected it. And, believe me, that responsibility scared me to death! I was not equipped. What would I say? How would I even begin to turn everyday conversations to spiritual issues? So, I began my quest to learn how to effectively share the gospel. I was trained with my local church, which was very helpful. I also read Will Metzger's book, *To Tell the Truth*,[1] which also helped me tremendously in learning practical ways to share the gospel. Yet, even though those things have helped me quite a bit, I must tell you that the greatest help has been the Spirit of God and the Word of God. These have been my greatest companions and helps in sharing the truth of Christ.

Sharing the gospel of Jesus Christ was also a responsibility of the disciples. In the portion of John's letter we've been studying, Jesus has informed His disciples that He will be leaving. Who, then, would take up this great responsibility and privilege of sharing the truth with the world? It would be the disciples. And I just imagine the disciples had thoughts like: "How will I be an effective witness? I mean, I'm just a mere man

---

1 Will Metzger, *To Tell the Truth* (Downers Grove: Inter Varsity Press, 1984).

and I'm not prepared. Who is going to help equip me?" (And remember, the disciples didn't have any evangelism training programs!) As we come to the end of John 15, Jesus encourages His disciples by first reminding them of His own example of being a witness, and then reminding them that the Spirit will be a witness. But then He tells them that they too will be witnesses. There will be three witnesses: Christ, the Spirit, and the disciples, all witnessing to who Christ is and what He came to do. Let's read John 15:22-27 and unfold this great mystery.

> "If I had not come and spoken to them, they would have no sin, but now they have no excuse for their sin. He who hates Me hates My Father also. If I had not done among them the works which no one else did, they would have no sin; but now they have seen and also hated both Me and My Father. But this happened that the word might be fulfilled which is written in their law, 'They hated Me without a cause.'
>
> But when the Helper comes, whom I shall send to you from the Father, the Spirit of truth who proceeds from the Father, He will testify of Me. And you also will bear witness, because you have been with Me from the beginning."

We learned in our last chapter that there are five reasons why the world hates and persecutes Christians: the world hated Christ first (v 18); believers are not of the world (v 19); believers are not greater than their Lord (v 20); believers bear the name of Christ (v 21a); and the world does not know Christ (v 21b). Our outline for this chapter will include three witnesses: *The Witness of Christ* (vv 22-25); *The Witness of the Spirit* (v 26); and *The Witness of the Disciples* (v 27). Let's look, first, at the witness of Christ. How did He witness?

The Witness of Christ *John 15:22-25*

> "If I had not come and spoken to them, they would have no sin, but now they have no excuse for their sin." (John 15:22)

Notice first that Jesus had to come, as evidenced by the words *if I had not come*. Jesus didn't sit around and wait for the unbelieving world to come to Him; He had to get up and go. He passes this same thought on to His disciples in Matthew 28:19-20 when He says, "'Go therefore and make disciples of all the nations, baptizing them in the name of the Father and of the Son and of the Holy Spirit, teaching them to observe all things that I have commanded you; and lo, I am with you always, even to the end of the age.' Amen." The disciples are commanded to go, just as Jesus went, and you and I are commanded to do the same. I hope you don't try and soothe your conscience like I did by thinking that others will just plop themselves at your front door to hear the gospel.

Not only did Jesus go, but He also had to open His mouth. He had to speak. He says *if I had not come and spoken to them*. The words *spoken to them* indicate that Jesus declared the will of God, audibly making known God's requirements. In fact, Matthew's Gospel reports that Jesus began His public ministry by saying, "Repent, for the kingdom of heaven is at hand" (Matthew 4:17b LSB). And that was just the beginning of many things Jesus spoke to them. He was always speaking and compelling the lost world to repent; He spoke words to arouse their consciences to their sin and their need for a Savior. Likewise, the disciples would need to go and speak, as do you and I. And we would do well to make sure we are also preaching the message of repentance that Jesus preached. Often, our "gospel" is nothing more than "God has a wonderful plan for your life," or something trivial like that. We must compel men and women to repent of their sins!

In Matthew 28, which we just looked at, Jesus said that the disciples not only needed to go, but they also needed to teach (which would mean they needed to open their mouths and speak) all things whatsoever He had commanded them. Opening our mouths is a command, a requirement, for each of us, if we are to testify of Jesus Christ and all that He commanded. *This is the first way Christ witnessed to the world—His words.*

Jesus then says that if He had not come and spoken to them, *they would have no sin*. What does He mean by this? Jesus is not saying that they would be sinless, but that they would not have guilt for a particular sin. If He had not come and spoken to them regarding their sin, they would not be as guilty as they are now. Christ spoke to them of their sin and their need to repent, but they rejected Him. *Sin* here is not referring to missing the mark, failing to meet God's righteous standard; rather, it is referring to the specific sin of rejecting Christ. They willfully sinned by rejecting Him as the Messiah. The greatest sin man can commit is to be given the knowledge of Jesus Christ as Lord and Savior and then reject it. Remember, back in our introductory chapter, we looked at John 1:11, where John records for us, "He came to what was His own, and those who were His own did not receive Him" (LSB). Jesus came to His own, the Jewish nation, and they rejected Him. H. A. Ironside illustrates this point with this story.

> Once in inland Africa, there was a missionary who had hung a little mirror on a tree outside of his home. The wife of an African chief happened to visit this mission station and saw the mirror and glanced into it. She had come straight out of her pagan environment and had never before seen the hideous paintings on her face or her hardened features. She was startled at what she saw and asked the missionary, "Who is that horrible looking person inside the tree?" The missionary explained it was her face. She could not believe it until she held the mirror in her hand. When she saw and understood it was her, she asked the missionary if she could buy it from him. After much insistence by the woman, the missionary sold it to her. After the sale, she threw it down and it broke in several pieces. She said, "I will never have it making faces at me again."[2]

That's what Jesus is saying here. The Jews had their sin exposed and they did not like what they saw, so instead of dealing with their sin, they killed the Lord of glory, trying to get rid of the guilt of sin which He had exposed. Instead of looking at their hearts and changing, they threw the truth away and hated the one who is Truth. They sinned willfully against the light that was given them, and they were guilty. According to the writer of Hebrews, that is a very serious thing. Hebrews 10:26-27 (LSB) says, "For if we go on sinning willfully after receiving the knowledge of the truth, there no longer remains a sacrifice for sins, but a terrifying expectation of judgment and the fury of a fire which will consume the adversaries." This is the blasphemy against the Holy Spirit that is spoken

---

2 H. A. Ironside, *Addresses on the Gospel of John*, https://www.brethrenarchive.org/media/364645/ironside-h-a-_-john.pdf. Accessed 10/5/2023.

of in Matthew 12:32. There is no forgiveness for this sin, the sin of rejecting the gospel of Christ.

Jesus goes on to say *but now they have no excuse for their sin*. They now have no cloak, no covering, for their sin; there is no *excuse* for them. Paul echoes this truth regarding the world's rejecting of truth, in Romans 1:20 (LSB), "For since the creation of the world His invisible attributes, both His eternal power and divine nature, have been clearly seen, being understood through what has been made, so that they are without excuse." The proof is so clear that they cannot plead ignorance. They cannot hide their sin. There is simply no excuse. They had been given the light, they had been given privileges, and yet they rejected the light and the privileges. They had no excuse! This exposure of their sin led them to hate the Lord, but little did they realize, their hatred was for the very God they claimed to worship. Look at verse 23:

> "He who hates Me hates My Father also." (John 15:23)

The Jews, remember, claimed God as their Father. In John 8:41, they stated, "we have one Father—God," and yet they hated Jesus, who was God in the flesh. So, Jesus reminds His disciples of the world's hatred again but now adds that to hate Him is to hate the Father also: *He who hates Me hates My Father also*. As we have already seen, Jesus and the Father are one. To glorify one is to glorify the other. To love one is to love the other. To receive one is to receive the other. To see one is to see the other. And, to hate one is to hate the other. The word *hate* here means to detest. It is impossible to hate only one member of the Trinity. One commentator helps us here: "The Jews professed that they loved God, and that on the ground of that love they hated Christ; the God, however, whom they loved was not the true God, but a phantom which they named God. The fact that they rejected Christ, in spite of all His words of spirit and truth, showed them to be the enemies of the Father."[3] Man cannot rightly say, "I love God," and yet reject His Son Jesus Christ and the work He was sent to do!

---

[3] J. C. Ryle, *Expository Thoughts on the Gospels*.

In verse 24, Christ now tells His disciples that not only did He use words to witness, but He also used works.

> "If I had not done among them the works which no one else did, they would have no sin; but now they have seen and also hated both Me and My Father." (John 15:24)

Jesus adds that not only did He come and speak to the world, but He also did *among them the works which no one else did*. John uses the word *works* 27 times in his Gospel, and 18 of those apply to the works Jesus did. These works that Christ did were not like anyone else's. No man has done such works. No other person has ever done the miracles that Jesus did. It is said that in the years Jesus was on earth, He probably performed more miracles than Moses and Elijah and all the prophets put together. And Jesus appealed to them to believe on Him because of His works. *This is the second way in which He witnesses: by His works.* (Consider the following verses: John 5:36; 10:38; 14:11.) Jesus had done more miracles before their eyes than anyone else, and yet they remained in unbelief and hatred toward Him. Their hatred for Him led them to ascribe His works to the power of evil. In fact, they claimed He had a demon (see John 7:20; 8:48-59; and 10:20). They attributed His works to Satan! So He came, He spoke, He worked miracles, and they still rejected Him. The disciples will also go and speak and do miracles, and they too will experience rejection and hatred. And ladies, we also must go and speak and do the works that Christ has called us to do, and we will be rejected too. What was the result of Christ doing works in their midst? *But now they have seen and also hated both Me and My Father*. These two verbs, *seen* and *hated*, are in the perfect tense, which indicates a permanent attitude of seeing and hating. The world saw Him, and they did not know they were seeing the Father; they hated Him, and they did not realize they hated the Father. They compounded sin upon sin.

But it's important that these words not overwhelm the disciples. Why? Because this is a fulfillment of prophecy, Jesus says in verse 25. This rejection was not a mistake.

> "But this happened that the word might be fulfilled which is written in their law, 'They hated Me without a cause.'" (John 15:25)

Jesus has already mentioned to them once in the upper room, in John 13:18, that Judas' betrayal was a fulfillment of Scripture, and when we studied that verse we learned that it was a fulfillment of Psalm 41:9. Now, Jesus says that this hatred of Him is a fulfillment of the *word* that is *written in their law*, the law they supposedly so strictly adhered to. In pointing to *their law*, Jesus indicates that this was the Jews' law; it was theirs, and it was given especially to them for their guidance. They should have been warned by this—but they read their own law with blind eyes! Jesus says it is written in their Scriptures: *they hated Me without a cause*. Where is this found? Psalm 35:19 is one of those Scriptures which states, "Let those who are wrongfully my enemies not be glad over me; nor let those who hate me without cause wink maliciously" (LSB). Also, in Psalm 69:4, we have, "Those who hate me without cause are more than the hairs of my head; those who would destroy me are powerful, being wrongfully my enemies; what I did not steal, I then have to restore" (LSB). The Scripture was indeed fulfilled.

What possible reason could there be for anyone to hate the Lord? He had never injured anyone. He had never said anything evil or thought anything evil of anyone. And yet, they hated Him, without anything in Him being worthy of hatred. No one on earth has been more hated than Jesus, and yet He is hated without a cause, without a justifying reason. Other men are hated, but there is usually an obvious reason. People like Hitler, Charles Manson, Saddam Hussein, Osama Bin Laden, Muammar Gaddafi, are understandably hated—but Jesus Christ? As Pilate asked, in Matthew 27:23, "What evil has He done?"

At this point, the thought of their Lord being hated might be causing some fear in the eleven disciples. This news alone might be enough to shatter the disciple's faith and discourage them, so the Lord reminds them of the encouragement of the Helper and the fact that the disciples will have the Holy Spirit with them. Both the Spirit and the disciples will need to testify of Jesus. Jesus spoke, and they hated Him. Jesus did works, and they hated him. Now, He is leaving them, and they too will speak and do works and be hated, but not without a Helper. So, we move from the witness of Christ to the witness of the Spirit. How did the Spirit witness? By testifying of Christ, as we see in verse 26.

The Witness of the Spirit *John 15:26*

> "But when the Helper comes, whom I shall send to you from the Father, the Spirit of truth who proceeds from the Father, He will testify of Me." (John 15:26)

Jesus encourages His disciples that *when the Helper comes*, He will testify of Christ. The *Helper* is the Holy Spirit, the Comforter, the One who has been called to help and to encourage. This Helper will be sent by Jesus *from the Father* (look back to John 14:16 and 26 to refresh your memory). The Son says He will pray for this gift of the Spirit and the Father will give Him; He *will proceed from the Father*. Jesus also calls Him *the Spirit of truth*. We saw this back in John 14:17. He is the Spirit *of truth*, because Jesus is truth, and the Father is truth—they are three, yet one. I think it is interesting that Jesus uses the word *truth* here to describe the Spirit, as He would be testifying to the truth, in contrast to the world, which is full of lies. In fact, Romans 1:25 tells us the unbelieving world has "exchanged the truth of God for the lie." And so, Jesus says, this Spirit of truth will come and testify of the truth. This will be one of His ministries when He comes; Jesus says *He will testify of me*. To *testify* is to bear witness. And the first instance we have of this witness of the Holy Spirit is found in Acts 2. *This is the witness of the Spirit—He will testify of Christ.* But Christ did not intend that He and the Holy Spirit be the only witnesses. The third witness was to be the disciples.

The Witness of the Disciples *John 15:27*

> "And you also will bear witness, because you have been with Me from the beginning." (John 15:27)

Jesus tells the Eleven that they *also will bear witness of Him*; they also will testify of Him. In Acts 1:8, right before Jesus ascends up into Heaven, the last words He says to His disciples are these: "but you will receive power when the Holy Spirit has come upon you; and you shall be My witnesses both in Jerusalem, and in all Judea and Samaria, and even to the end of the earth" (Acts 1:8 LSB). This was one of the main reasons Christ chose them and sent them forth: to be witnesses of Him. No other men would have more authority to be such solid, profound witnesses. Why? Jesus says *because you have been with Me from the beginning.* This simply means that they had been with Him from the *beginning* of His public work (see Matthew 4:17-22; Luke 1:1-4; and Acts 1:1-8). An interesting side note is that when the other 11 were choosing a successor for Judas, they felt it necessary that the one requirement be that he belong to the company of the disciples who had been with Jesus from the beginning: "Therefore it is necessary that of the men who have accompanied us all the time that the Lord Jesus went in and out among us—beginning with the baptism of John until the day that He was taken up from us—one of these must become a witness with us of His resurrection." (Acts 1:21-22 LSB).

The testimony of the Spirit and of the disciples goes out to the world as one. The disciples are the Spirit's instruments. He and they are joined together and thus the testimony of Jesus Christ is delivered.

Summary

We have three witnesses—Christ, the Spirit, and the disciples—all testifying to the truth of the gospel of saving grace. The method is go, speak, and do works. The response many times will be hatred and persecution, but some will be saved. Some will see the light of the gospel.

Ladies, we too must be witnesses for our Savior. Perhaps some of you have the same thought I had as an early Christian: "I will just live the gospel and the world will see that I am a Christian." Perhaps some of you are ashamed of the gospel. Perhaps some of you just don't know what to say or you're afraid you will make mistakes. We too must go. We too must speak. And we too must live out the gospel before the world by our good works.

Let's consider each of these three areas, by way of closing. First, the going. Jesus had to come. The disciples were commanded to go. You and I are also commanded to go. Are you willing to go? When the Spirit of God prompts you and says, "Go and tell that neighbor about Jesus Christ," do you go? Are you willing to lay aside your schedule and your time to go? And are you willing to go wherever and whenever He wants you to go? You must have a willing heart to go.

Secondly, you must open your mouth and speak. Are you willing? Are you prepared? When you're at a gathering with family members and the Holy Spirit says, "Speak to them about Jesus Christ; tell them the gospel," do you? Will Metzger says in his book, *To Tell the Truth*, "To remain silent and let others put their interpretation upon our actions is wrong. God himself did not do this.... Likewise we must speak—and speak of Christ. We must speak even when we do not know much about the Bible. We must speak even when it is inconvenient. God is bigger than our sins, our ignorance, and our pride. He will honor His words in our mouth."[4] Maybe you're thinking, "I don't know what to say." Then I highly encourage you to get involved in an evangelism training class like *Evangelism Explosion*[5], or read Will Metzger's book, *To Tell The Truth*. But do something. As Romans 10:14-15 (LSB) says, "How then will they call on Him in whom they have not believed? How will they believe in Him whom they have not heard? And how will they hear without a preacher? And how will they preach unless they are sent? Just as it is written, 'How beautiful are the feet of those who proclaim good news of good things!'"

Lastly, ladies, we must do works. Jesus did His works before the unbelieving world, the Spirit did works, and the disciples did works. Are you doing works? Are you living your life in such a way that people see that you are a Christian? Does your life reflect holiness? Are you showing the love of Christ to your neighbors, or do they hear you and your husband screaming at each other or see you out in your yard yelling at your kids? Do you show compassion when you know an unbeliever might be sick or in need of something? Would the world be left without excuse as they witness your lifestyle before them? Again, Metzger says, "At times our actions do speak louder than our words.... God didn't send a tract, He

---

4 Will Metzger, *To Tell the Truth*, 23.

5 D. James Kennedy, *Evangelism Explosion 4th edition* (Carol Stream: Tyndale House Publishers, 1999).

prepared a body. Likewise, God has prepared our bodies to demonstrate Him. Much of Jesus' witnessing was in response to a question following an act of kindness or a miracle."[6] Others should look at our lives and say, "There is something very different about her; she is not like the world." We must go, we must speak, and we must do the work before the lost world. Are you willing to go, to speak, and to do the work?

---

6 Will Metzger, *To Tell the Truth*, 23.

QUESTIONS TO CONSIDER

1. Read John 15:22-27. (a) What caused the world to hate the Lord? (b) What causes the world to hate you?

2. Memorize John 15:26.

3. Jesus says, in John 15:22, that if He had not spoken to them (the world) they would have no sin. (a) Read John 5:31-47; 6:25-59; 7:16-53; and 12:37-50. What things did Jesus say to the unbelieving world that would have exposed their sin, and what was their response to His words? (b) What does the phrase, "they would have no sin," mean in John 15:22 and 24? (c) How does the world respond to your words?

4. (a) What does Jesus say about His works in the following passages? John 5:17-20, 36; 10:25-26; (b) Why do you think His works caused a response of hate from the Jews? (c) In what ways have your works caused hatred from the world?

5. In what ways did the Holy Spirit "testify of Christ" (John 15:26) when He came in Acts 2?

6. The disciples were told that they too would be witnesses for Christ. Find two or three examples in Acts where this was true and note what you learn about their witness.

7. Can you effectively share the gospel of Jesus Christ with a lost person? What would you say?

8. Please come with a prayer request regarding how you might be a better witness for the Lord.

Warning: Persecution Is Coming!
John 16:1-4

THE week I was studying for this chapter, I was communicating with two of my friends who both attend churches other than my own in my hometown. Both of them shared with me how their churches had recently spent time praying for the persecuted church. November 13th had, evidently, been set aside as the International Day of Prayer for the Persecuted Church. It is a special day, designed to focus on the needs of Christians around the world who are being persecuted for their faith. It is a time to ask God to strengthen their faith and grant them strength and courage when they feel weak, tired, or scared.

Persecution is not a popular topic among Christians today. The biggest reason it is not a popular topic is because most believers recoil from conflict, pain, and suffering. If you think I'm wrong, just ask the person next to you or your closest Christian friend, if they would prefer some form of persecution this week or if they would rather receive a tremendous blessing or an answer to prayer from the Lord. But, an even less popular topic among Christians would be martyrdom. And for this you don't need to ask anyone; just ask yourself, "Self, would you like to be put to death this week because of your faith in Christ Jesus?" Don't give "self" too long to answer that question, because "self" might surprise you!

Persecution and martyrdom. These are hard topics to contemplate, are they not? We 21st century American Christians don't have to think of persecution or martyrdom too often. But that was not the case for the beloved eleven disciples. They not only had to think about persecution and martyrdom, but they also had to endure it. In the passage we'll study in this chapter, Christ forewarns His disciples of persecution and martyrdom by saying in John 16:1-4,

> "These things I have spoken to you, that you should not be made to stumble. They will put you out of the synagogues; yes, the time is coming that whoever kills you will think that he offers God service. And these things they will do to you because they have not known the Father nor Me. But these things I have told you, that when the time comes, you may remember that I told you of them. And these things I did not say to you at the beginning, because I was with you."

There is an unfortunate chapter division between John 15 and 16. The reason it's unfortunate is that in John 15 the Lord has been speaking of the hatred of the world against Himself, against the Father, and against the disciples. And here, in chapter 16, He is simply continuing to speak about that very same hatred and how it will manifest itself in shocking ways. But, remember that there is also encouragement in Christ's words; He's just spoken in the proceeding verses of the dear Comforter, the Holy Spirit, so the disciples will not go through this persecution alone. As they go out and bear witness, testifying of the grace of the gospel, they will be persecuted, yes, but the Comforter will be with them.

In our last chapter, we learned of three witnesses who all testify to the truth of the gospel of saving grace: Christ Himself, the Holy Spirit, and the disciples. The method, we learned, is to go, to speak, and to work. And the response, many times, will be hatred and persecution. Thankfully, though, some will be saved, some will see the light of the gospel. Our outline for this chapter will show us: *The Lord's Mercy by Warning of Persecution* (vv 1, 4); *The World's Method of Persecution* (v 2); and *The World's Motive Behind the Persecution* (v 3). Let's look at the mercy of our Lord in warning of impending persecution, in verse 1.

The Lord's Mercy by Warning of Persecution   *John 16:1, 4*

> "These things I have spoken to you, that you should not be made to stumble." (John 16:1)

You might be wondering what things Christ is referring to when He says *these things*. He is referring back to the opposition and hatred from the world that He's been talking about. (*These things*, by the way, is used five times in the first six verses of John 16.) Jesus says these things *I have spoken to you, that you should not be made to stumble.* The word *stumble*, or offend, means to do something which leads to the fall or ruin of someone. The figure is that of a trap in which a crooked stick holds the bait and springs the trap when it's touched. Christ is saying, "I am telling you these things so that you may not be caught unaware. I am telling you now so that you will realize that being my disciple means hatred from the world. Don't let this fact trip you up as a disciple of Jesus Christ. When these things happen to you, don't let them cause you to apostatize!" Hadn't Jesus forewarned them of this already in Matthew 10? When Christ gave the disciples their "marching orders," He told them it would be difficult. He told them that they would be delivered up to the council, that they would be scourged, that they would be hated and persecuted. And then He reminded them in Matthew 10:24 (LSB) that "A disciple is not above his teacher, nor a slave above his master." He also told them in Matthew 16:24-26 (LSB), "If anyone wishes to come after Me, let him deny himself, and take up his cross and follow Me. For whoever wishes to save his life will lose it; but whoever loses his life for My sake will find it. For what will it profit a man if he gains the whole world and forfeits his soul? Or what will a man give in exchange for his soul?" The cost of discipleship is losing one's life for the sake of Christ and, at times, that could literally entail one's actual physical life!

This is not the only thing Jesus warned His disciples about while they were all in the upper room. He also warned them of Judas' betrayal (John 13:18-19); He warned Peter of his denial (John 13:38); He warned all of them that the prince of the world was coming (John 14:29-30); He warned them of the seriousness of not abiding in Him (John 15:6) and many other things. What a loving Savior we have, Who warns His children of such things! What mercy He manifested!

That same mercy Jesus showed to His disciples is also shown to us, as we too will suffer for His name, because all who desire to live godly in Christ Jesus will suffer persecution. But aren't you glad that you have been forewarned? Isn't it a gracious and loving thing for our Lord to warn the disciples and to warn us of such coming suffering? And yet, even with this warning and the admonition to not be tripped up, in less than 24 hours we see the disciples being offended and forsaking their Lord, according to Matthew 26:56 (LSB): "'But all this has taken place in order that the Scriptures of the prophets would be fulfilled.' Then all the disciples left Him and fled."

However, here in John 16, in the upper room, we see the love and mercy of Jesus, Who loved those disciples to the end. He knew that they would be offended, and yet, He didn't say, "I don't know why I'm telling you guys this. You're going to mess up in just a few hours anyway! I'm just wasting my breath!" No, Christ is very long-suffering. His mercy is shown in warning them of impending persecution.

Just the day before I wrote this chapter, I was speaking to a pastor's wife, trying to encourage her as she was enduring much suffering for Christ. I gently reminded her that this was promised by Jesus, and Jesus even said, "Woe to you when all men speak well of you (Luke 6:26a LSB). Now, in verse two, Christ is going to get a little more graphic as to what form of persecution His disciples should expect. Here we see the world's method of persecution.

The World's Method of Persecution   *John 16:2*

> "They will put you out of the synagogues; yes, the time is coming that whoever kills you will think that he offers God service." (John 16:2)

Who is Jesus talking about when He says *they will put you out of the synagogues*? When Jesus says *they*, who is He referring to? This persecution came from Christ's people, the Jews, who professed to be the people of God. And what is the method of persecution? What will they do? There are two forms of persecution that Christ mentions here. First of all, the disciples will be *put ... out of the synagogue*. This literally means "they will make you out-of-synagogue men." This means they would be separated from the synagogue, excommunicated from it. This word is only used in John 9:20-22; John 12:42-43; and here. So what did it mean to be *put out* of the synagogue? There were three degrees of excommunication or banishment among the Jews.

The first degree was only a rebuke pronounced upon the offender for up to 30 days. This did not necessarily mean exclusion from attending and participation in the synagogue worship, but exclusion from the fellowship of the congregation and the blessings and privileges that went along with that.

The second degree was exclusion from the assembly and from communication with others for another 30 days. This degree was accompanied by curses and severe restrictions.

The final degree was a ban of indefinite duration. It involved an exclusion from all the rights and privileges of the Jewish people, both civil and religious, and the offender was considered as dead.

The first two degrees were primarily disciplinary; the third was a cutting off from the congregation. The definition of this Greek term denotes one who has been excommunicated from the commonwealth of the people of God and has been given over to the curse. We see this very thing warned of in Ezra 10:8 (LSB), "and that whoever would not come within three days, according to the counsel of the prince and the elders, all his possessions should be devoted to destruction and he himself separated from the assembly of the exiles." In fact, Jesus actually warns the Pharisees, in Matthew 23:34, that they will do this to His people: "On account of this, behold, I am sending you prophets and wise men and scribes; some of them you will kill and crucify, and some of them you will flog in your synagogues, and persecute from city to city" (LSB). The Jews who persecuted the disciples regarded them as blasphemers and as seeking to overthrow the temple service and the entire religious system that God had established.

Ladies, this would be a very hard thing for the disciples. To the Jews, the synagogue held a very special place in their lives. This would not just be a denial of church membership. This would mean no participation in worship, no sacrifices, not even the reading of the Scriptures. And remember, during this time, the Scriptures could only be found and heard in places of worship. So, this would mean to the disciples that they would lose all their religious benefits. But they wouldn't only be losing religious privileges; they would lose social and economic privileges as well. Friends would shun them and treat them as pagans. They would lose their jobs and be exiled from their families and lose the privilege of an honorable burial. These words that Jesus says would be hard words for the disciples to hear, because this persecution would come from their own religious leaders.

And what should be their response to this? Jesus tells them in another place what their response should be. In Luke 6:22-23 (LSB), He says, "Blessed are you when men hate you, and exclude you, and insult you, and scorn your name as evil, for the sake of the Son of Man. Be glad in that day and leap for joy, for behold, your reward is great in heaven. For their fathers were doing the same things to the prophets." Rejoice and leap for joy?! This would not be an easy thing for them to do! Peter is listening to these words, and even though he will go on to deny the Lord just a few hours from this moment, he will later on in his life and ministry pick up his pen and write, in 1 Peter 4:12-13 (LSB), "Beloved, do not be surprised at the fiery trial among you, which comes upon you for your testing, as though some strange thing were happening to you. But to the degree you are sharing the sufferings of Christ, keep on rejoicing, so that also at the revelation of His glory you may rejoice with exultation." Peter came to learn that part of the cross he was called to take up was suffering and fiery trials.

The second part of this persecution would come in the form of murder. Jesus says, *Yes, the time is coming that whoever kills you will think that he offers God service*. How could they think that killing Jesus' followers would be doing God a service? The word for *think* here in the Greek is interesting. It means to incorrectly think, which involves error. Their thinking was absurd and it involved error. But, nonetheless, they think that they are doing God a service. *Service*, here, means a divine service or an act of worship; it is a term used of service that a priest rendered at the altar in the temple of God. These persecutors thought that killing the disciples would actually be serving God! It's amazing, isn't it, that people could actually think that murder would be an act of worship to God? It displays how perverted one's worship can become. The apostle Paul felt this way prior to his conversion. When he was speaking to King

Agrippa, in Acts 26:9-11, Paul explains,

> "Indeed, I myself thought I must do many things contrary to the name of Jesus of Nazareth. This I also did in Jerusalem and many of the saints I shut up in prison, having received authority from the chief priests; and when they were put to death, I cast my vote against them. And I punished them often in every synagogue and compelled them to blaspheme; and being exceedingly enraged against them, I persecuted them even to foreign cities."

And to the church of Galatia, he says, "For you have heard of my former conduct in Judaism, how I used to persecute the church of God beyond measure and tried to destroy it" (Galatians 1:13 LSB). Paul was like many of the Jews who thought that persecution of Christians to their death was morally justified. They had a zeal for God, but not according to knowledge, as Romans 10:2 says.

The amazing thing is that this prophecy was fulfilled as most all of Christ's disciples and apostles were martyred by the enemies of their Master. According to historical tradition, Matthew suffered martyrdom when he was slain in a city in Ethiopia. Mark died in Alexandria after being dragged through the streets of the city. Luke was hung on an olive tree in the land of Greece. Peter was crucified in Rome with his head facing downward. In John 21:18, the Lord told Peter how he would die, that when he was young he clothed himself and went where he wanted to go, but when he would grow old someone else would clothe him and carry him where he did not want to go, and stretch forth his hands, indicating crucifixion as the means by which he would die. James, the brother of Jesus, was thrown from a pinnacle of the temple and then beaten to death. Bartholomew was flayed alive. Andrew was bound to a cross, where he preached to his persecutors until he died. Jude was shot to death with arrows. Matthias was stoned and then beheaded. Barnabas was stoned to death. Thomas was martyred in India. John, the writer of the epistle we're studying, was put in boiling oil and afterwards was banished to the Isle of Patmos. The apostle Paul, after various tortures and persecutions, was beheaded in Rome by Emperor Nero. And, even as we move to second and third generation of Christians, we find it no different. One church historian records:

> The most horrible recorded instances of torture were usually inflicted, either by the populace, or in their presence, in the arena. We read of Christians bound in chains of red-hot iron, while the stench of their half-consumed flesh rose in a suffocating cloud to heaven; of others who were torn to the very bone by shells, or hooks of iron; of holy virgins given over to the lust of the gladiator or to the mercies of the pander; of two hundred and twenty-seven converts sent on one occasion to the mines, each with the sinews of one leg severed by a red-hot iron, and with an eye scooped from its socket; of fires so slow that the victims writhed for hours in their agonies; of bodies torn limb from limb, or sprinkled with burning lead; of mingled salt and vinegar poured over the flesh that was bleeding from the rack; of tortures prolonged and varied through entire days. For the love of their Divine Master, for the cause they believed to be true, men and even weak girls, endured these things without flinching, when one word would have freed them from their sufferings.[1]

Jesus says, "Yes, the time is coming that whoever kills you will think that he offers God service" (John 16:2).

The thought of their dying for the sake of Christ must have been frightening for the eleven disciples. But now that they are in Heaven, that sacrifice must seem insignificant to them. Heaven is exceedingly better than this world of sin and sorrow. In fact, do you know that those who have been martyred for their faith in the Lord Jesus are specifically mentioned in Revelation 6:9-11 and Revelation 20:4? Revelation 6:9-11 says,

> When He opened the fifth seal, I saw under the altar the souls of those who had been slain for the word of God and for the testimony which they held. And they cried with a loud voice, saying, "How long, O Lord, holy and true, until You judge and avenge our blood on those who dwell on the earth?" Then a white robe was given to each of them; and it was said to them that they should rest a little while longer, until both the

---

1 William Edward Hartpole Lecky, "History of European Morals From Augustus to Charlemagne: Vol. 1.," 467-468, *Project Gutenberg*, https://www.gutenberg.org/cache/epub/39273/pg39273-images.html. Accessed 9/29/2023.

number of their fellow servants and their brethren, who would be killed as they were, was completed.

And Revelation 20:4 states,

> And I saw thrones, and they sat on them, and judgment was committed to them. Then I saw the souls of those who had been beheaded for their witness to Jesus and for the word of God, who had not worshiped the beast or his image, and had not received his mark on their foreheads or on their hands. And they lived and reigned with Christ for a thousand years.

Now, you might be thinking to yourself, "Other than thinking they were worshipping God, what would have led these people to do such horrific things to Christ's followers?" That's a good question. And our Lord answers that in verse three, and here we see the world's motive behind their persecution.

The World's Motive Behind the Persecution   John 16:3

> "And these things they will do to you because they have not known the Father nor Me." (John 16:3)

When Jesus says *these things they will do*, it indicates certainty. These prophecies of coming persecution will happen. The motive behind the persecution is because they have not known the Father. In fact, Jesus has already mentioned this to them in the upper room, in John 15:21. But here, He says they will do this not only *because they have not known the Father* but also because they have not known Him—He adds, *nor Me*. If Jesus had just said because they did not know the Father, that might have been confusing. Why? Because the Jews knew God according to knowledge, but they rejected Jesus as Messiah and God in the flesh. "To be ignorant of Me," Jesus is saying, "is to be ignorant of the Father." As Paul states in Romans 10:2 (LSB), "For I testify about them that they have a zeal for God, but not according to knowledge."

The word for *known* here means to know experientially. We saw back in John 14:17 that the disciples knew Jesus experientially; they had a relationship with Him. But these that will go on to kill His followers and put them out of the synagogue do not know Him; they do not have a relationship with Him or with His Father. The Jews did not understand that Jesus and the Father are one. This is a huge reason why we see hatred of Christians even today: the world is ignorant of God and of Christ. If the Jews had really known who Jesus is, they would not have persecuted the early Christians the way they did, nor would they have crucified the Lord of glory. Having established this fact, Jesus now turns from the motive for why they would do such horrible things to, once again, His warning of what is to come. Here, again, we see the Lord's mercy by warning of persecution in verse 4.

The Lord's Mercy by Warning of Persecution *John 16:1, 4*

> "But these things I have told you, that when the time comes, you may remember that I told you of them. And these things I did not say to you at the beginning, because I was with you." (John 16:4)

The *I* in this sentence is emphatic in the Greek. It's as though Jesus is saying, "Remember that I myself, your Master, told you these things. And why have I told you these things?" So that *when the time shall comes, you may remember that I told you of them*. Just as His hour had come, as John 13:1 indicates, so their hour would also come. Jesus is saying, "Remember, be mindful, when it comes, that I told you it would come." He is telling them ahead of time, and He does not allow His disciples to fall into trials without giving them sufficient warning. But He will also give them the sufficient grace that they will need to bear these things. He is effectively strengthening them here by forewarning them. That's what a loving Lord does. They would not be able to honestly say, "Why didn't He warn us of this?" Often, we as parents do the same thing for our children. We forewarn them of things to come.

I think of all the things I forewarned my children of when they were growing up in our home. Things like the results of marrying a non-believer, committing fornication, getting involved with wrong friends, getting caught up in sin, and yes, even the cost of being a disciple. Our children have had to learn the loneliness and difficulty of sometimes standing alone. But that is what a loving parent will do, warn and prepare our children for life in a hostile world. Hopefully, our kids have remembered these warnings and are passing them on to their own children. They came from a heart of love, just as Christ warned His disciples from a heart of love.

What is so wonderful about our Lord is that His timing of when to say these things is perfect! He says *And these things I did not say to you at the beginning, because I was with you.* He did not tell them these things at the beginning of His ministry with them. Can you imagine what would have happened if He had told them the day He met them: "Guess what, guys? You're going to be persecuted and put out of the synagogue and killed." He knew that to tell them this truth at that point would have hindered the joy of the time they had with Him for those three and a half years. There was not a need then to tell them then, but now, at this point, there is, because He will soon be departing.

Ladies, we see the mercy of Christ in the timing of this painful prophecy, and by this we all can learn the importance of timing. You wouldn't tell your newborn child, "Now baby, don't marry a non-Christian, and it's a rough life out there, and don't commit fornication, and don't do drugs." They wouldn't comprehend a word you were saying! Having the right timing means we must be discerning and wise and seek the face of God. But there was another reason Jesus did not tell His disciples these things at the beginning; He says, *because I was with you.* While He was with them, it would have been premature to speak about the persecutions they would encounter. He didn't give them this warning any earlier because the world's persecution had been against Him, not them. All along, they must have seen the antagonism He encountered, and He had protected them in the midst of all that. But He will be gone soon, and they will have to stand alone without Him. They will feel the hatred He felt, they will suffer the persecution He suffered; they will die unjustly the way He died.

Summary

We have seen the Lord's mercy by warning the Eleven of persecution, in verses 1 and 4. In verse 1, His mercy is displayed in warning them of the persecution to come and to not to be tripped up by it. In verse 4, His mercy is manifested in encouraging them to remember that He had warned them of this and that His warning was perfectly timed.

We have seen the world's method of persecution, in verse 2. They will do two things: they will put the disciples out of the synagogue and will kill them.

And we have seen the world's motive behind the persecution, in verse 3. The reason unbelievers will do these things is because they do not know the Father and they do not know Jesus.

Persecution and martyrdom are indeed unpleasant topics, but, nonetheless, they are a reality. You might be objecting to this statement, thinking, "Well, yes, this is true for those eleven disciples, but not for us." It is true that we here in the United States have been spared from serious persecution thus far, but in other parts of the world, martyrdom is very real. In fact, in the 20th century alone, there were close to 100 million martyrs. There were more people martyred for their faith in Jesus Christ in the 20th century than in all the previous 19 centuries combined. More people died in circumstances related to their faith in the 20th century than in all the 20th century wars combined. Just recently, I read the following from a worldwide persecution watch list:

> Christians remain one of the most persecuted religious groups in the world. While Christian persecution takes many forms, it is defined as any hostility experienced as a result of identification with Christ. Christians throughout the world continue to risk imprisonment, loss of home and assets, torture, beheadings, rape and even death as a result of their faith. Trends show that countries in Africa, Asia and the Middle East are intensifying persecution against Christians, and perhaps the most vulnerable are Christian women, who often face double persecution for faith and gender. Every day we receive new reports of Christians who

face threats, unjust imprisonment, harassment, beatings and even loss of family because of their faith in Jesus. Every month 255 Christians are killed; 104 are abducted; 180 Christian women are raped, sexually harassed or forced into marriage; 66 churches are attacked; 160 Christians are detained without trial and imprisoned.[2]

When we consider the reality of these persecutions, we might ask, "When will these atrocities against Christians end?" We know the answer to that question, don't we? It won't end until Jesus comes again and takes His beloved ones to Heaven. But the bigger question we ought to be asking is, "Why don't we see more martyrdom, especially in our country?" We're promised such persecution here in this text as well as in 2 Timothy 3:12, "Yes, and all who desire to live godly in Christ Jesus will suffer persecution." The answer lies in the fact that we live in a "Christianized" nation. But the day may come here in America (and it may be sooner than we think) when either we or our children may be martyred for the faith. Are we ready? Who will be the martyrs of the 21st century, and who will be their persecutors? We must make up our minds that we will endure the battles, the opposition, the conflicts, the wounds, the persecution, and, perhaps, even the death that may come to us because of our faith in the Lord Jesus! J. C. Ryle once said, "We never can tell what is before us in life. But of one thing we may be very sure: we must carry the cross if we would wear the crown."[3]

---

[2] "Joint Statement by Open Doors International and Global Christian Relief," *Open Doors International*, www.opendoorsus.org. Accessed 3/12/2019.

[3] J. C. Ryle, *Expository Thoughts on the Gospels*.

QUESTIONS TO CONSIDER

1. (a) Read John 16:1-6. How many times are "these things" (KJV) mentioned, and what did Jesus mean by each one? (b) What does the future hold for the disciples, according to these verses? (c) What encouragement does Christ give His disciples in these verses? (d) Write down some of the ways in which Christ's words to the disciples were fulfilled in the book of Acts.

2. Memorize John 16:2.

3. (a) Read Matthew 10 and note the kinds of persecution the Lord predicts for His disciples. (b) How would Matthew 10 also be an encouragement to the disciples?

4. Read Acts 6:8 – 7:60. (a) Who was the martyr mentioned in this passage? (b) What did he say that caused him to be hated and eventually killed? (c) How does his sermon compare to many modern-day sermons?

5. Read Acts 12. (a) Who else was martyred for his faith? (b) Who was behind this wicked act? (c) How did the Jews react? (d) Whom did Herod then want to kill? (e) What happened to Peter and what happened to Herod?

6. (a) In Acts 23:12, who wanted to kill Paul? (b) Read on through verses 13-35 of Acts 23. How did the Lord providentially rescue Paul? (c) Why do you think the Lord rescued Peter and Paul, yet allowed Stephen to be martyred? (d) What do these passages teach you about the providence of God in your own life?

7. (a) Are you willing to suffer persecution for Christ? At work? In your neighborhood? With your family? In your church? (b) If the time ever comes for you to die for your faith, what do you think you will do? (c) What comfort will you find in the Word?

8. (a) In looking at John 16:1-4, we see the love of Christ in warning His beloved children of the things that were going to happen to them. If Jesus so loved them and us to forewarn us as His children about coming persecution, should we instruct our children in these truths? (b) How would you explain to your child or to a new believer about what Christ has said concerning persecution for His sake?

9. Come with a prayer request for either yourself, if you are going through persecution, or for someone you know who is suffering because of Christ's sake.

The Threefold Work of the Spirit in the World
John 16:5-11

IN R. A. Torrey's book, *The Person and Work of the Holy Spirit*, Torrey recounts a story from his own experience in his ministry at Chicago Avenue Church. Mr. Torrey had been burdened over the fact that there had been very little conviction of sin in their meetings. There had been conversions, to be sure, but few were coming with an apparently overwhelming conviction of sin. One night, one of the officers of the church said, "I am greatly troubled by the fact that we have so little conviction of sin in our meetings. While we are having conversions and many additions to our church, there is not that deep conviction of sin that I like to see. So I suggest that we, the officers of the church, meet every night to pray that there may be more conviction of sin in our meetings." They did just that, and a few days later on a Sunday evening Torrey noticed a man in the congregation that he had not seen before. The man was very flashy in his dress, with a big diamond blazing from his shirt. After the service Torrey went to the room where they would meet with any inquirers and there was the man with the flashy shirt. He was terribly upset.

"I don't know what is the matter with me. I never felt this way in my life. I was starting out this afternoon to go to Cottage Grove Avenue to meet some men and spend the afternoon gambling. But as I passed the park some of your men were having an open-air meeting and I stopped to listen. I saw one man testifying whom I had known in a life of sin, and I waited to hear what he had to say. When he finished I went on down the street. I had not gone far when some strange power took hold of me and brought me back and I stayed through the meeting. Oh, I don't know what is the matter with me. I feel awful. I never felt this way before in my life."

"I know what's the matter with you," Torrey replied. "You are under the conviction of sin, for the Holy Spirit is dealing with you."[1]

Torrey then pointed the man to Christ, and the man asked Jesus to forgive his sins and was born again. It was the beginning of many striking conversions in the Chicago Avenue Church.

Wouldn't it be great if we had more of this going on in our churches today?!

The conviction of the Holy Spirit is a wonderful thing for the unbeliever. This is the topic that Christ brings to the attention of His disciples in the passage we will be studying in this chapter. He wants His disciples to know that convicting an unbeliever of their sin is not their ministry; it is the Spirit's. Let's look at what the Lord says to the Eleven in John 16:5-11.

> "But now I go away to Him who sent Me, and none of you asks Me, 'Where are You going?' But because I have said these things to you, sorrow has filled your heart. Nevertheless I tell you the truth. It is to your advantage that I go away; for if I do not go away, the Helper will not come to you; but if I depart, I will send Him to you. And when He has come, He will convict the world of sin, and of righteousness, and of judgment: of sin, because they do not believe in Me; of righteousness, because I go to My Father and you see Me no more; of judgment, because the ruler of this world is judged."

In our last chapter, we saw the Lord's mercy by warning of persecution (vv 1, 4); the world's method of persecution (v 2); and the world's motive behind the persecution (v 3). Our outline for this chapter will include: *The Reminder of Christ's Departure Out of the World* (vv 5-6); *The Reminder of the Spirit's Coming to the World* (v 7); and *The Threefold Work of the Spirit in the World* (vv 8-11). Let's look first at the reminder of Christ's departure from the world.

---

1 R. A. Torrey, *The Person and Work of the Holy Spirit* (New York: Cosimo Classics, 1911), 72-73.

Reminder of Christ's Departure Out of the World *John 16:5-6*

> "But now I go away to Him who sent Me, and none of you asks Me, 'Where are You going?'" (John 16:5)

The words *but now I go away* are a contrast to the words *I was with you* that are found in verse 4. *Now* means at this very moment. And where is Jesus going? He says *to Him who sent Me*. Jesus had already mentioned this to His disciples in John 14:2-3: "In My Father's house are many mansions; if it were not so, I would have told you. I go to prepare a place for you. And if I go and prepare a place for you, I will come again and receive you to Myself; that where I am, there you may be also." But now Jesus follows His statement with something very puzzling: *and none of you asks Me, "Where are You going?"* Why is this puzzling? It's puzzling because Peter asked Jesus in 13:36 where He was going, and Thomas asked Jesus about the way in John 14:5. So what does Jesus mean by this statement? Both of these disciples had asked, but they had not pursued the question. They were not persistent. Peter went straight from, "Where are you going?" to "Why can't I follow you?" Thomas really never pursued the question either; he just wanted to know how to get to wherever Jesus was going. They were too concerned with the thought of their own impending loss, and their sorrow crowded out their pursuit of the question. Peter was diverted immediately and made no real attempt to find out where Jesus was going. He had been concerned with the thought of Jesus leaving and not so much with where He was going. Both Peter and Thomas asked but thought they were going to go with Jesus. Once they understood that Jesus was leaving them and they would be without Him, none of them pursued the question, "Where are you going, Lord?" any further. Instead, they were consumed with their own grief. They were thinking of themselves and the dangers in front of them. Remember, Jesus had just lovingly forewarned them of the fact that they would be put out of the synagogue and even killed.

My friend, self-interest blinds men! And we do the same thing, don't we? When you and I are going through troubling times and we are really sorrowing, we may ask another person a question, but with no real intent to pursue an answer because we are drowning in our own sorrows.

In the midst of our sorrows, we must die to ourselves and reach out to others. This is a challenge at times, to be sure, but it is not impossible. The disciples were too absorbed in their own grief to minister to Jesus, who was facing the cross very soon. They were still thinking of Christ's departure. Christ knew this about them, so He says,

> "But because I have said these things to you, sorrow has filled your heart." (John 16:6)

Their sorrow, their sadness and heaviness, was so intense that the thought of how this would glorify the Father was absent from their minds and hearts. It's as if the Lord is saying, "Sorrow has filled your heart, the heart that I have been endeavoring to comfort. You men are not looking at the end of my departure, or on the fullness of my glory, or on the addition to your own blessedness, but on your own loss and disappointment." They did not see how they could go on without Jesus. They knew that parting would indeed be a painful time for them. Again, this is a reminder for all of us: beware of being so swallowed up by sorrow that we forget the needs of others. (In fact, remember in the Garden of Gethsemane, in Luke 22:45, when Jesus is praying, He finds them sleeping because of their sorrow.) This must have been disheartening for our Lord, who was obviously joyful at the thought of returning home to His Father. His disciples were not sharing in His joy at this moment (consider John 14:28). But the Lord is gracious and patient with them during this confusing time; even though they are absorbed in themselves, He still is absorbed in them, and reminds them again that He will not leave them as orphans. And with that, He now reminds His disciples of the Spirit's coming to the world, in verse 7.

The Spirit's Coming to the World *John 16:7*

> "Nevertheless I tell you the truth. It is to your advantage that I go away; for if I do not go away, the Helper will not come to you; but if I depart, I will send Him to you." (John 16:7)

Even though they are filled with sorrow, Jesus tells them the truth. This is a great example for us to follow. Even though we make it our aim to comfort those who are sorrowing, we still must tell them the truth, as Jesus does here. We must always speak the truth in love, as Paul says in Ephesians 4:15. I have been around people who are trying to comfort others who are going through difficult times, and they will say something like, "Oh, I just can't tell them the truth about that right now! It would devastate them! I'll just lie a little."

Ladies, we must always be truthful, even when others are sorrowing and going through troubling times. Of course, Jesus is truth, so it makes sense that He would tell the truth. But what Jesus says here is emphatic in the Greek: "Verily, verily, I say whether you believe me or not, it is true." And what is He telling them the truth about? *It is to your advantage that I go away*. It is profitable, it is advantageous, it is better, it is good if I go away. God takes the acts of wicked men and uses them for His purposes. Joseph said to his brothers, "As for you, you meant evil against me, but God meant it for good in order to do what has happened on this day, to keep many people alive." (Genesis 50:20 LSB). Notice here that Jesus does not say it is to His own advantage, but it is for their advantage that He goes away. Jesus' foremost motive and desire was for them. Though the disciples thought Jesus' going away was disastrous, it was really for their profit. Jesus says it is not only better for them if He goes away, but He also says *for if I do not go away, the Helper will not come to you*. The words *go away* mean to depart on a journey with a definite purpose, the purpose here being the sending of the Holy Spirit. This departing would, of course, include His death, resurrection, and ascension. The Holy Spirit could not come until Jesus left. One writer helps us understand Jesus' words this way, "Unless I go away, that is, unless I die, nothing will be done—you will continue as you are and everything will remain in its old state: the Jews under the law of Moses, the heathen in their blindness—all under sin and death. No Scripture would be fulfilled, and I should have come in vain."[2]

Now, I don't know about you, but I don't like change much. And some of the disciples may have been thinking along those same lines, "But why do things have to change? Why is the presence of the Holy Spirit more

---

[2] Martin Luther, quoted in A. W. Pink, *Exposition of the Gospel of John*.

valuable than Jesus?" Let's consider some valuable reasons for Jesus' departure and the Spirit's coming:

1. Jesus could only be bodily present at one place at a time, whereas the Holy Spirit can be everywhere. This means the Holy Spirit can comfort all believers in all places at all times, but the Lord Jesus could only be bodily present to comfort a few and only in one place.

2. With the Spirit's coming, the disciples would be able to do those "greater works" that Christ told them they would do after He went to the Father (John 14:12). The Spirit would carry forth those works by dwelling within them and enabling them to do His work.

3. With Christ's leaving and the Spirit's coming, the disciples would learn to walk by faith and not by sight. This would be a real test for them, as it is for you and me. One man has said of this need, "We shall never see the absolute necessity of the Holy Ghost's coming until we see the inconvenience of His not coming."[3]

Have you asked yourself what your life would be like today without the Holy Spirit? And, when you think about it, isn't it often true that when God takes away one blessing, He gives us a greater one in its place, even if we aren't able to see it right away?

Jesus goes on to say *but if I depart, I will send Him to you.* Now, what does this mean? Jesus said back in 14:26 that it would be the Father who would send the Spirit. Is this a contradiction? No, it is not, because as we have already learned in our study, the two are one—the Father and the Son are one. There is perfect cooperation.

Christ now goes on to speak of what the Spirit's work will be in the world, and He describes it as threefold.

---

3 Bishop Andrews, quoted in J.C. Ryle, *Expository Thoughts on the Gospels*.

The Threefold Work of the Spirit in the World   John 16:8-11

> "And when He has come, He will convict the world of sin, and of righteousness, and of judgment." (John 16:8)

The words *and when He has come* are in the future tense. Does that mean that the Holy Spirit had not yet come at all? We see throughout the Scriptures that He has been present, that He had indeed come in some way, but not in the sense of indwelling believers in an ongoing and permanent manner. After Pentecost, He would come with larger power and influence. But what is it that the Holy Spirit will do when He comes? What will be His purpose? Here, Jesus says that the Spirit's purpose is threefold—to *convict the world of sin, and of righteousness, and of judgment.* This is His work in the world before conversion.

Let's consider the first work of the Spirit in the world. First, *He will convict the world of sin.* There are two meanings to this word *convict.* The first is a judicial act; it means to convict with a view toward judgment. In other words, to convict someone is to render them guilty of something. It is to cross-examine for the purpose of convincing or refuting an opponent. The term was especially used in legal proceedings, where it conveys the idea of cross-examining someone until that person would see and admit his error. The Holy Spirit is responsible for convicting the world of its sin, with a view toward sin's just punishment in hell. When the Jews crucified Jesus, they did not think they were sinning; they thought they were serving God. But when Peter preached the story of the crucifixion in Acts 2, they were "cut to the heart," it says in verse 37. The Holy Spirit convicted them. They suddenly realized their sin and were convicted that they had crucified the Lord. A second meaning of the word *convict* is to convince, to prove, or to persuade a person to do something by presenting reasons for that action. The Holy Spirit convinces a person that he needs Jesus Christ. He wants to convince you so that He doesn't have to convict you. Jesus had been doing this job up until now, but Jesus wants the disciples to understand that with the Spirit's coming, convicting and convincing will be one of His primary works.

What will the Spirit convict the world of? He will convict the world of three things: of *sin*, of *righteousness*, and of *judgment*. Let me briefly define each one of these and then elaborate on them. *Sin* is missing the mark, missing the true goal and scope of life. It is an offense in relation to God with emphasis on the resulting guilt. By contrast, *righteousness* refers to one's need to be made right with God in light of one's sin. Righteousness is the opposite of sin, and it is to be yearned for after conviction. *Judgment* is a separation, a sentence, which is as certain to come as condemnation, because of one's sin and lack of righteousness. Christ goes on to repeat these three works of the Spirit in the world and gives a reason behind each one. Let's look at the first one, sin, in verse 9.

>"of sin, because they do not believe in Me;" (John 16:9)

Sin, in general, we already defined, but Jesus gives the particular sin the world is guilty of, which results in condemnation. The sin is unbelief. Jesus says *because they do not believe in Me.* The sin of the world is not sins, plural, the many sins each has committed, but the specific sin of not believing on Jesus Christ. It is not the sin of adultery, or the sin of pride, or the sin of stealing that Jesus says the world is guilty of here; what the world is guilty of, ultimately, is the sin of refusing to believe that Jesus is the Son of God. In John 5:40 (LSB), Jesus says, "and you are unwilling to come to Me so that you may have life." In John 1:11, which we looked at in our introductory chapter, it says, "He came to what was His own, and those who were His own did not receive Him" (LSB). Hebrews 3:18-19 (LSB) says, "And to whom did He swear that they would not enter His rest, but to those who were disobedient? So we see that they were not able to enter because of unbelief." Paul says in 2 Thessalonians 2:11-12, "And for this reason God sends upon them a deluding influence so that they will believe what is false, in order that they all may be judged who did not believe the truth, but took pleasure in unrighteousness."(LSB) R. A. Torrey has written that "When the Holy Spirit touches a man's heart, he no longer looks upon unbelief as a mark of intellectual superiority, he does not look upon it as a mere misfortune; he sees it as the most daring, decisive and damning of all sins and is overwhelmed with a sense of his awful guilt in that he had not believed on the name of the only begotten Son of God."[4]

---

4 R. A. Torrey, *The Person and Work of the Holy Spirit*, 77.

Does this mean, then, that the Holy Spirit doesn't convict of particular sins in any way? No, it does not mean that; note what Jesus says in verse 10 about the second area in which the Spirit convicts.

> "of righteousness, because I go to My Father and you see Me no more;" (John 16:10)

This seems to refer to the *righteousness* or innocence of Jesus Himself, that is to make men think earnestly on the subject of righteousness, to show them how utterly rotten their own righteousness is. Remember what the centurion said after Jesus had given up the spirit in Luke 23:47? "Certainly this was a righteous Man." When we see the righteousness of Christ and compare it to our own righteousness, we are convicted—or, at least, we should be! "Go away from me Lord, for I am a sinful man," Peter said in Luke 5:8 (LSB). When the prophet Isaiah saw the righteousness of God, he cried, "Woe is me, for I am ruined! For I am a man of unclean lips, and I live among a people of unclean lips; for my eyes have seen the King, Yahweh of hosts" (Isaiah 6:5 LSB). Both of these men were exposed to the holiness and righteousness of God and it profoundly affected them.

Christ clarifies that this convicting the world of righteousness is *because I go to My Father and you see Me no more.* Righteousness can only be found in Christ. He was once here on the earth, but He makes it clear in this text that He is going to the Father. The disciples will not visibly see righteousness anymore, in the sense that Christ's physical body will no longer be present with them, but the Spirit will carry on that work of showing the world what righteousness is. Jesus mentions this reality to His disciples in just a few verses from this moment. In John 16:14-15, He says of the Holy Spirit, "He will glorify Me, for He will take of what is Mine and declare it to you. All things that the Father has are Mine. Therefore I said that He will take of Mine and declare it to you."

In addition to convicting the world of sin and of righteousness, the third convicting work of the Spirit will be in regard to judgment, as we see in verse 11.

> of judgment, because the ruler of this world is judged. (John 16:11)

It is the Holy Spirit's ministry to convince the world that there is a *judgment* to come. God is just and He will execute justice on that Day. In Ecclesiastes 3:11, Solomon states that God has placed eternity in men's hearts. Don't let anyone try to convince you that they don't believe in the hereafter. God has put eternity in man's heart. I've even heard my husband, when sharing the gospel with someone who tells him they don't believe in a hereafter, say, "Oh, yes, you do! You know there is life after death." It is the Holy Spirit who gives us that inner conviction that we will all stand before the judgment seat of Christ. Peter says, in 2 Peter 2:9, "then the Lord knows how to rescue the godly from trial, and to keep the unrighteous under punishment for the day of judgment" (LSB).

Why will the Spirit convict the world of judgment? Jesus says *because the ruler of this world is judged.* (Jesus already pronounced that the ruler of the world was coming, in John 14:30.) *The ruler of this world* is Satan, and he will be judged. Consider Satan's final judgment as it is mentioned in Revelation 20:7-10 (LSB):

> And when the thousand years are finished, Satan will be released from his prison, and will come out to deceive the nations which are in the four corners of the earth, Gog and Magog, to gather them together for the war; the number of them is like the sand of the seashore. And they came up on the broad plain of the earth and surrounded the camp of the saints and the beloved city, and fire came down from heaven and devoured them.
>
> And the devil who deceived them was thrown into the lake of fire and brimstone, where the beast and the false prophet are also, and they will be tormented day and night forever and ever.

My friend, if Jesus can destroy the biggest sinner ever, how shall anyone else escape?

Summary

We have seen the reminder of Christ's departure from the world, in verses 5 and 6: "I go away to Him who sent Me." We have also seen the reminder of the Spirit's coming to the world, in verse 7: "I will send Him to you." And we see the threefold work of the Spirit in the world, in verse 8-11: "He will convict the world of sin and of righteousness and of judgment."

You might be wondering to yourself, "This is all well and good, but what does this have to do with me? If the Spirit is the one who does this work in the world, then what does this have to do with me?" It has much to do with you and me, because we are not exempt from being mouthpieces for the Spirit's work. In fact, if you did the *Questions to Consider* that accompany this chapter, then you spent some time considering how these three elements—sin, righteousness, and judgment—show up in Peter's sermon in Acts 2. What was the result of that sermon? Verse 37 says, "Now when they heard this, they were cut to the heart, and said to Peter and the rest of the apostles, 'Men and brethren, what shall we do?'" My friend, the Spirit used a mouthpiece; the Spirit used Peter as His mouthpiece. It was the same mouth that had made many a blunder, to be sure, but it was, in that moment and for many years to come, being powerfully used by the Spirit.

Consider also the account in Acts 24:24-27, where the apostle Paul is standing before Felix using these same three elements that Peter uses: "But as he was discussing righteousness, self-control, and the judgment to come, Felix became frightened and answered, 'Go away for the present, and when I find time I will call for you'" (Acts 24:25 LSB).

Even Jonathan Edwards, who preached that famous sermon, *Sinners in the Hands of an Angry God*, was said to have been frail and sickly, his voice thin and weak, and his eyesight dim. Yet, some thought his sermon important enough to spend all night in prayer. And what was the result? The elders during the sermon threw their arms around the pillars in the church and cried, "Lord save us as we are slipping down into hell!" It is said that the distressed and convicted multitude wept all around him. That is how God works, by the power of the Holy Spirit working through instruments like you and me—strong like Peter; short and stout like Paul, or weak like Jonathan Edwards. We are vessels for use by our God!

Are you a clean vessel, which God can use? Are you sharing the gospel on a regular basis with the lost, allowing the Holy Spirit to work through you to convict the world of sin, of righteousness, and of the judgment to come? If not, why not? God the Holy Spirit will convict, but He needs a mouthpiece. Will you be His mouthpiece? Remember, they cannot hear unless there is a preacher, as Paul says in Romans 10:14.

Just this past year, when I was visiting with a friend of a relative of mine who is now gone, I was struck with the sober reminder that we must be bold to share the truth of Christ. That woman's words have haunted me: when I asked her if she thought my relative was a believer, she told me that she did not know, but doubted so, and that she deeply regretted that in the many decades they were friends they never had any spiritual conversation, and that she had never shared with her that she had concerns about her soul. Dear one, the time is short. We have the aid of the Holy Spirit to help us, but we must go and we must speak.

QUESTIONS TO CONSIDER

1. Read John 16 and list all the things you find in that chapter that pertain to what the Holy Spirit does. Thank Him for each one.

2. Memorize John 16:7.

3. Read John 13:36 and John 14:5. How does what you read in those verses reconcile with what Jesus says in John 16:5?

4. Read Acts 2:14-47 and answer the following questions. (a) Through whom is the Spirit preaching? (b) How did Peter's sermon bring conviction of sin, of righteousness, and of judgment? Cite specific examples. (c) What happened as a result of this conviction? (d) According to Hebrews 3:7-19, what happens when man does not respond to the Spirit's conviction?

5. According to John 16:8, one ministry of the Holy Spirit is to convict the world of righteousness. Read Matthew 5:17-48 to see what Jesus says about righteousness. How is true righteousness described in these verses?

6. (a) What do the following verses say about judgment? Acts 17:31; Hebrews 9:27; 10:26-27; James 2:13; 1 Peter 4:17; and Jude 14-16. (b) According to Revelation 20:7-10, when will the prince of this world finally be judged? (c) What judgment will take place after that, according to Revelation 20:11-15? (d) How does these truths help you to understand what Jesus says in John 16:11?

7. *Briefly* share how the Holy Spirit worked in your life to convict you of sin and bring you to salvation.

8. How do you see the Holy Spirit convicting the world of sin, of righteousness, and of judgment in the world today?

9. Write down a prayer request for a lost soul that you know needs to respond to the convicting work of the Spirit of God.

The Spirit's Ministry to the Eleven
John 16:12-15

JAMES Ryle (not to be confused with J. C. Ryle) claimed that he awoke from a strange dream one night and heard the Lord tell him, "I am about to do a strange, new thing in My church. It will be like a man bringing a hippopotamus into his garden. Think about it." Ryle did think about it, and he concluded that God was telling him He was going to return the power of His prophetic word by His Holy Spirit into the churches that no longer have any place for it. Ryle said, "Not only is the hippo in the garden the unusual thing God will do prophetically within His church but it also heralds His release of a prophetic voice into the world through His church, bringing in a great last-days harvest." Ryle has also claimed that the Lord revealed other bizarre truths to him, one of those being that the secret of the Beatles' success was that they had received an anointing from God. He also claimed that he dreamed once that he was literally inside the Lord and had the ability to look through His eyes and to see what He was seeing without being seen.[1]

James Ryle is only one of countless pastors who believe that they receive truth directly from God, apart from Scripture. They claim that the Word of God is much broader than the Scriptures, that it includes visions, dreams, voices, and the like. Is that what Jesus meant when He said to the disciples that the Spirit of truth would guide them into all truth and show them things to come? James Ryle would take these verses out of context and answer that question with a resounding "Yes!" But what do these verses really mean? Well, let's find out as we look at John 16:12-15.

> "I still have many things to say to you, but you cannot bear them now. However, when He, the Spirit of truth, has come, He will guide you into all truth; for He will not speak on His own authority, but whatever He

---

1 John MacArthur, "Looking For Truth in All the Wrong Places," *Grace to You*, https://www.gty.org/library/blog/B170607/looking-for-truth-in-all-the-wrong-places. Accessed 10/4/2023.

hears He will speak; and He will tell you things to come. He will glorify Me, for He will take of what is Mine and declare it to you. All things that the Father has are Mine. Therefore I said that He will take of Mine and declare it to you."

Our outline for this chapter will include: *The Sensitivity of Christ to the Eleven* (v 12) and *The Spirit's Ministry to the Eleven* (vv 13-15). In our last chapter, we learned of the reminder of Christ's departure out of the world (vv 5-6); the reminder of the Spirit's coming to the world (v 7); and the threefold work of the Spirit in the world (vv 8-11), which is to reprove (convict and convince) them of sin, of righteousness, and of judgment. In this chapter, Jesus shifts from speaking about what the Holy Spirit's ministry to the world will be, to what the Holy Spirit's ministry will be to the eleven disciples. Even though many churches have abused the work of the Holy Spirit, as James Ryle has, the Spirit does have a vital role in our lives. As Charles Haddon Spurgeon has said, "Some people hardly know whether there be any Holy Ghost. Let the Father and the Son be equally adored; but be careful in reference to the Holy Spirit, for the failure of the church towards the Holy Trinity lies mainly in a forgetfulness of the gracious work of the Holy Spirit."[2] Let's begin by looking at the sensitivity of Christ toward the eleven disciples:

The Sensitivity of Christ to the Eleven   *John 16:12*

> I still have many things to say to you, but you cannot bear them now. (John 16:12)

When Jesus says He *still* has many things to say, He means to communicate that there were things on His heart that He had a continued desire to say to His disciples. *Many things* indicates that there were a number of items still on His heart that He wanted to share. What things would Christ want to share with them if the time were right? The text doesn't tell us, but it could be that Jesus wanted to say more regarding the work of the Spirit or concerning His death and resurrection and ascension. Perhaps He wanted to elaborate on more doctrinal issues. Maybe He

---

2 Charles H. Spurgeon, "The First Fruit of the Spirit," The Spurgeon Center, https://www.spurgeon.org/resource-library/sermons/the-first-fruit-of-the-spirit/. Accessed 9/27/2023.

wanted to share more about the persecution they would endure, His love for them, His leaving them, or His apprehension about His soon-coming crucifixion. There was so much He still could have said, but Christ was sensitive to His disciples. We see Him here taking into consideration their present condition and the fact that they are sorrowful over His coming departure. Knowing where they're at, He doesn't want to weigh them down with an extra heavy load.

I can recall a very difficult time in my own life when I was so blessed by other believers who were especially sensitive to me, being careful not to weigh me down with more burdens than I could bear. I was so grateful for the many who were looking for ways to ease my load, rather than increasing it. During that time, the Lord taught me a lot about being sensitive to others and that "snapping out of it" isn't always possible.

Christ understands what His disciples are able to endure at this moment. He also understands that, in this moment, there isn't time for Him to say much more to them because Judas and all those coming with him are on their way. In fact, the rest of what Christ says to the Eleven takes only about 2-3 minutes to communicate, and so we see that the time really is short. He affirms to them that, yes, He does have some others things He wants to say to them, His friends, *but*, as He says, *you cannot bear them now.* The word *bear* is used in John 19:17 when John mentions Jesus' carrying of His cross: "They took Jesus, therefore, and He went out, bearing His own cross, to the place called the Place of a Skull, which is called in Hebrew, Golgotha" (LSB). It is also the word that Jesus used to rebuke the Jewish religious leaders in Luke 11:46 (LSB): "But He said, 'Woe to you scholars of the Law as well! For you weigh men down with burdens hard to bear, and you yourselves will not even touch the burdens with one of your fingers.'" The picture is that of a weight laid on a man who is unable to carry it. Jesus was saying that the disciples were not able to bear everything He still wanted to say to them; they were unable to carry, spiritually speaking, the things that were on Christ's heart. This verse should be a learning tool for all of us, as we must be sensitive to those whom God places in our path that we have the privilege and responsibility of discipling or counseling. We don't want to overwhelm them with too much doctrine or too much information at once. It is line upon line, precept upon precept. We need to be careful how much truth we attempt to give to others at any given time (see 1 Corinthians 3:1-2 and Hebrews 5:11-14).

It's the same principle we see in the physical realm. We don't give newborn babies meat, do we? No, we give them milk. And we don't teach first graders algebra; we teach them simple addition and subtraction. Yet, a teenager should be able to digest algebra and have a capacity for mathematics far beyond simple addition and subtraction. We, too, need to be sensitive to where people are in their walks with God and to be patient with them in their learning. Jesus certainly was. For example, in teaching a new believer about the things of the Lord, you would not want to start by teaching them about the Babylonian captivity or the destruction of Jerusalem. Instead, you would start them out on some fundamentals of the faith, like their relationship with Christ, prayer, Bible reading, and other means of grace. On the other hand, those who have been in the faith for some time need more than the milk of the Word, because they should be able to digest some of the deeper things of God's Word. Had Christ told the disciples in this moment that the Jewish sacrifices were going to be done away with, the priesthood abolished, and the celebration of the feast days done away with, they perhaps would not have been able to bear that. Too much at one time may have overwhelmed them to the point of grief or rejection. But there would come a time when they would be able to digest these things. I know, for me, there are some doctrines that I have only just been able to digest in the last few years. So, when we look at this verse and the example we see Jesus setting for us, we can conclude that, like Him, we must be sensitive to others' spiritual, emotional, and even their physical conditions as we impart the truths of God's Word to them.

Well, Jesus did have a lot of things to say, but He was not going to be able to say them to the disciples just yet. They couldn't bear those things at this moment, but soon they would be able to. But who would teach them these things? I'm so glad you asked! Jesus tells them, as He has already told them, who their instructor will be after He leaves. The Holy Spirit will be the One who will teach them. He will be someone who is just like Jesus—another Comforter! He will teach them all these things, these things that they are unable to bear right now! So, we turn from the sensitivity of Christ toward the Eleven to the Spirit's ministry to the Eleven, in verses 13-15. It is a threefold ministry. (Interestingly enough, we learned in our last chapter, from John 16:8-11, that the Spirit also has a threefold ministry in the world.)

The Spirit's Ministry to the Eleven — John 16:13-15

> "However, when He, the Spirit of truth, has come, He will guide you into all truth; for He will not speak on His own authority, but whatever He hears He will speak; and He will tell you things to come." (John 16:13)

First of all, we see that the Holy Spirit is called *the Spirit of truth*. This is not the first time He has been given this title; we also see this title show up in John 14:17 and 15:26. *So, when the Spirit comes, what will He do? The first thing He will do is: Show them the truth.* Jesus puts it like this: *He will guide you into all truth.* This means He will *guide you* along the way, He will show you the way, He will lead you. Notice that the Spirit does not drive; He leads. As it has been said, "Leaders don't force people to follow, they invite them on a journey." It suggests a pilgrimage and a process, a moving forward. It is the same word that the Ethiopian eunuch used in Acts 8 when Philip asked him if he understood what he was reading in Isaiah, to which the Ethiopian eunuch responded, "Well, how could I, unless someone guides me?" (Acts 8:31b LSB).

What will the Spirit guide them or lead them *into*? He will guide them into *all truth*. It does seem logical that the Spirit of truth would lead others into all truth, doesn't it? Obviously, this is not referring to the truths related to science and history and math, that is, facts about our world that you and I know to be true. Rather, the *truth* here that Christ is referring to is spiritual truth. Jesus is saying that the Spirit would give the disciples insight into and understanding of things pertaining to spiritual truth. This would include all the truth necessary for salvation and Christian living. In fact, the Greek literally reads, "guide into all the truth," as if it specifically meant the truth concerning Christ, who is *the* truth! In fact, several Bible translations (RSV, ESV, NASB, and LSB) translate these words as "the truth," which would be referring to truth centering on Christ. The Holy Spirit is the guide or the leader who points the way to the truth, Christ being Himself both the Way and the Truth. Consider John 15:26, "But when the Helper comes, whom I shall send to you from the Father, the Spirit of truth who proceeds from the Father, He will testify of Me." Also consider John 16:14, which states, "He will glorify Me, for He will take of what is Mine and declare it to you." Just as the Spirit of truth leads us to truth, so the father of lies, Satan, leads us to lies and evil of every kind. In fact, 1 John 4:6 (LSB) says, "We are from God. The one who knows God hears us; the one who is not from God does not hear us. From this we know the spirit of truth and the spirit of error."

As we think about this wonderful promise, dear sisters, I would ask you to consider whether you allow the precious Holy Spirit to guide you into all truth, or do you guide yourself or allow yourself to be guided by the voices of others? The apostle John tells us that we must be so careful about this. Listen to his words in 1 John 4:1 (LSB): "Beloved, do not believe every spirit, but test the spirits to see whether they are from God, because many false prophets have gone out into the world." In order for the Spirit of God to guide us, there must be a willingness on our part to follow His directions. I think we often rush to other sources before waiting for that still small voice to guide us into all truth. We listen to these other sources and say to ourselves, "Hmm ... that sounds good," and we swallow what they say, hook, line, and sinker! Men today are claiming bizarre things which they say the Spirit is doing that are, in fact, contrary to the Word of God. Things like: the Holy Spirit led me to be disobedient to my parents, to get a divorce, to not read my Bible for a while, to not go to church, to have premarital sex, to not give money to the Lord.

I actually had a lady approach me during a conference I was doing and tell me that the Lord told her to fornicate before she got married! I don't know what "lord" she was listening to, but it wasn't the Lord of truth! I had another woman tell me once that she divorced her husband because she prayed that if it wasn't God's will, He would stop her—and yet this particular woman did not have biblical grounds for divorce. God's will is clearly revealed in the truth of His Word and yet she was listening to the father of lies. Ladies, things like this are blasphemous and dangerous!

There are countless women who listen to false teachers and false ideas, and because they don't have enough biblical knowledge or discernment to discard such nonsense, they fall prey to ungodly ideas! We must be careful to measure everything we read and hear with God's Word. The Spirit of Truth will always be consistent with God's Word because it is Truth!

Jesus goes on to say regarding the Holy Spirit: *for He will not speak on His own authority, but whatever He hears He will speak; and He will tell you things to come*. Notice that the Holy Spirit doesn't go off on His own in some independent, arrogant way. The Spirit does not act independently of the other Persons of the Trinity. There is not competition within the Trinity. Each knows their role. He doesn't seek to talk about Himself as that is not His role. But if He doesn't speak about Himself, then who does He speak about? Jesus tells us: *whatever He hears He will speak*. The Father would tell the Spirit what to teach the disciples about Jesus. In this, we see the interdependence of the Persons of the Trinity. Lenski says, "'He shall hear' is, as in the case of Jesus, a human term for a divine act, picturing the divine Persons as communicating with each other after the manner of human persons. Being one in essence, each is in the other, and nothing known to the one is ever hidden from the other."[3]

The second ministry of the Spirit is that He will show things that are to come. Jesus says of the Holy Spirit: *He will tell you things to come*. This means that the Spirit will tell or declare freely, openly, or eminently the things that are coming. In John 14:26, the Lord said that the Spirit would help the disciples remember the past, and now the Lord says that the Spirit will show them the future as well as the things already begun concerning the work of the Kingdom. In Ephesians 3:5, in speaking of the mystery of Christ, Paul says, "which in other generations was not made known to the sons of men, as it was now revealed to His holy apostles and prophets in the Spirit" (LSB). How were future things to be revealed? Paul says it is by the Holy Spirit. In Acts 2, we see the apostle Peter speaking prophetic words which pertained to the end times. How did Peter get this information? He received it from the Holy Spirit. 1 Timothy 4:1-3

---

[3] R. C. H. Lenski, *The Interpretation of St. John's Gospel: 11-21*, 1091.

is another passage which deals with the prophetic truth of the things that the Spirit reveals: "But the Spirit explicitly says that in later times some will fall away from the faith, paying attention to deceitful spirits and doctrines of demons, by the hypocrisy of liars, who have been seared in their own conscience, who forbid marriage and advocate abstaining from foods which God created to be shared in with thanksgiving by those who believe and know the truth" (1 Timothy 4:1-3 LSB). Probably one of the greatest fulfillments of what Jesus is saying here is found in the book of the Revelation, which John received on the Isle of Patmos. What a revelation from the Spirit of things to come! (We would do well to consider 2 Peter 1:19-21 to remind ourselves of this more sure Word of prophecy that we have—God's Holy Word!)

The third ministry of the Spirit to the Eleven is seen in verses 14 and 15. *The third ministry of the Spirit is that He will show them Christ.* Let's listen to what Jesus says:

> "He will glorify Me, for He will take of what is Mine and declare it to you." (John 16:14)

The Spirit *will glorify* Christ, which means that the Spirit will honor and praise Christ. It is always the Spirit's ministry to point to Christ. He wants to make us like Christ; that is why He reveals Christ to us. As Paul says in 1 Corinthians 12:3 (LSB), "Therefore I make known to you that no one speaking by the Spirit of God says, 'Jesus is accursed,' and no one can say, 'Jesus is Lord,' except by the Holy Spirit." It is sad that today so many of our churches are seeking to glorify the Spirit, because even Jesus says that the Spirit's work is to glorify Christ. J. C. Ryle writes, "Any religious teaching which does not tend to exalt Christ, has a fatal defect about it. It cannot be from the Spirit."[4] (By the way, this quote is from J. C. Ryle—quite a bit different from the James Ryle I wrote of at the beginning of this chapter!)

How will the Holy Spirit glorify Christ? Jesus says the Spirit *will take of what is Mine and declare it to you.* He shall *take of* or from Jesus and

---

4 J. C. Ryle, *Expository Thoughts on the Gospels.*

announce or communicate it to you. The Holy Spirit receives Christ's commission and instruction as an ambassador for Christ; in this way, the Spirit does the will of Christ and completes the work of Christ. Barnes says, "This is always the work of the Spirit. All serious impressions produced by Him lead us to the Lord Jesus, and by this we may easily test our feelings. If we have been truly convicted of sin and renewed by the Holy Ghost, the tendency of all his influences has been to lead us to the Savior; to show us our need of Him; to reveal to us the loveliness of His character, and the fitness of His work to our wants; and to incline us to cast our eternal interests on His almighty arm, and commit all to His hands."[5] Jesus repeats this truth but in a little different way in verse 15, and with this we bring our chapter to a close.

> "All things that the Father has are Mine. Therefore I said that He will take of Mine and declare it to you." (John 16:15)

These are things that Christ has said before. *All things that the Father has are Mine.* (See Luke 10:21-22; John 3:35; 13:3; 17:10; Colossians 1:15-19.) *Therefore*, because *all things* that Jesus *has* belong to *the Father*, the Holy Spirit *will take* all that and *declare it* to the disciples. This verse gives us a wonderful glimpse into the inner revelation of the Godhead. All three Persons are working together in a harmonious way. The Spirit is a vital part of the believer's life, a vital truth we must remember. Too often, He is the Person of the Godhead that we tend to either forget, on one extreme, or overemphasize, on the other.

Summary

We have learned of the sensitivity Christ showed to the Eleven (v 12). We have also learned of the ministry of the Spirit to the Eleven: to show them the truth (v 13a), to show them things to come (v 13b), and to show them Christ (vv 14-15).

What can we learn from these verses that is applicable to our lives? I think there are some practical principals we can glean from this chapter,

---
5 Albert Barnes, *Barnes' Notes,* 348.

and they all begin with the words, "Be sensitive."

1. *Be sensitive to others.* Be sensitive to the needs of others, to their burdens, and especially to where they are in their spiritual walks. Do not burden others with more spiritual truth than they can carry at the moment, or with more burdens then they can carry, especially if they are going through difficult times like the disciples. Learn from Christ's example in verse 12.

2. *Be sensitive to the Spirit.* We need to be sensitive to the Holy Spirit's leading, and we need to let Him be our guide. We need to let Him guide us into truth, and we need to shun error. We should possess an attitude like that of the Berean believers, who searched the Scriptures daily to see whether the things that they were learning were true or not (Acts 17:10-12). When you hear or read something that doesn't sound right, check it out. And even if it does sound right, still check it out. Make sure that everything you read that claims to be biblical truth actually is biblical truth!

3. *Be sensitive to give glory to whom glory is due.* In our personal lives and in our churches, we need to make sure that we are not merely glorifying the Spirit, but that we are glorifying Jesus. "If anything calling itself Christian teaching makes its approach to us and does not exalt and glorify Christ, it is not of the Holy Spirit."[6]

May God help us to be sensitive to others, to be sensitive to the Spirit, and be sensitive to give Christ all the glory!

---

[6] John Phillips, *Exploring the Gospel of John* (Grand Rapids: Kregel Publications, 1989, 2001), page 308 Used by permission.

QUESTIONS TO CONSIDER

1. (a) Read John 14-16 and write down what you observe regarding the Holy Spirit. (b) In what ways are these observations an encouragement to you? (c) What new truths have you learned about the Spirit from these chapters? (d) How have these truths changed your life?

2. Memorize John 16:13.

3. In what ways could John 16:12 be helpful to you when giving advice to someone going through troubling times?

4. (a) According to the following verses, what work does the Holy Spirit do in the life of a believer? John 16:12-15; Romans 8:14, 16, 26; 1 Corinthians 12:5-13; Ephesians 5:18-21; Titus 3:5. (b) Share a time when the dear Holy Spirit ministered to you in one of these ways. (c) According to Ephesians 4:30 and 1 Thessalonians 5:19, what are believers commanded not to do? (d) What do these verses mean?

5. (a) In John 16:14, Jesus says that the Holy Spirit will glorify Jesus. Read any chapter (one chapter is sufficient) in the book of Acts to see how the Spirit's coming did indeed glorify the Lord. (b) Why do you think some churches today focus so much on glorifying the Spirit and not the Lord? (c) What is the danger in that? (d) Is there a balance? If so, what is the balance?

6. Jesus tells the disciples that the Holy Spirit will show them things to come (John 16:13). Read the following verses and write down what the Holy Spirit revealed and to whom it was revealed. Acts 11:28; Acts 21:10-11; 1 Timothy 4:1-3; 2 Peter 1:14.

7. What work does the Holy Spirit need to do in your life? Write it down to share as a prayer request.

Sorrow Turned to Joy!
John 16:16-24

MOST of us have lived long enough to experience some sort of sorrow that profoundly affects our lives. That sorrow may come in the form of a loss of some kind: the loss of a job, a marriage, a child, a parent, a dear friend, one's health, or even finances. That sorrow could also come in the form of an unexpected change or event: attacks like that of September 11, a son who is sent suddenly to a foreign country to fight in a war, or a friend who unexpectedly turns on you and hurts you deeply. When sorrows confront us, we often grapple with questions that are difficult to answer: Is this emotion of sorrow that I'm experiencing a sin? Should I be able to just "snap out of it" (my *former* discipleship motto) when sorrow has come my way? Should I remain in this state of sorrow? Just how long should I sorrow?

Sorrow is an emotion given to us by God. In fact, Jesus Himself told the eleven disciples in the garden of Gethsemane that His soul was exceedingly sorrowful, even unto death. In the verses we'll consider in this chapter, Jesus tells the Eleven that they too will be sorrowful, but they will not remain in that sad state. Let's listen in on His words to the Eleven in John 16:16-24.

> "A little while, and you will not see Me; and again a little while, and you will see Me, because I go to the Father."
>
> Then some of His disciples said among themselves, "What is this that He says to us, 'A little while, and you will not see Me; and again a little while, and you will see Me'; and, 'because I go to the Father'?" They said therefore, "What is this that He says, 'A little while'? We do not know what He is saying."
>
> Now Jesus knew that they desired to ask Him, and He said to them, "Are you inquiring among yourselves about what I said, 'A little while, and you will not see Me; and again a little while, and you will see Me'?

> Most assuredly, I say to you that you will weep and lament, but the world will rejoice; and you will be sorrowful, but your sorrow will be turned into joy. A woman, when she is in labor, has sorrow because her hour has come; but as soon as she has given birth to the child, she no longer remembers the anguish, for joy that a human being has been born into the world. Therefore you now have sorrow; but I will see you again and your heart will rejoice, and your joy no one will take from you.
>
> "And in that day you will ask Me nothing. Most assuredly, I say to you, whatever you ask the Father in My name He will give you. Until now you have asked nothing in My name. Ask, and you will receive, that your joy may be full."

In our last chapter, we learned of the sensitivity of Christ to the eleven disciples. We also learned of the Spirit's ministry to the Eleven, which included showing them the truth, showing them things to come, and showing them Christ. In this chapter and the next one, we will examine Christ's final words to His disciples. These will be the last things He says to them in the upper room before He prays to the Father and goes to the cross. Our outline for this chapter will include: *Confusing Words* (vv 16-19); *Clarifying Words* (vv 20-22); and *Comforting Words* (vv 23-24). Let's look at these confusing words, these mysterious words, Christ says to His disciples.

Confusing Words — *John 16:16-19*

> "A little while, and you will not see Me; and again a little while, and you will see Me, because I go to the Father." (John 16:16)

When Jesus says *a little while*, He is referring to a small space of time. And, indeed, it will be that in just a few hours from this moment the disciples will not see Christ anymore! Jesus is communicating to them: "In just a short space of time, men, you will not see Me because I am going to be crucified. I am going to die. You will not see Me then." The word for *see* here, in the first part of verse 16, is *theoreo* in the Greek, which means to be a spectator. In fact, we get our English word theater from it. It communicates the idea of seeing something or someone face to face. In a little while, the disciples will not see Jesus face to face. But Jesus then follows these words by saying *and again a little while, and you will see Me*. What does this mean? Some think that this is a reference to Christ's return, but that doesn't seem to fit this context because the disciples will not be around when Christ comes back the second time. Even now, they are in Heaven, and indeed they are with Him at this very moment. Others think this is a reference to the time following the resurrection of Christ when the disciples will see Him for forty days. It is true that the disciples will see Jesus again after the resurrection, but this interpretation of Jesus' words doesn't seem to fit in the context of what He says next: *because I go to the Father*. The disciples will see Him indeed for 40 days, but then Jesus will be going to the Father. How were the disciples going to see Him again? When we focus in on the immediate context, it becomes clear what Christ is saying. Look back at John 14:16 and 19 for what Christ is saying. Remember, we discovered in John 14:16 that the Greek word for another is *allos*, which is another of the same kind. The Holy Spirit will be someone just like Christ. The disciples will see Jesus again via the manifestation of the Holy Spirit. Also, we know this is what Christ is speaking of here because the Greek word here for *see* is not the same one used in the first part of verse 16. Here, in the latter part of verse 16, the Greek word for see is *horao*, which means to comprehend. The disciples were going to see Jesus but in a new way. So, when He tells them they will see Him again, He is not talking about seeing His physical body again; He is talking about seeing Him, or comprehending Him, in a new way, that is, through the person of the Holy Spirit. What a comfort that must have been to the Eleven! Jesus gives them hope to help alleviate their sorrow! Did the disciples understand these words? No. They were still confused, and we know that from verses 17 and 18.

> Then some of His disciples said among themselves, "What is this that He says to us, 'A little while, and you will not see Me; and again a little while, and you will see Me'; and, 'because I go to the Father'?" They said therefore, "What is this that He says, 'A little while'? We do not know what He is saying." (John 16:17-18)

It appears that only *some* of the disciples were confused, as it says *some of His disciples said among themselves*. Perhaps, the rest of the disciples were beginning to understand what Christ was saying. When it says they *said among themselves*, it means they were speaking in low, muffled tones, not wanting to ask Jesus openly. *Among themselves* is in the imperfect tense in the Greek language, which indicates that considerable dialogue took place among the disciples for some time without them being able to arrive at an answer.

As verse 18 shows us, these confused disciples go on asking these questions among themselves. Did they not know that Jesus knew they were asking this question among themselves? Did they not realize He knew even the intent of their thoughts? He certainly did, as John tells us in verse 19,

> Now Jesus knew that they desired to ask Him, and He said to them, "Are you inquiring among yourselves about what I said, 'A little while, and you will not see Me; and again a little while, and you will see Me'?" (John 16:19)

The words *now Jesus knew* are important words because they remind us that Jesus is all-knowing, as we have seen John reiterate throughout the Gospel of John. (Consider John 2:23-25; 4:17-18; 6:64; 13:1.) Even the disciples testify in verse 30 of this same chapter: "Now we are sure that You know all things, and have no need that anyone should question You. By this we believe that You came forth from God."

Isn't it wonderful that Christ shows His mercy here to His disciples by taking the initiative to help them in their embarrassment? They wanted to ask Him a question but did not venture to express their desire. They're not any different than you and me. I can't tell you how many times, when a gathering is happening at our church, I have asked someone else to ask a question of someone out of embarrassment or fear of being thought silly. This is why most of us do not ask the questions we have, and it's probably the same reason the disciples did not ask. The ironic thing is that, usually, there are others in the audience who have the same question but also will not ask. One difference, for sure, for us is that the pastors of our local churches usually do not know the questions in the minds of their people, but Jesus knew the disciples desired to ask Him what He meant by His mysterious words. In verses 20-22, in contrast to what seemed to be confusing words, Jesus provides the disciples with some clarifying words.

Clarifying Words *John 16:20-22*

> "Most assuredly, I say to you that you will weep and lament, but the world will rejoice; and you will be sorrowful, but your sorrow will be turned into joy." (John 16:20)

Jesus says to the disciples *most assuredly*, which conveys the idea that this will indeed happen. And what is it that will indeed happen? *You will weep and lament.* Why will they weep and lament? Because Christ is soon to be taken away from them and crucified. (See Mark 16:9-11 and Luke 24:13-20, especially verse 17.) The word *weep* means to wail aloud, to sob with loud, unrestrained weeping, while the word *lament* means to audibly express lament, to wail, to utter wailing cries and moans for the dead. In Jesus' day, these verbs were used of the loud wailings and lamentations which were customary in the days following someone's death. We see this with David, in 2 Samuel 1:17, after Jonathan dies: "Then David chanted with this funeral lament over Saul and Jonathan his son" (LSB). This demonstration of grief would at times even take the form of a poem, such as the beautiful lamentation David composed in 2 Samuel 1:25-27 (LSB): "How have the mighty fallen in the midst of the battle! Jonathan is slain on your high places. I am distressed for you, my brother Jonathan; you have been very pleasant to me. Your love to me was more wonderful than the love of women. How have the mighty fallen, and the weapons of war perished!" David wept and lamented over his dear friend Jonathan, and soon the disciples will weep and lament over their dear friend Jesus who will die the terrible death of crucifixion.

But while the disciples are weeping and lamenting, Jesus says *the world will rejoice*. Why would the world *rejoice*? Because they would think that the death of Jesus would be a time to celebrate. In fact, the word for *world* here refers particularly to the Jews who sought His death and who would soon be rejoicing at it. We have already seen, in John 16:2, that the world would soon think that to kill the disciples would be doing God a service! Rejoicing at the death of the Savior is a sad statement, indeed, but their rejoicing will only be temporary. Jesus said in Luke 6:25b (LSB), "Woe to you who laugh now, for you shall mourn and cry." The world may laugh now, but there is coming a day when they will be weeping in hell. The disciples, on the other hand, will soon be weeping, but on that same future day, they will be rejoicing in Heaven, as Jesus also says in Luke 6:21b (LSB), "Blessed are those who cry now, for you shall laugh."

Jesus reminds them again *and you will be sorrowful, but your sorrow will be turned into joy*. They will be *sorrowful*, which means to grieve. This Greek word for *sorrowful* is the most common word used to express grief and is the opposite of the Greek word for rejoice. It does not necessarily require that this grief be outwardly expressed, though it can be, depending on how a person chooses to express their grief. There are many times in my life when I have expressed grief in the silence of my own heart, and no one else has known about it but the Lord and me. Sorrow can be expressed outwardly with loud emotions, but often a heart can be grieving and breaking inside as well.

In contrast to this sorrow, Jesus assures His disciples that *your sorrow will be turned into joy*. Notice that *joy* does not replace the *sorrow*; rather, the sorrow is *turned into joy*. The cross would indeed be sorrowful for them, but later on it would become a source of great joy. How would their sorrow turn into joy? The first answer is found in Matthew 28:8 and John 20:20. Matthew 28:8 (LSB) tells us, "And they left the tomb quickly with fear and great joy and ran to report it to His disciples." And John 20:20 (LSB) tells us, "And when He had said this, He showed them both His hands and His side. The disciples then rejoiced when they saw the Lord." These verses clearly show us that the disciples' sorrow will be turned into joy by the resurrection of their Lord. But, also, their sorrow would be turned into joy by seeing the Lord again via the ministry of the Holy Spirit within them. Look at John 16:22: "Therefore you now have sorrow; but I will see you again and your heart will rejoice, and your joy no one will take from you." The day the Holy Spirit comes is the day their sorrow is truly and fully turned into joy. The joy they would have in seeing Jesus after the resurrection would be temporary—only 40 days—and then He would be gone again. But they would have lasting joy when the Holy Spirit comes to reside within them for good.

Ladies, may I pause here and say to you that the Lord wants to do the same thing in each of our lives? He wants to turn our sorrow into joy!

To use Paul's words in 2 Corinthians 6:10, Jesus means to make us "as sorrowful, yet always rejoicing." In the midst of his sorrow, the Psalmist rejoiced in Psalm 30:5 (LSB), "For His anger is but for a moment, His favor is for a lifetime; weeping may last for the night, but a shout of joy comes in the morning." If we could see the end of our sorrows, the outcome of all our afflictions, we too would rejoice, as Job did in Job 23:10: "But He knows the way I take; when He has tested me, I shall come forth as gold." In the midst of our sorrow, we need to remember that there is joy to be found even there. No sorrow is too great that we cannot also find something to rejoice in. God is always at work in our lives—and we can take joy in that! The puritan John Owen, who had 10 out of 11 of his children die in infancy with the one daughter who survived to adulthood dying as well, writes about the joy we have in understanding that God is making us more like Christ: "There is a secret joy and spiritual refreshment rising in the soul from a sense of its renovation into the image of God."[1]

In verse 21, Jesus further clarifies His Words by using one of the greatest examples of human sorrow and joy to illustrate how God can and does turn sorrow into joy:

> "A woman, when she is in labor, has sorrow because her hour has come; but as soon as she has given birth to the child, she no longer remembers the anguish, for joy that a human being has been born into the world." (John 16:21)

Many of us know from experience exactly what Christ is saying here. Childbirth is painful! In fact, the word for *labor* means to break, crush, press, compress, squeeze. It is a grievous affliction or distress. Remember, God told Eve in Genesis 3:16 that in sorrow she would bring forth children. But the sorrow does not remain, or at least it shouldn't. Why? *For joy that a human being has been born into the world*! I can't even remember the 36 hours of labor pain that I had with my firstborn, Charles, but I know it was real at the time. So real, in fact, that I would like to forget my unsanctified behavior during that time! There is no joy at the time

---

[1] John Owen, "Gospel Grounds and Evidences of the Faith of God's Elect," *Christian Classics Ethereal Library,* 33, https://www.ccel.org/ccel/o/owen/faith/cache/faith.pdf. Accessed 9/28/2023.

of the pain, is there? It is tremendously difficult—it's *anguish*, as Jesus says here—but then the joy does come. Two of the greatest joys of my life have been the births of my two children! So, what is Christ saying to the Eleven here? He's saying that, just as giving birth to a child first brings sorrow and anguish yet afterward brings abundant joy, so too will the death of Christ first bring weeping and wailing but afterward bring great joy. Joy because salvation has come! God in the flesh bringing salvation to mankind!

The image that Christ gives here is used to provide a familiar and touching illustration of the truth that pain is often necessary in order to experience the joys of life. Think about it in your own life. When have you had the most joy in your life, the most growth? I would venture to say it was a time when you had also experienced the most pain. The Lord has just allowed me to go through a lengthy time of sorrow, which is still going on in many ways, and yet the inward joy I now possess is indescribable. It is a bittersweet time. And so, Christ goes on to say,

> "Therefore you now have sorrow; but I will see you again and your heart will rejoice, and your joy no one will take from you." (John 16:22)

At this moment the disciples were sorrowing; we know that from John 16:6. And soon they are going to enter a deeper period of pain and sorrow. But that sorrow will not last, as Christ goes on to say: *but I will see you again and your heart will rejoice*. It is true that Christ will indeed see them very soon, just after the resurrection. But, in this context, it seems that He is referring to their seeing Him through the Holy Spirit's presence within them. And when this happens, their hearts *will rejoice*. And when we think about it, today the disciples are seeing Him in Heaven, and you and I know, without a doubt, that they are rejoicing!

Jesus then says some profound words: *and your joy no one will take from you*. What does He mean by this? He is speaking of the promise of the indwelling Holy Spirit. He will abide within them forever. He will be a forever comforter and a lasting source of *joy*! Isn't that one of the fruits of the Spirit, according to Galatians 5:22-23? "But the fruit of the Spirit is love, joy, peace, patience, kindness, goodness, faithfulness, gentleness, self-control. Against such things there is no law" (LSB). Though man may try to take away our joy, though the enemy may attempt to take away our joy, no one can ever succeed in taking it from us because of the Spirit within us! He is our constant source of joy! Hallelujah!

In verses 23-24, Christ continues speaking to the eleven disciples, and He transitions into a word of comfort for them. The things He has just spoken have been confusing and saddening, but here He offers to them words that are comforting. And, in these words, we find for ourselves a profitable discipling principle: When we have bad news or hard things that we need to say to those we disciple, we should always give them hope. And here we see our Lord doing just that. Jesus says,

Comforting Words *John 16:23-24*

> "And in that day you will ask Me nothing. Most assuredly, I say to you, whatever you ask the Father in My name He will give you." (John 16:23)

Now, what *day* is Jesus referring to when He says *that day*? He's referring to the day He had already spoken to them about, the day the Spirit would come, the day of Pentecost (see 14:20). In *that day*, Jesus says, they *will ask Me nothing. Ask* here, in the beginning of verse 23, is not in the sense of requesting something in prayer, but that of asking a question. They will ask Him no questions, not one thing. Why wouldn't they ask Him anything? Because He would be ascended into Heaven and He would cease to be bodily available to them for their questions. But, also, they will have gained a fuller understanding of what is going to happen. On the day of Pentecost, things would become much clearer to them. They will then have Someone else to help them answer their questions, that Someone being the Holy Spirit, as mentioned in John 14:26 and John 16:13.

But Christ goes on to say something which seems like a contradiction, but it is not: *Most assuredly, I say to you, whatever you ask the Father in My name He will give you*. He has already given them this promise in John 14:13-14 and 15:7, 16. But what is He saying here about asking when He has just said that they won't ask Him anything? When Jesus says they will ask Him nothing, the meaning of the Greek term *ask* has to do with the asking of a question, rather than the asking of a favor. Remember, the disciples had been asking Him one question after another. But, with His ascending into Heaven and the coming of the Spirit on the day of Pentecost, they would ask Jesus no questions, because He would not be there. Besides, the Holy Spirit would then become their teacher, as Jesus has been telling them. Here, in the latter part of verse 23, Christ is introducing a new thought by using a different Greek word for *ask*. The meaning of this term has to do with begging, and it refers to the seeking of something from a superior by one who is inferior. There is a reason for these different terms with different meanings. Instead of asking Jesus questions about this or that, the disciples would instead petition the *Father* in prayer in the *name* of Christ for whatever they need. Jesus goes on to further explain what He means, and with this we close.

> "Until now you have asked nothing in My name. Ask, and you will receive, that your joy may be full." (John 16:24)

Up *until now*, the disciples had addressed their prayers to God, without making mention of Jesus' name. But that was to soon change, as Christ would become the mediator between them and God. *Ask*, here, is the word for petition or request made by an inferior to a superior. To ask in Jesus' name means to ask on the basis of His merit and in harmony with His will. *Ask, and you will receive*, Jesus says. And the tense here indicates that the one asking is to keep on asking, continuously, habitually. It is the same Greek tense used in Matthew 7:7-8 (LSB): "Ask, and it will be given to you; seek, and you will find; knock, and it will be opened to you. For everyone who asks receives, and he who seeks finds, and to him who knocks it will be opened."

So, what will happen when the disciples ask, when they pray? First, Jesus says, they *will receive*. But, second, their *joy* will *be full*. The word *full* means to fill, as a net is filled with fish in Matthew 13:48; as a house is filled with a perfumed smell in John 12:3; and as Jesus describes the valleys being filled in, in Luke 3:5. When we, as Christians, pray, we have fullness of joy! Prayer results in joy being filled. Through constant fellowship with God in prayer and through the receiving of answers to their prayers, whatever was lacking in the disciples' joy would be supplied until the cup of their joy would be filled to the brim. It makes sense, doesn't it? We even see the apostle Paul connecting these two concepts—prayer and rejoicing—in 1 Thessalonians 5:16-17, when he says, "Rejoice always, pray without ceasing." If we cease to pray, we will likely cease to rejoice. We must pray without ceasing so that we may rejoice always. The person who prays little and coldly must not expect to know much of joy. What comforting words these must have been to the Eleven, and what comfort they are to you and me.

Summary

We have learned of some confusing words from our Lord (vv 16-19). Do you sometimes find the Word of the Lord to be confusing? Does this lead you to further questioning and studying of the Word of God, or does it lead you to further questioning and doubting of God? Do you walk by faith in those confusing times, or do you walk in confusion?

We have also learned about some clarifying words from our Lord (vv 20-22). While Christ has explained that He would be leaving the disciples, He also assures them that their sorrow would soon be turned into joy. When you study Scriptures that once were confusing but now are clearer, do you give thanks to God for opening your eyes to see the truth?

Lastly, we have learned of some truly comforting words from our Lord (vv 23-24): that we can ask the Father in Jesus' name and be assured that He will give to us what we've requested. As we keep on asking, and keep on receiving, our joy will be made full. How has God's Word comforted you during your time as a believer? Are you thankful for the comfort that God's Word gives to you?

John MacArthur summarizes these verses in a wonderful way:

> Again, we can't help but see the beauty and magnificence of the person of Jesus Christ. What a Savior! He knew the cross was coming; He could already see with His mind's eye the nails tearing into His limbs, the thorns puncturing His brow, the spear into His internal organs, the

jeers of the mocking people, and the spit and laughter of the killers. He could already feel the loneliness of being separated from God, and the pain of bearing every sin of mankind. But even in anticipation of all that, He wanted most of all to make the disciples happy. That tells me He really cares for us. In the midst of all that He must be doing to uphold the universe, He cares that we have joy. Right up to His death on the cross, Christ did everything to assure us full joy. He provided a glorious prayer, fellowship with the Father, and He sent His Holy Spirit to live within us—all because He wants us to have joy. It must break the Lord's heart when a Christian becomes bitter or cynical and doesn't take hold of the joy he could have. God forgive us if we are not overwhelmed with the sweet joy that is ours because of the cross and with the way He can turn sorrow into joy.[2]

---

2 John MacArthur, *The MacArthur New Testament Commentary: John 12-21* (Chicago: Moody Publishers, 2008), 218-219.

QUESTIONS TO CONSIDER

1. (a) What did Jesus say to the disciples in John 16 that may have caused them sorrow, and what joy can be found in each of those things He said? (b) What does Christ mean when He says in verse 20 that their sorrow would be turned into joy?

2. Memorize John 16:22.

3. In John 16:16-18, it is clear that the disciples did not understand what Jesus was trying to say to them. (a) Look up the following passages and note what else the disciples had difficulty understanding. Mark 9:9-10; Luke 9:44-45; Luke 18:31-34; John 12:12-16; John 14:5; John 14:22. (b) What lessons do you learn for your own life from these passages?

4. (a) What does Psalm 139 tell you about God's omniscience? (b) How does this correlate with John 16:19? (c) Why do we try to hide things from God when He sees all and knows all? (d) Analyze your thoughts and prayers this week. Are you honest with God in your thoughts and prayers, or do you try to hide from Him?

5. (a) Choose someone from the Scriptures who had sorrow and yet their sorrow was turned into joy. What can you learn from their example about sorrow being turned to joy? (b) How does this give you hope?

6. (a) What illustration does Jesus use in John 16:21 to explain to the disciples that their sorrow would be turned into joy? (b) Why do you think Christ uses this particular illustration?

7. (a) What are you currently sorrowing over? (b) How do you see God using this current sorrow in your life? (c) What joy do you see in the sorrow?

8. Consider your answers to Question 7 and write your need in the form of a prayer request to share.

Christ's Final Words to the Eleven

John 16:25-33

MOST of us have lived long enough to experience the death of someone we love. I have experienced the death of my grandparents, my parents, some of my siblings, my husband, friends, and a number of parishioners in the churches my husband pastored over the years. Some of these deaths stand out in my mind more than others, for various reasons. But there was one particular church member's death, many years ago, that jolted me. I had just begun a discipling relationship with her when she found out she had cancer. She died a month later. The Lord blessed me with the wonderful privilege of being with her and caring for her in her dying process. When she found out she had cancer, I had several conversations with people that went something like this: "Suppose you knew you had only six months to live, what would you do? What would you change? What would you say to those people who are the closest to you?" The answers were always interesting, stimulating, and thought-provoking. I think all of us would answer these questions by saying that, faced with our own impending death, we would get together with those closest to us and we would share the things that are on our hearts—the things that, perhaps, we haven't yet said but probably should. I remember saying things to my dying friend in those final days with her that I probably would not have shared had she not been facing death.

As we have been studying these past few chapters of John's Gospel, we have been looking not at Jesus' last six months with His disciples, but His last hours with them. He has been sharing with them the things that are on His heart. It has been a time of tenderness with His disciples as He stooped to wash their dirty feet; a time of warning, especially in light of upcoming persecution; a time of instruction regarding the coming ministry of the Holy Spirit; and a time of assuring them of some wonderful promises. But now, we have come to the final minutes He has with them before Judas comes with his kiss of betrayal. These are the final words recorded for us that Jesus says to His own in the upper room. They are the final words of Jesus to the Eleven before He goes to the cross and before He goes back to the Father. What's on Christ's mind as He faces death? The final things that are on His mind are prayer, love, faith, and peace. And, in all of this, the Person that seems to be foremost on Jesus' mind is His Father—Jesus refers to the Father eight times in these verses alone! Let's listen in on these final words in John 16:25-33.

> "These things I have spoken to you in figurative language; but the time is coming when I will no longer speak to you in figurative language, but I will tell you plainly about the Father. In that day you will ask in My name, and I do not say to you that I shall pray the Father for you; for the Father Himself loves you, because you have loved Me, and have believed that I came forth from God. I came forth from the Father and have come into the world. Again, I leave the world and go to the Father."
>
> His disciples said to Him, "See, now You are speaking plainly, and using no figure of speech! Now we are sure that You know all things, and have no need that anyone should question You. By this we believe that You came forth from God."
>
> Jesus answered them, "Do you now believe? Indeed the hour is coming, yes, has now come, that you will be scattered, each to his own, and will leave Me alone. And yet I am not alone, because the Father is with Me. These things I have spoken to you, that in Me you may have peace. In the world you will have tribulation; but be of good cheer, I have overcome the world."

In our last chapter, we saw that Christ said some confusing words in verses 16-19: "A little while you will see me, and in a little while you won't see me." We also saw Christ offer some clarifying words in verses 20-22: He explained that even though He was leaving them, their sorrow would soon be turned into joy. And, lastly, we also saw Christ encourage his disciples with some comforting words in verses 23 and 24: They were to ask the Father in His name and He would answer their prayers. In fact, they were to keep on asking and they would keep on receiving as well, as the means by which their joy would be made full. Our outline for this chapter will include: *Christ's Proclamation of His Incarnation* (vv 25-28); *The Disciples' Profession of Their Faith* (vv 29-31); and *Christ's Promise of Peace* (vv 32-33).

Let's consider Christ's proclamation of His incarnation as we finish chapter 16 of John's Gospel.

Christ's Proclamation of His Incarnation   John 16:25-28

> "These things I have spoken to you in figurative language; but the time is coming when I will no longer speak to you in figurative language, but I will tell you plainly about the Father." (John 16:25)

Christ begins by saying *these things I have spoken to you*. So, naturally, one asks, "What things is He talking about?" *These things* would be all the things He has spoken in the upper room. And Jesus says He has *spoken* them in *figurative language* or proverbs. In the Greek, this language conveys the idea that the words Jesus has spoken have been veiled, have been allegories, wayside sayings, pointed statements, or dark sayings. The Hebrew meaning of this term refers to an iceberg that is largely hidden under the water's surface. Christ is saying, in effect, "I have been speaking to you in veiled statements," and He is referring in general to what He has been saying to them in the upper room, but more specifically He is referring to His statements about the Father. We know this because He clarifies what He is referring to by using the phrase *about the Father*. He has been speaking in figurative language about His coming and going to the Father. Christ could not speak plainly to them about all of this; He had to use figurative language because they were unable to bear it and lacked understanding. He had just told them in John 16:12, "I still have many things to say to you, but you cannot bear them now." He had been speaking to them in veiled language, in proverbs, but He goes on to say *but the time is coming when I will no longer speak to you in figurative language, but I will tell you plainly about the Father*. The time is here, is close at hand, when His speaking to them regarding the Father will not be in the figurative language He's been using but will, instead, be in plain language. What does Jesus mean here? Some think that Jesus means that He will explain things concerning the Father more fully in the 40 days He will have with them after His resurrection and before His ascension. However, when we take into account the bigger context of all Jesus has been talking about, it appears that this is, again, in reference to the day of Pentecost when the Holy Spirit comes. Remember, Jesus has been telling them that the Spirit, One who is just like Christ, will come and reveal things to them. He will be their teacher. And, once He has come to be their teacher, then they will understand more clearly about the Father. When we read from Acts all the way through to the Book of the Revelation at the end of the New Testament, we see the revelation that came from the Spirit about the Father. We can't know anything about the Father without knowing His Word and having the blessed Holy Spirit as our teacher. In verse 26, Jesus continues on with what will happen at Pentecost and says,

> "In that day you will ask in My name, and I do not say to you that I shall pray the Father for you;" (John 16:26)

What *day* is Jesus talking about? Again, the answer is the day of Pentecost, as we have already seen referenced back in verse 23. *In that day you will ask in My Name*. After Pentecost, the prayers of the disciples will be in Jesus' name. But then Jesus says *and I do not say to you that I shall pray the Father for you*. Now, you might have read this and said to yourself, "I do not understand this, because Romans 8:34, Hebrews 7:25, and 1 John 2:1 tell us that Jesus is at the right hand of the Father interceding for us. So, what does Jesus mean here?" He means that when the Holy Spirit comes, the disciples would be able to go directly to the Father in the name of Jesus (see John 16:23-24). Jesus is not saying here that He wouldn't pray for us or for the disciples, as that would be a contradiction to so many other statements in the Word of God. He's saying, "You won't need Me to pray to God for you. You're able to go directly to Him yourself. You don't have to have Me beg to God on your behalf; you can just go to Him in My Name. You belong to Me, and the Father loves Me so much that whatever you ask in My name, for My sake, He will do it for you." It would then be up to the disciples to come into the Father's presence themselves. With the Holy Spirit's coming, they would have full access to the Father. One man offers these helpful thoughts:

> That does not rule out the Lord's high priestly ministry or His advocacy of our needs. When Satan comes as the accuser, the Lord is there. When any question is raised about our human frailty and shortcomings, our sins and falls and failures, the Lord is there to raise His pierced hands

as token that His precious blood has not lost anything of its power. What the Lord is teaching here is that the Father loves us as much as the Son loves us, and reaches out to us as much as He, Jesus reaches out to us.[1]

Ladies, this is a wonderful privilege that we should not take for granted. Think of it: We have full access to the Father! And you know why that is? Jesus tells us in verse 27.

> "for the Father Himself loves you, because you have loved Me, and have believed that I came forth from God." (John 16:27)

There will be no need for Jesus to intercede for the disciples because *the Father Himself loves* them. Now, Jesus uses an interesting word here for *love*. It is not *agape*, which we see so often in the New Testament; rather, it is *phileo*, which is a love that entails a tender affection and common interests with others. Why does Jesus use the word *phileo* here for love and not *agape*? Because God not only loves you and me with *agape* love but also with a deep affection type of love, because He has an interest in us. (Remember, He has already called the disciples friends, in John 15:15.) In this context, this *phileo* love refers to a deep, fatherly affection God has for those who love Jesus. He is our Abba Father, our daddy, a term that communicates intimacy. He knows us just like we know our children and so we can go to Him boldly and freely and talk to Him.

You might be wondering, "Why does the Father love the disciples and love us so?" I'm glad you asked! Jesus gives us two reasons why. First, He says, *because you have loved Me*. Love is rewarded with love. Jesus already mentioned this to them back in John 14:23: "If anyone loves Me, he will keep My word; and My Father will love him, and We will come to him and make Our home with him." The second reason why the Father loves them so is because they *have believed that I came forth from God*. That is, they believed that Christ was God in the flesh. In verse 28, Christ reminds them again of this belief, that He is God in the flesh. They believe in His incarnation.

---

[1] John Phillips, *Exploring the Gospel of John,* 313.

> "I came forth from the Father and have come into the world. Again, I leave the world and go to the Father." (John 16:28)

In this verse, Christ is simply reiterating something He has already said to the disciples. He had said this very thing in John 14:2 and 28 and 16:5. But in this particular verse, Christ lays out four essential elements of the redemption: 1. *I came forth from the Father*—His Incarnation. 2. *I have come into the world*—His humiliation and mission. 3. *I leave the world*—His passions. 4. *I go to the Father*—His Ascension. It's as if Christ is giving the ABCs of the Father's divine plan of salvation. And we see in verses 29-31 that this statement from Christ causes the disciples to speak up and give their profession of their faith.

The Disciples' Profession of Their Faith   *John 16:29-31*

> His disciples said to Him, "See, now You are speaking plainly, and using no figure of speech!" (John 16:29)

It appears that the disciples had come to understand what Jesus was saying. It appears they were finally beginning to grasp what He'd been explaining to them. But, of course, we know that they will not fully understand until the day of Pentecost. It appears, at least for a while, that they took their mind off their own problems long enough to be excited about what Jesus was saying. Why did they now understand it when they had not understood before? I do not know. But I do know that, in my own life, it sometimes takes several attempts at learning new things before I get them. Or, someone can convey a truth in a different way, and then I will finally get it. The disciples continue in verse 30 with their profession of their faith:

> "Now we are sure that You know all things, and have no need that anyone should question You. By this we believe that You came forth from God." (John 16:30)

This is the disciple's last profession of their faith before Jesus' death. It is similar to several other confessions in the Gospel accounts: to John's confession (John 1:29 LSB, "On the next day, he saw Jesus coming to him and said, 'Behold, the Lamb of God who takes away the sin of the world!'"); to Nathanael's confession (John 1:49 LSB, "Nathanael answered Him, 'Rabbi, You are the Son of God; You are the King of Israel.'"); to Nicodemus' confession (John 3:2 LSB, "this man came to Jesus by night and said to Him, 'Rabbi, we know that You have come from God as a teacher; for no one can do these signs that You do unless God is with him.'"); to Peter's confession (Matthew 16:16 LSB, "And Simon Peter answered and said, 'You are the Christ, the Son of the living God.'"); and to Thomas' confession (John 20:28 LSB, "Thomas answered and said to Him, 'My Lord and my God!'").

The disciples here are quite sure in their belief. It's as though they're saying, "You have now told us plainly, so now there's no more need for any more questions!" Oh, really?! Jesus certainly has some doubt about their bold profession of belief in who He is, as evidenced by what He says in verse 31.

> Jesus answered them, "Do you now believe?" (John 16:31)

This is a question of doubt. The Greek suggests a crisis. Jesus seems to be warning His disciples of their apparent self-confidence. Did they not know that Jesus knew what was in their heart? Did they think they were above denying Him? There is a lesson in this verse for each of us. We may think we are very strong in a particular area of our Christian walk, and yet, my friend, we should take heed least we fall. Does not pride come before destruction? I remember vividly at the writing of this chapter that I was struggling with some plaguing thoughts, thoughts that I had been dead to since I embraced Christ's Lordship. I had assumed that these thoughts would never again be a part of my life. But their return was a warning to me that I am still in the flesh and I had better be soberminded and aware and watch and pray. The spirit is oh, so willing, but the flesh is oh, so weak! The disciples seemed to be confident here, as evidenced by Jesus' saying to them *you now believe?* The disciples had not estimated the weakness of their own flesh, the power of the devil, and the weakness of their faith. When we are under pressure and the fear of man and strong temptation, we can easily fail. The disciples had not learned the importance of wearing the armor of the Lord and standing steadfast in the day of battle. Albert Barnes reminds us, "When we feel strong in the faith we should examine ourselves. It may be that we are deceived; and it may be that God may even then be preparing trials for us that will shake our faith to its foundation."[2] We must be on the alert and not be ignorant of Satan's devices, for he is a roaring lion, seeking whom he may devour. Because Jesus understands this risk, He goes on to tell His disciples that very soon they will be offended and forsake Him, and, yet, as troubling as that is, He leaves them with a promise once again, a promise of peace.

Christ's Promise of Peace   *John 16:32-33*

> "Indeed the hour is coming, yes, has now come, that you will be scattered, each to his own, and will leave Me alone. And yet I am not alone, because the Father is with Me." (John 16:32)

Jesus reminds the disciples that *the hour is coming*. The long looked-for hour is so close that it has virtually come, as evidenced by the words *yes, has now come*. The time for Jesus' arrest is near. Judas and his band of captors are coming. The word *indeed* points to the fact that this indeed will happen. And what does Jesus say will happen when the hour comes? They *will be scattered*, which means to be offended. In fact, it will happen that very night, according to Matthew 26:31 (LSB): "Then Jesus said to them, 'You will all fall away because of Me this night, for it is written, "I will strike down the shepherd, and the sheep of the flock shall be scattered."'" Matthew will say later on that this was a fulfillment of Scripture, in Matthew 26:56 (LSB): "'But all this has taken place in order that the Scriptures of the prophets would be fulfilled.' Then all the disciples left Him and fled.." The Scripture that was fulfilled was Zechariah 13:7. "'Awake, O sword, against My Shepherd, against the Man who is My Companion,' says the LORD of hosts. 'Strike the Shepherd, and the sheep will be scattered; then I will turn My hand against the little ones.'" Also, Isaiah 63:3 indicates the same thing: "I have trodden the wine trough alone, and from the peoples there was no man with Me. I also trod them in My anger and trampled them in My wrath; and their

---

[2] Albert Barnes, *Barnes' Notes*, 331.

lifeblood is sprinkled on My garments, and I stained all My clothes" (LSB).

Jesus says they *will be scattered, each to his own*, which means each will flee for himself. Essentially, each will look out for his own interest. In fact, after Jesus' death, the disciples go back to their employment of fishing, according to John 21:1-14. Instead of preaching, they would be fishing. They would stop working for the Kingdom. The disciples would soon flee from the One they have just confessed to believe in. They will each be looking out for their own interests and be caught up in their own little world. They will leave Him alone; leave Him to die without human sympathy or compassion.

But notice that Jesus doesn't rebuke them for what they will do. He says *and will leave Me alone. And yet I am not alone*. He is thinking of them again and trying to comfort them. Amazing! And why won't Jesus be alone? He says *because the Father is with Me*. He has already mentioned this in John 8:29 (LSB), when He said, "And He who sent Me is with Me; He has not left Me alone, for I always do the things that are pleasing to Him." The Father has not left His Son alone. Even though Peter, James, and John would fall asleep on Jesus, the Father would be there with Him. Even though Judas and the others would come soon, and the disciples would soon flee, yet the Father would be with His Son. Even though Caiaphas, Herod, and Pilate would bully Jesus and harass Him, the Father would be with Him. Peter will soon swear and deny Him, yet the Father will be with Him. The crowd will mock Him, He will be scourged and spit upon and have His beard plucked out, yet the Father will be with Him. And, ladies, you and I have the same promise when we are facing what seems like our darkest hour. We are never alone. The Psalmist says in Psalm 27:10 (LSB), "For my father and my mother have forsaken me, but Yahweh will take me up." In Hebrews 13:5, we are assured by Jesus' promise to us: "I will never leave you nor forsake you." He will never, no, never, no, never leave us! As Jesus Himself said to the Eleven in Matthew 28:20, "And lo, I am with you always, even to the end of the age." It has been said that one of the martyrs, who was burned at the stake, took special comfort in this verse here in John 16. And, ladies, these verses should be of great comfort to all of us who have been forsaken by friends and family or find ourselves with that very real possibility. If we are honest, we would confess that there have been many times we too have felt that God has forsaken us and, yet, we have this promise that He will never leave us or forsake us. We are not alone, for the Father *is* with us.

I remember visiting my husband's mentor, Dr. Stewart, before the Lord took him home several years ago. He was reminiscing about all his friends who had gone to Heaven already—H. A. Ironside, J. Vernon McGee, Dr. John Walvoord, and even his wife. But then He said something I have never forgotten: "I have the Lord and He is enough." Christ intends to comfort His disciples—and us—with this same truth. And in His very last words to the Eleven, once again, He speaks words of comfort for their troubled hearts.

> "These things I have spoken to you, that in Me you may have peace. In the world you will have tribulation; but be of good cheer, I have overcome the world." (John 16:33)

What are *these things* Jesus is referring to? The entire Upper Room Discourse. And why has Christ *spoken* these things to them? Not to glorify Himself, but once again, for their benefit, *that in Me you may have peace*. The entire discourse was given so that they would have peace. *Peace* is rest, and it is in contrast with strife. It is the idea of contentment and trust in God, in spite of our circumstances. This promise of peace, interestingly, comes after the announcement that they soon will abandon Him in His final hour. Jesus is still loving them to the end and thinking of them, even though soon they will be thinking only of themselves. What a loving Lord! In spite of the fact that He would be leaving, that Judas would soon betray Him, that Peter would deny Him, that the prince of this world was coming, that there would be false branches and painful pruning, that the world would hate them and persecute them, that they would be put out of the synagogue and eventually killed—in spite of all this, and all their sorrow—He has spoken all these things, so that they would have peace. Christ did not want them to be troubled. He had already said this to them in John 14:1 and 27. But, notice that Christ is careful to say on what basis they would have peace: *in Me*! Without being in Him, there is no way the disciples could have peace. The world does not have peace, as can be seen in the next phrase, which is a contrast to what has come before it: *in the world you will have tribulation.* In the world they would have tribulation. Christ has already warned them of this, in John 15:19-21 and 16:1-4. The word for *tribulation* means to break, crush, press, compress, and squeeze. It is a word that denotes trouble or fear. Jesus had told the disciples, in chapters 15 and 16, that they would be hated, persecuted, put out of synagogue, and murdered. But that should not discourage them. He says *but be of good cheer*, be of courage, be courageous in the face of danger. And He's told them before that they should rejoice and, yes, even leap for joy when under persecution.

The disciples might be thinking, "How can we be of good cheer?!" Christ answers that. He says, I have overcome the world. I have conquered the world; I have prevailed over it; I have won the victory! The word *overcome* always refers to spiritual victory. Jesus told the disciples in John 14:30, "I will no longer talk much with you, for the ruler of this world is coming, and he has nothing in Me." And in 1 John 4:4, John tells us, "You are of God, little children, and have overcome them, because He who is in you is greater than he who is in the world." Peace and joy should fill the disciples' hearts, and ours, when we realize that Jesus has overcome the world. It should not matter what the circumstance is in our lives; for the believer, a peaceful heart should prevail over a troubled heart because Jesus has overcome the world! He has been victorious over death and Satan! Martin Luther says: "thus is the 'good night' said, and the hand shaken.... Let not your heart be troubled. Be of good cheer."[3]

Summary

We have learned of Christ's proclamation of His incarnation (vv 25-28): I came from God and I am going back to God, and then you will see Me plainly. We have learned of the disciples' profession of their faith (vv 29-31): We see all things clearly now, and we believe and know that you came from God. We have also learned of Christ's promise of peace

---
3 Martin Luther, quoted in J. C. Ryle, *Expository Thoughts on the Gospels.*

(vv 32-33): You will leave me alone, but I leave you with peace. You will have tribulation in the world, but you will have My peace.

Christ's final words to the disciples are words of comfort and encouragement. In this, we can learn a lesson from our Lord regarding final words. Have you ever asked yourself, "What will be my final words?" Some of us may not have time to think about our final words, because we may be ushered into eternity in a flash, without warning. Others of us may have the time, as my friend did, to say the things that are on our hearts. Perhaps each of us should have the mindset that one puritan had when he wrote this prayer: "May I speak each word as if my last word, and walk each step as my final one. If my life should end today, let this be my best day."[4]

---

4 Arthur Bennett, *The Valley of Vision,* 221.

QUESTIONS TO CONSIDER

1. (a) Read John 16 and list all the promises you find. (b) What was Jesus' final promise to the eleven disciples? (c) What do you think was the reason for this particular promise being given at this particular time?

2. Memorize John 16:32.

3. (a) What does Jesus tell His disciples in John 16:26? (b) Do Romans 8:34; Hebrews 7:25; and 1 John 2:1 contradict John 16:26? (c) How do you resolve this apparent tension?

4. (a) What do the following verses say about God's love? Deuteronomy 7:6-10; Jeremiah 31:3; John 3:16; John 16:27; Romans 5:5; Romans 8:35-39; Ephesians 2:4-7; 1 John 4:7-10; 1 John 4:16; 1 John 4:19. (b) What comfort do these verses give? (c) What are some of the ways the Father has expressed His love to you recently? Take the time to thank Him for each of His expressions of love.

5. (a) What had Jesus been telling the world as well as the disciples, according to John 6:33; John 6:61-62; John 7:29; John 8:42? (b) Why do the disciples appear to finally "get it" in John 16:28-30? (c) How does this give you hope for the lessons Christ has repeatedly brought about in your own life?

6. Jesus tells the disciples in John 16:33 to be of good cheer because He has overcome the world. In the following passages, whom does Jesus tell to be of good cheer, and why? Matthew 9:2; Matthew 9:20-22; Matthew 14:22-27; Mark 10:49-52; and Acts 23:11. (b) What do these passages teach you?

7. (a) What are the disciples sure of in John 16:30? (b) What does Jesus say will happen in John 16:31-32? (c) What does this teach you about being over-confident in your flesh? See 1 Corinthians 10:12-13. (d) What steps can you take to make sure you do not become over-confident in your own flesh? (Use Scripture to demonstrate your answer.)

8. (a) What has Christ said in the upper room which should have brought peace to the disciples? (b) In what ways do these things bring you peace?

9. (a) How did Christ overcome the world? (John 16:33). Demonstrate your answer from the Scriptures. (b) How are you overcoming the world?

10. How is John 16:32-33 a personal comfort to you during difficult times?

11. (a) How have you been challenged as a result of this chapter? (b) Put your need in the form of a prayer request.

22

The High Priestly Prayer, Part 1: Christ Prays for Himself
John 17:1-5

JOHN 17, which is the last chapter in our study of Jesus' Upper Room Discourse, is one of the most moving prayers in all the Word of God. It is the prayer before the cross, which some have called the High Priestly Prayer. Matthew Henry says that John 17 is "the most remarkable prayer following the most full and consoling discourse ever uttered on earth."[1] Martin Luther writes, "This is truly, beyond measure, a warm and hearty prayer. He opens the depths of His heart, both in reference to us and to His Father, and He pours them all out. It sounds so honest, so simple; it is so deep, so rich, so wide, no one can fathom it."[2] Melanchthon writes, "There is no voice which has ever been heard, either in heaven or in earth, more exalted, more holy, more fruitful, more sublime, than the prayer offered up by the Son to God Himself."[3] John Brown says, "The seventeenth chapter of the Gospel of John, is without doubt, the most remarkable portion of the most remarkable book in the world .... What concentration of thought and affection are there in these few sentences. How 'full of grace' and 'full of truth.' How condensed, and yet how clear the thoughts—how deep, yet how calm, the feelings which are here, as far as the capabilities of human language permit, worthily expressed!"[4] "This remarkable model prayer contains none of the things that take up so much room in our prayers. All its items of petition and praise are of a spiritual nature. Like Moses at the burning bush, we would do well to remove the shoes from our feet. The place whereon we now stand is holy ground."[5] John Knox, the Scottish Reformer, had John 17 read to him every day during his final illness, and in the closing moments of his life,

---

[1] Matthew Henry, quoted in A. W. Pink, *Exposition of the Gospel of John*.
[2] Martin Luther, quoted in A. W. Pink, *Exposition of the Gospel of John*.
[3] Philip Melanchthon, quoted in A. W. Pink, *Exposition of the Gospel of John*.
[4] John Brown, quoted in A. W. Pink, *Exposition of the Gospel of John*.
[5] John Phillips, *Exploring the Gospel of John*, 317.

he testified that these verses continued to be a great comfort and a source of strength for his conflict. Clearly, this prayer has been a source of sweet comfort to Christ's people since the day He offered it up to His Father.

As we approach this prayer, and specifically look at its first five verses in this chapter, you might find yourself wondering, "Where was Jesus at when He prayed this prayer? And where were the eleven disciples? Were they still in the upper room?" While the precise location of Jesus and His disciples while this prayer is being offered isn't all that important, it appears that they were probably still in the upper room. The reason I say that is that there is nothing in chapters 16 or 17 to indicate that Christ or His disciples had left the room they'd been in during the earlier part of the evening. As we highlighted earlier in this study, it appears from John 18:1 that they did not leave the upper room until after this prayer was over. This prayer seems to have been offered up in the hearing and for the instruction of the Eleven. Lenski says, "Jesus utters this prayer aloud for the simple reason that He wants His disciples to hear His communication with the Father. For His own person a silent prayer might have sufficed. To the last His interest includes His disciples."[6] And, of course, we have learned in our study of the Upper Room Discourse that everything Jesus did and said was for the benefit of His disciples. This is the longest prayer of Jesus that is recorded for us in the Scriptures, and it is the longest prayer in the New Testament, and yet it can be recited in its entirety in just three minutes. Let's read the prayer in its entirety in John 17.

> Jesus spoke these words, lifted up His eyes to heaven, and said: "Father, the hour has come. Glorify Your Son, that Your Son also may glorify You, as You have given Him authority over all flesh, that He should give eternal life to as many as You have given Him. And this is eternal life, that they may know You, the only true God, and Jesus Christ whom You have sent. I have glorified You on the earth. I have finished the work which You have given Me to do. And now, O Father, glorify Me together with Yourself, with the glory which I had with You before the world was.
>
> "I have manifested Your name to the men whom You have given Me out

---

6 R. C. H. Lenski, *The Interpretation of St. John's Gospel,* 1114.

of the world. They were Yours, You gave them to Me, and they have kept Your word. Now they have known that all things which You have given Me are from You. For I have given to them the words which You have given Me; and they have received them, and have known surely that I came forth from You; and they have believed that You sent Me.

"I pray for them. I do not pray for the world but for those whom You have given Me, for they are Yours. And all Mine are Yours, and Yours are Mine, and I am glorified in them. Now I am no longer in the world, but these are in the world, and I come to You. Holy Father, keep through Your name those whom You have given Me, that they may be one as We are. While I was with them in the world, I kept them in Your name. Those whom You gave Me I have kept; and none of them is lost except the son of perdition, that the Scripture might be fulfilled. But now I come to You, and these things I speak in the world, that they may have My joy fulfilled in themselves. I have given them Your word; and the world has hated them because they are not of the world, just as I am not of the world. I do not pray that You should take them out of the world, but that You should keep them from the evil one. They are not of the world, just as I am not of the world. Sanctify them by Your truth. Your word is truth. As You sent Me into the world, I also have sent them into the world. And for their sakes I sanctify Myself, that they also may be sanctified by the truth.

"I do not pray for these alone, but also for those who will believe in Me through their word; that they all may be one, as You, Father, are in Me, and I in You; that they also may be one in Us, that the world may believe that You sent Me. And the glory which You gave Me I have given them, that they may be one just as We are one: I in them, and You in Me; that they may be made perfect in one, and that the world may know that You have sent Me, and have loved them as You have loved Me.

"Father, I desire that they also whom You gave Me may be with Me where I am, that they may behold My glory which You have given Me; for You loved Me before the foundation of the world. O righteous Father! The world has not known You, but I have known You; and these have known that You sent Me. And I have declared to them Your name, and will declare it, that the love with which You loved Me may be in them, and I in them."

Before we go over our outline for this prayer, let's remind ourselves of what we learned in our last chapter. As we ended chapter 16, we considered, first, Christ's proclamation of His incarnation, from verses 25-28: I came from God and I am going back to God, and when I do you will see Him plainly. Second, we saw the disciples' profession of their faith, from verses 29-31: We see all things clearly now; we believe and know you came from God. Lastly, we considered Christ's promise of peace, from verses 32-33: You will leave Me alone, but I leave you with peace; you will have tribulation in the world, but you will also have My peace.

As we consider the entirety of Christ's High Priestly Prayer, which spans all of John 17, we will divide it into three parts: *Christ's Prayer Regarding Himself* (vv 1-5), which we'll consider in this chapter; *Christ's Prayer for the Eleven Disciples* (vv 6-19), which we'll consider in our next chapter (It must have been truly encouraging to the eleven disciples to hear this prayer, as the bulk of Jesus' prayer was for them. I know I am very encouraged to hear others praying for me!); and *Christ's Prayer for Future Believers* (vv 20-26), which we'll consider in our final chapter. Imagine that! Jesus prays for future believers—for you and me!

In this chapter, we will cover the first five verses of Christ's prayer. As we look at His prayer for Himself, we see three elements present, and they will form our outline for this chapter: *The Posture of Christ's Prayer* (v 1a); *The Petition of Christ's Prayer* (vv 1b, 5); and *The Purpose of Christ's Coming* (vv 2-4). Let's look first at the posture of His prayer, in verse 1.

The Posture of Christ's Prayer   John 17:1

> Jesus spoke these words, lifted up His eyes to heaven, and said: "Father, the hour has come." (John 17:1a)

John begins by saying that *Jesus spoke these words*. What words is John speaking about here? He is referring to the words Christ has spoken in the upper room, recorded for us in chapters 13-16 of John's Gospel. So, after Jesus finished speaking His final words to His disciples, He then lifted up His eyes to Heaven to pray. We know that Jesus was in constant communion with the Father, and yet He had specific times of prayer, as we can see throughout the Gospel accounts. This is an important practice for you and I to consider; we, too, should be in an attitude of praying without ceasing, but we should also have specific times set aside for prayer, as our Lord did. You might be wondering, "If Jesus was God, why did He need to pray?" There are many reasons that Christ needed to pray: He prayed in order to demonstrate His humility, His humanity, His submission to the Father, and also, specifically, here in this passage, to model for the disciples (and us) how to pray.

Notice the posture of Jesus while He is praying. John says *He lifted up His eyes to heaven*. To *lift up* one's *eyes* to Heaven is an indication of purity of heart on the part of the one offering the prayer—in this case, our Lord. We have an interesting account of this very posture in Luke 18:13 (LSB), where we read, "But the tax collector, standing some distance away, was even unwilling to lift up his eyes to heaven, but was beating his chest, saying, 'God, be merciful to me, the sinner!'" Sin separates us from God and makes it difficult to lift our eyes to Heaven. But that was not the case for our Lord; He had nothing to hide. They tell us that when a person won't look you in the eye, it's generally the sign of a guilty conscience. Additionally, lifting up the eyes was one of many common postures of prayer we see in the Word of God. Consider Psalm 121:1-2 (LSB), "I will lift up my eyes to the mountains; from where shall my help come? My help comes from Yahweh, who made heaven and earth." Also, Psalm 123:1 (LSB), "To You I lift up my eyes, the One enthroned in the heavens!" But lifting up the eyes is just one of many postures of prayer we have recorded for us in God's Word. There is no set place, no set time, and no set posture prescribed in the Scriptures for prayer. And I think we must always remember that God is not so much interested in the posture of our bodies as He is with the posture of our hearts.

Notice the place that Jesus lifted His eyes to: *to Heaven*. It seems only logical that Jesus would lift His eyes to Heaven. Why? His throne was there; His angels were there; His rest was there; and His Father was there. He lifted up His eyes to pray to the place that is His home. These tender words that John records for us certainly indicate the love from the Son to His Father.

The first word that Jesus says in His prayer is *Father*. This is a word He will use six times throughout this prayer; we'll see it again in verses 5,

11, 21, 24 and 25. Wasn't it to the Father that Jesus told His disciples to address their prayers? Luke records for us, in Luke 11, that one of Jesus' disciples asked the Lord to teach them to pray, to which He replied, in Luke 11:2, "When you pray, say: Our Father in heaven, hallowed be Your name. Your kingdom come. Your will be done on earth as it is in heaven." Jesus is praying in John 17 to the very One to Whom He had told the disciples to pray. It's interesting that, in the 70 recorded prayers of Jesus in the New Testament, each time He uses the word Father, except on the cross, when He cried, "My God, My God, why have You forsaken Me?" (Mark 15:34b LSB).

After Jesus addresses the Father, He then says *the hour has come*. What hour is Jesus talking about? He is talking about the hour of His death, the hour of the cross, the hour when He would die for the sins of the world. Essentially, He's saying, "the hour is now here for me to die!" Up until this point, His hour had not yet come, but now it had. Jesus knew this was the hour, as we discovered in our first chapter in the upper room: "Now before the Feast of the Passover, when Jesus knew that His hour had come that He should depart from this world to the Father, having loved His own who were in the world, He loved them to the end" (John 13:1). Here, in John 17, this is the seventh and last time Jesus refers to His hour coming (see also John 2:4; 7:30; 8:20; 12:23; 12:27; 13:1; see also 16:32, where His mention of this hour coming refers to the disciples scattering).

The Petition of Christ's Prayer   *John 17:1, 5*

"Glorify Your Son, that Your Son also may glorify You," (John 17:1b)

As our Lord faces His final hour, what is on His mind? It is not the pain, the agony, or the separation from God, and it is not even leaving the disciples whom He loved so deeply. The preeminent thought on His mind was the glory of His Father, as is evident by the statement *glorify Your Son, that Your Son also may glorify You.*

Here we see the second element in Christ's prayer: His petition. This is the only petition Jesus asks for Himself. His petition is for the Son to be glorified so that the Son would glorify the Father. This is very similar to what He will request in verse 5. "And now, O Father, glorify Me together with Yourself, with the glory which I had with You before the world was." What is Jesus asking here when He asks the Father to *glorify Your Son*? The word *glorify* means to render the glory that is due. Jesus is asking to be given glory by the Father for the purpose of then giving to the Father the glory that is due to Him. How would Jesus receive glory that would, in return, glorify His Father? This would happen by Jesus going to the cross, going down into the grave, being resurrected, and then ascending into Heaven to be seated at the right hand of His Father (see Philippians 2:5-11). Jesus looked past the pain to the glory. Hebrews 12:2 draws our attention to this very reality: "fixing our eyes on Jesus, the author and perfecter of faith, who for the joy set before Him endured the cross, despising the shame, and has sat down at the right hand of the throne of God" (LSB). Why does Jesus want to be glorified? He wants to be glorified not for Himself but so that He can glorify His Father. This was Jesus' desire while He was on earth: to glorify the Father. Consider John 12:27-28 (LSB): "'Now My soul has become dismayed; and what shall I say, "Father, save Me from this hour"? But for this purpose I came to this hour. Father, glorify Your name.' Then a voice came from heaven: 'I have both glorified it, and will glorify it again.'" This statement in John 17 demonstrates for us the equality of the Son and the Father, because no other person could rightly say, "Glorify Your Son, that Your Son also may glorify You."

This request for the Father to glorify Jesus was answered, and we will see how when we get to verse 5. But, ladies, this brings me to a question for all of us. As you think about your own prayers, is glorifying the Father the thing that is primarily on your mind when you pray? It should be! Remember what Christ has already said in John 14:13-14? "And whatever you ask in My name, that I will do, that the Father may be glorified in the Son. If you ask anything in My name, I will do it."

In verses 2-4, we come to the third element in Christ's prayer regarding Himself, and this is where we see His purpose in coming. He mentions three purposes in this prayer.

The Purpose of Christ's Coming   *John 17:2-4*

> "as You have given Him authority over all flesh, that He should give eternal life to as many as You have given Him." (John 17:2)

Jesus mentions here that the Father has *given Him* [Jesus] *authority over all flesh*. This means Jesus has power or permission over all mankind. He has power over every person, whether they are rich or poor, educated or uneducated; He has power over everyone, even you and me. He not only has power over all flesh, all of mankind, but we know He has power over all of creation. Paul reminds us in Colossians 2:10 that Christ is "the head of all principality and power." And, again, Paul reminds us in Ephesians 1:22, "And He put all things in subjection under His feet, and gave Him as head over all things to the church" (LSB). In 1 Peter 3:22, the apostle Peter tells us that Christ "who is at the right hand of God, having gone into heaven, after angels and authorities and powers had been subjected to Him" (LSB).

God the Father gave Jesus authority over all flesh, even the authority to give life eternal. *This is His first purpose for coming: that He should give eternal life to as many as the Father has given.* This is a powerful statement Christ gives here because, left to ourselves, we all would be alienated from God. But Christ has the power to awaken our dead spirits so that we can respond to Him in faith. This is another way that Christ brought glory to the Father: by saving the souls that the Father has chosen. Since Christ has power to give us eternal life, it will be helpful to us to consider the question, "What is eternal life?" Simply put, eternal life is life without end, but it refers not only to the duration of life but to its quality as well. It is a quality of existence. It is a quality of life that will go on forever, but it is also something that we possess right now. Notice, though, that this eternal life is given to as many as God has given to Jesus. Jesus puts it this way: *that He should give eternal life to as many as You have given Him.* In John 6:37, Jesus said, "All that the Father gives Me will come to Me, and the one who comes to Me I will by no means cast out." And, again, in John 10:27-28, Jesus said, "My sheep hear My voice, and I know them, and they follow Me. And I give them eternal life, and they shall never perish; neither shall anyone snatch them out of My hand."

Considering what we've just read in verse 2, it is difficult for me to understand how anyone can deny the doctrines of election and predestination. They are simply self-evident. And while it is not our purpose to elaborate on that doctrine here, but to simply touch on it, one man helpfully states regarding this verse, "Here we touch the fringe of that robe of God's sovereignty in redemption. That God has given certain members of Adam's race to Christ and that Christ has given to those chosen ones eternal life, is perfectly clear."[7]

As Jesus continues speaking, in verse 3, He answers for us the question: "What is the nature of eternal life?"

> And this is eternal life, that they may know You, the only true God, and Jesus Christ whom You have sent. (John 17:3)

Eternal life, Jesus says, is to *know the only true God*, the One who cannot lie. He is *the only true God*, in contrast to all the false gods of this world. And notice that eternal life is not just to *know God*, but it is also to know *Jesus Christ*. A lot of people say they know and believe in God or a god, but do they know Jesus Christ? He is the Way, the Truth, and the Life. Eternal life is to know God, and we must know Him as He has revealed Himself through His Son Jesus Christ. As John would say in another one of his writings, 1 John 5:20 (LSB), "And we know that the Son of God has come, and has given us understanding so that we may know Him who is true; and we are in Him who is true, in His Son Jesus Christ. This is the true God and eternal life." Without knowing Jesus Christ, there is no eternal life.

Now, what does it mean to know God? The word *know* has two meanings. But, before I give you the two meanings, it's important to note that the Greek tense here indicates that this knowing is a continuing action. We don't fall in and out of salvation; we don't fall in and out of knowing the Father and knowing His Son. It is ongoing; Jesus already has made it clear that no one can pluck us out of the Father's hand. We are sealed until the day of redemption. With that in mind, let's consider the

---
7 John Phillips, *Exploring the Gospel of John,* 319.

meanings of the term *know*. The first meaning has to do with knowing someone or something intellectually. As it relates to knowing God, this refers to having a knowledge about God, about what God is like. To know God, we must know about him intellectually. But, we will never truly know what God is like apart from knowing His Son Jesus Christ, who is God the Son in human flesh. The term *know* can also have another meaning, one used in Genesis 4:1, where it says, "Now the man knew his wife Eve, and she conceived and gave birth to Cain" (LSB). Adam and Eve were one flesh; they were intimate in heart, mind, and soul; they knew one another. To know God, then, is not just merely to know about Him intellectually, but to have an intimate personal relationship with Him. We must be on intimate terms with Him and, again, this is impossible without knowledge of His Son Jesus Christ. This is a saving knowledge of God through His Son Jesus Christ. Ladies, our highest aim in life should be to know God and to know Jesus Christ. Is knowing God your deepest passion and desire? Would that we all could echo with the apostle Paul, "that I may know Him and the power of His resurrection and the fellowship of His sufferings, being conformed to His death" (Philippians 3:10 LSB)!

Christ goes on to state in His prayer that He was sent by God, as evidenced by the words *Jesus Christ whom You have sent*. Paul says in Galatians 4:4, "But when the fullness of the time came, God sent forth His Son, born of a woman, born under the Law" (LSB). God was the One who sent Jesus Christ, and this was all part of the divine plan. Now, before we go on to verse 4, an interesting fact to consider here is that this is the only place in the New Testament where our Lord calls Himself *Jesus Christ*. In verse 4, Jesus goes on to give us two more purposes of His coming.

> "I have glorified You on the earth. I have finished the work which You have given Me to do." (John 17:4)

The second purpose for which Christ came was to glorify God while on the earth. How did Jesus *glorify* God *on the earth*? There are several ways in which Jesus did this, but allow me give you just four:

1. *Jesus glorified God by keeping the law perfectly*. No one has ever kept

the law perfectly while on earth, except Jesus.

2. *Jesus glorified God by revealing His characteristics*. Being God in the flesh, Jesus was able to reveal who God is.

3. *Jesus glorified God by His miracles*. After Jesus heals a paralytic, Matthew records for us in Matthew 9:8, "Now when the multitudes saw it, they marveled and glorified God, who had given such power to men."

4. *Jesus glorified God by His death on the cross*. As Paul tells us in Philippians 2:8 Christ was obedient until death, even the death of the cross. My dear friend, can you say that your life has glorified God while you have been on this earth?

Christ goes on to mention a third purpose in His coming: to finish the work God gave Him to do. The word *finished* means to complete or accomplish. Jesus says in John 4:34b (LSB), to His disciples, "My food is to do the will of Him who sent Me and to finish His work." You might be wondering, "What was the work God gave Jesus to do?" Luke 4:16-21 gives us the answer to that question.

> So He came to Nazareth, where He had been brought up. And as His custom was, He went into the synagogue on the Sabbath day, and stood up to read. And He was handed the book of the prophet Isaiah. And when He had opened the book, He found the place where it was written:
> "The Spirit of the LORD is upon Me, because He has anointed Me to preach the gospel to the poor; He has sent Me to heal the brokenhearted, to proclaim liberty to the captives and recovery of sight to the blind, to set at liberty those who are oppressed; to proclaim the acceptable year of the LORD."
> Then He closed the book, and gave it back to the attendant and sat down. And the eyes of all who were in the synagogue were fixed on Him. And He began to say to them, "Today this Scripture is fulfilled in your hearing."

The Lord certainly had a lot of *work* to do, did He not? To finish the work which God had given Him would also have included His death. In fact, on the cross Jesus said, "It is finished" (John 19:30). Jesus had completed the work God gave Him to do by bringing the love of God to man, beginning at His birth and continuing all the way to His death on the cross. As He faces His death, Jesus has no sense of failure. Paul felt the same way as he faced his own death. Recorded for us in 2 Timothy 4:6-7 are these profound words: "For I am already being poured out as a drink offering, and the time of my departure has come. I have fought the good fight, I have finished the course, I have kept the faith" (LSB). (By the way, 2 Timothy 4:7 is what I would like inscribed on my tombstone!) Also, in Acts 20:24 (LSB), Paul says, "But I do not make my life of any account nor dear to myself, so that I may finish my course and the ministry which I received from the Lord Jesus, to testify solemnly of the gospel of the grace of God." Paul had finished the work God gave him to do. Christ had completed the work God had foreordained for Him to do. Jesus is not sitting in Heaven today wishing that He had done more while He was on the earth. His work is completed. It is finished. He has no regrets.

As women, we say, "A woman's work is never done," but Christ finished His work. If your life were suddenly to end today, could you say that you have finished the work God gave you to do? Before we can finish the work God has given us to do, we must first know what it is God wants us to be doing. Jesus knew that His purpose in life was to come and die for the sins of the world. What is your purpose, and are you fulfilling it? Several years ago, my husband challenged me to clarify my life's purpose, and I am glad he did. Knowing my purpose has made me more focused for Christ and His Kingdom.

In verse 5, Jesus ends the portion of His prayer regarding Himself with the same request He made back in verse 1—a request for glory.

The Petition of Christ's Prayer *John 17:1, 5*

> And now, O Father, glorify Me together with Yourself, with the glory which I had with You before the world was. (John 17:5)

What is Jesus saying here? Jesus is saying that He possessed God's attributes—His glory, both inward and outward—before ever coming to the earth. When Christ came to the earth, He laid these aside, in a sense. If He had not done so, no one would have been able to approach Him. So, what Jesus is praying for here is that the original glory He possessed—*from before the world was*—might be restored to Him. And God did answer that request by giving Jesus an exalted name and position, as we see in the following verses: Ephesians 1:20-23; Philippians 2:9-11; Hebrews 1:2-3; 1 Peter 1:21; Revelation 5:12. We learn from this verse that suffering for God is the highway to glory. Christ had to suffer immensely before returning to the Father, before returning to the glory He had with the Father before the world was. J. C. Ryle says, "A lazy wish to go to glory without working is not according to Christ's example."[8]

Summary

We have learned about the posture of Christ's prayer (v 1a): He lifted up His eyes to Heaven. We have considered the petition of Christ's prayer (vv 1b, 5): that the Son would be glorified with the glory He had before the world was. And we have seen the purpose of Christ's coming (vv 2-4): to give eternal life to those whom God gave Him, to glorify God while on the earth, and to finish the work God gave Him to do.

We have come to the end of the portion of Christ's prayer that is for Himself. This entire prayer can be prayed in just three minutes, yet it is powerful. This entire prayer can be prayed in just three minutes, yet it is not listless. This entire prayer can be prayed in just three minutes, yet it is not cold or selfish. This entire prayer can be prayed in just three minutes, yet it is not shallow (like, "God bless this mess! Amen!"). What can we learn from this prayer? We can learn that even during our darkest hour, perhaps even our final hour, we can still seek to glorify God. What was foremost on Christ's mind before the cross? That He would be glorified, so that, in return, the Father would be glorified. The hour had come, and that was what was on Christ's mind. Not the pain, the agony, and the suffering that He would soon encounter. Not the fact that the disciples were going to forsake Him and flee. Not the fact that the world

---

8 J.C. Ryle, *Expository Thoughts on the Gospels*.

would rejoice at His death. Instead, on His mind and in His prayer was the glory of the Father and of the Son.

Is the glory of God what is foremost on your mind when you pray? Does your prayer life reflect a desire for God to be glorified? Something to ponder, for sure. But, in addition to that, when your hour does come, what will be on your mind? The thought of leaving your loved ones behind? The suffering you're going through in the dying process? A clinging to this world and all it has to offer? Also something to think about, isn't it? Would to God that we would all think about how we can glorify the Father in our final hours—that He might receive the glory due Him in our death and in our life!

QUESTIONS TO CONSIDER

1. (a) Read all of John 17 and write down all the petitions that are in the Lord's prayer to the Father. (b) How do these compare to the petitions that are typically in your prayers?

2. Memorize John 17:1.

3. Compare the Lord's prayer in John 17 to the Lord's Prayer in Matthew 6:9-13, listing the similarities and the differences.

4. (a) What do you learn from Jesus' posture of lifting His eyes to Heaven to pray? (b) Look up the following verses and note who prayed and what their posture was in prayer (it may be helpful to search the surrounding verses to discover who is praying): Numbers 16:20-22; 1 Kings 19:1-4; 2 Chronicles 7:1-3; Psalm 4:4; Psalm 134:2; Daniel 6:10; Matthew 26:39; Mark 11:25; Luke 22:41; John 11:41; 1 Timothy 2:8. (c) What do these verses teach you about praying? (d) Are you judgmental of people whose posture in prayer differs from yours? (e) In what unusual postures and/or places have you prayed?

5. (a) Read the following verses and write down when, where, why, and for what or whom Jesus prayed (if it is stated; it may be helpful to search the surrounding verses to discover some of these answers). Matthew 11:25-26; Matthew 27:46; Mark 1:35; Mark 6:45-46; Luke 3:21-22; Luke 5:16; Luke 6:12-13; Luke 9:18; Luke 9:28-29; Luke 23:33-34, 46; John 11:41-44; John 12:27-29. (b) What things have you prayed for this week? (c) As finite creatures, why is it necessary for us to pray?

6. Jesus says in John 17:4 that He has finished the work which God gave Him to do. (a) What work has God called you personally to do? (b) What work have you neglected that would cause you to have regrets if this were your last day (i.e., making restitution, sharing the gospel with one who is lost, etc.)?

7. Jesus says in John 17:4 that He has glorified God while He was on the earth. (a) How did Christ bring glory to God while on the earth? Demonstrate your answer from the Scriptures. (b) In what ways is your life bringing glory to God? (c) In what areas of your life are you not bringing glory to God? (d) How will you work on those? Why not find someone who will pray for you and hold you accountable in those areas?

8. (a) What are the strengths and weaknesses of your own prayer life? (b) What changes would you like to see in your prayers as a result of studying the High Priestly Prayer in the coming chapters? Write down your answer in the form of a prayer request.

The High Priestly Prayer, Part 2: Christ Prays for the Eleven Disciples
John 17:6-19

WE have come to the second chapter in our study of the High Priestly Prayer. I trust that you have been evaluating your own prayers as you meditate on this beautiful prayer of Christ's. One of the areas of our prayer lives that is essential for us to consider is our intercession for others. Often our intercession for others has hints of selfish motives or self-interest. For example: "God, I pray for my husband that he will be more sensitive to me." Notice the selfishness as evidenced by the word *me*? Or, "I pray that my child will behave tonight at our friend's house," the motive being, of course, so that I don't look like a bad parent. Or "Father, I hope my husband gets that raise so we can buy that new car or I can get that new dress." Or, "Lord, when are you going to take vengeance on her for what she did to me?" Much of our intercession for ourselves and for others could use a little refining.

As we come to the second portion of the High Priestly Prayer, we will see our Lord praying in a very different manner than some of His children. His prayers for the Eleven do not contain any elements of selfishness. He prays for *their* unity, *their* joy, *their* purity, *and their* sanctification. His prayers are unlike many of ours, and we would do well to model His example. As we look at these verses, let's put ourselves in the disciple's shoes and enter into how this must have encouraged their discouraged hearts at this time. Let's listen in on this portion of His prayer for the Eleven. Let's look at John 17:6-19.

> "I have manifested Your name to the men whom You have given Me out of the world. They were Yours, You gave them to Me, and they have kept Your word. Now they have known that all things which You have given Me are from You. For I have given to them the words which You have given Me; and they have received them, and have known surely that I

came forth from You; and they have believed that You sent Me.

"I pray for them. I do not pray for the world but for those whom You have given Me, for they are Yours. And all Mine are Yours, and Yours are Mine, and I am glorified in them. Now I am no longer in the world, but these are in the world, and I come to You. Holy Father, keep through Your name those whom You have given Me, that they may be one as We are. While I was with them in the world, I kept them in Your name. Those whom You gave Me I have kept; and none of them is lost except the son of perdition, that the Scripture might be fulfilled. But now I come to You, and these things I speak in the world, that they may have My joy fulfilled in themselves. I have given them Your word; and the world has hated them because they are not of the world, just as I am not of the world. I do not pray that You should take them out of the world, but that You should keep them from the evil one. They are not of the world, just as I am not of the world. Sanctify them by Your truth. Your word is truth. As You sent Me into the world, I also have sent them into the world. And for their sakes I sanctify Myself, that they also may be sanctified by the truth."

As we began our study of the High Priestly Prayer in our last chapter, we saw the posture of Christ's prayer, in verse 1, which was lifting up His eyes to Heaven. We then saw the petition of His prayer, in verses 1 and 5, which was that the Son would be glorified with the glory He had before the world was. Lastly, we saw the purpose of Christ's coming, in verses 2-4, which was threefold: to give eternal life to those God gave Him, to glorify God while on the earth, and to finish the work God gave Him to do. In this chapter we will learn of Christ's *Six Summary Statements About the Eleven Disciples* (vv 6-8) and *Six Selfless Supplications for the Eleven Disciples* (vv 9-19). Let's begin by looking at the first two summary statements regarding the eleven disciples, in verse 6.

6 Summary Statements About the 11 Disciples *John 17:6-8*

"I have manifested Your name to the men whom You have given Me out of the world. They were Yours, You gave them to Me, and they have kept Your word." (John 17:6)

*The **first** summary statement Christ makes concerning His disciples is this: Christ manifested God's name to the disciples.* Jesus states in His prayer *I have manifested Your name to the men whom You have given Me out of the world.* How had Jesus *manifested* God's name to them? This doesn't mean that Jesus just went around using God's name so everyone would know it. The word *name* is often used to designate a specific person and their character. And the word *manifest* means to make visible and clear. So, when Jesus says He has manifested God's name to the eleven disciples, He is saying that He had made known God's person and character to them. Jesus had already spoken of this in the upper room in John 14:9: "Jesus said to him, 'Have I been with you so long, and yet you have not known Me, Philip? He who has seen Me has seen the Father; so how can you say, "Show us the Father"?" The disciples had seen the Father manifested in the person of Jesus Christ. And notice that this manifestation was to the men that, Jesus says, *You have given Me out of the world.* These men originally belonged to God, just as everything belongs to Him, because He created everything. These eleven disciples belonged to the Father, and the Father gave them to Jesus. It's the same for you and me. We first belonged to God and then God gave us to Jesus. It's hard to imagine that depraved and sinful Susan Heck is a gift from God to the Son! How humbling! But this is a fact that Christ repeats several times in these verses (see verses 2, 9, 12, 24). He viewed the disciples as a gift from His Father. Do you look at those you pour your life into as a gift from God? Many times, we look at them as burdens—but they are gifts, and they should be gifts that we cherish.

Christ repeats this statement again in a little different way: *They were Yours, You gave them to Me, and they have kept Your word.* God created all men and, therefore, they are His, and in His goodness and kindness He chose some of them to eternal life, as we saw in verse 2. How do you and I know if we are a gift that has been given from the Father to the Son? How do we know we are chosen? We know by *Jesus' **second** summary statement about the eleven disciples: The disciples kept God's Word.* The word for *kept* means to pay attention to, to observe. It would be like paying attention to a traffic law and obeying it. The keeping of God's Word is a sign of a true disciple of Jesus Christ. John mentions this important truth in 1 John 2:3-5: "And by this we know that we have come to know Him, if we keep His commandments. The one who says, 'I have come to know Him,' and does not keep His commandments, is a liar, and the truth is not in him; but whoever keeps His word, truly in him the love of God has been perfected. By this we know that we are in Him" (LSB). The disciples did not keep the Word perfectly, just like you and I do not keep the Word perfectly, but their overall lives were marked by obedience to it.

Did you notice that Jesus did not mention one word in His prayers to the Father regarding the disciple's failures? He did not mention Peter's soon denial, or the fact they would all argue as to who would be the greatest in the Kingdom of Heaven. There's no mention of their soon forsaking Him and scattering. He could have prayed: "Father, can you believe that Peter, James, and John are going to fall asleep on me? Can you believe Judas turned me in for 30 pieces of silver? And what about all their endless questions? These sheep—they are driving me crazy! And now they are all going to forsake Me and flee?" These are not the prayers coming from our Lord's lips. He loved His disciples to the end and that love manifested itself even in how He prayed for them. Paul says in 1 Corinthians 13:5 about love, that "it does not act unbecomingly, does not seek its own, is not provoked, does not take into account a wrong suffered" (LSB). This encourages me because Jesus Christ is my Advocate who is pleading for me now. He is not accusing me to the Father; He is pleading for me, bringing out my righteousness because of God's righteousness! Praise the Lord!

Well, before we go on to verse 7, notice God's sovereignty as evidenced by the words, *You have given Me*, right alongside man's responsibility as evidenced by the words *they have kept Your word*. Jesus then gives a third summary statement in verse 7.

> "Now they have known that all things which You have given Me are from You." (John 17:7)

Jesus' **third** *summary statement about the disciples is this: The disciples understood that Jesus is God.* Jesus says of His disciples that *they have known that all things which You have given Me are from You*. Now, at long last, they know; they have been taught, and now they believe. The disciples had finally recognized that the things which were given to Jesus had been given to Him from the Father. In fact, they had just said this in John 16:29-30: "His disciples said to Him, 'See, now You are speaking plainly, and using no figure of speech! Now we are sure that You know all things, and have no need that anyone should question You. By this we believe that You came forth from God.'" Now, they have believed that Jesus came from God and all things that Jesus has the Father has. This belief, perhaps, has grown in their hearts specifically because of the words Jesus has spoken to them in the upper room. Jesus gives the reason for the fact that they finally believe as well as the fourth summary statement, in verse 8.

> "For I have given to them the words which You have given Me; and they have received them, and have known surely that I came forth from You; and they have believed that You sent Me." (John 17:8)

*The **fourth** summary statement is this: Christ gave the disciples God's Words.* The term for *words* in this verse refers to doctrine. Jesus speaks of this in John 7:16 (LSB): "So Jesus answered them and said, 'My teaching is not Mine, but from Him who sent Me.'" And what did the disciples do with the words, the doctrine, that Jesus gave them? They received them, which is Christ's ***fifth** summary statement about the disciples: They received God's Words.* This is what a true disciple of Jesus Christ does with the words of God: a true disciple receives God's words. True disciples of Christ don't reject the Word; they do not reject sound doctrine that is from God. James mentions the importance of receiving God's Word in James 1:21 (LSB), when he says, "Therefore, laying aside all filthiness and all that remains of wickedness, in gentleness receive the implanted word, which is able to save your souls."

Jesus goes on to give us His ***sixth** summary statement regarding the disciples: The disciples believed that God sent Jesus.* He says they *have known surely*, or truly, for certain, without doubt, *that I came forth from You; and they have believed that you sent Me*. The word *sent* is referring to the mission which Jesus had come to fulfill and the authority which backed Him. He mentions this 5 times throughout His prayer, in verses 8, 18, 21, 23, and 25. The disciples finally believed this. What joy must have filled the Lord's heart as He reviewed these things to His Father! At this point, Christ now shifts from the summary statements regarding the eleven disciples to His six selfless supplications for them in verses 9-19.

6 Selfless Supplications for the 11 Disciples   John 17:9-19

> "I pray for them. I do not pray for the world but for those whom You have given Me, for they are Yours." (John 17:9)

When Jesus says *I pray for them*, He is saying, "I am making request for them." And then He goes on to say in His prayer to the Father that *I do not pray for the world*. He isn't praying for wicked, rebellious men. What is Jesus saying here? He's saying that His High Priestly intercession, at this moment, is concerned with those special eleven disciples who were given to Him. This does not mean that Christ never prays for the world, but that is not what He's doing at this point—not at this time and in this prayer. He did pray for the world when He prayed on the cross that the Father would forgive them because they did not know what they were doing, as we see in Luke 23:34. Also, if He meant that He never prayed for the world, it would be a contradiction to what He says in verse 20, where He prays for future believers who are now a part of the world. Jesus cares for the lost—that's why He is going to the cross, to die for the lost world. So, He's saying to His Father, for the disciples' benefit, that He is not praying for the world at this moment, *but* I am praying *for those that You have given Me, for they are Yours*. And then, in verse 10, Christ says something He has said throughout His earthly ministry.

> "And all Mine are Yours, and Yours are Mine, and I am glorified in them." (John 17:10)

This verse, once again, shows the equality of the Godhead: *all Mine are Yours, and Yours are Mine*. Specifically, it reveals to us that all that is the Father's is the Son's: all of His nature, His name, His attributes, His glory, and His people. Jesus then adds *and I am glorified in them*. Can you imagine how the disciple's hearts must have leaped for joy as He prayed this? I imagine they must have been wondering to themselves, "Christ says He is glorified in *me*?" As one man says: "Jesus did not see these men as they were just then, huddled around Him, half listening, minds wandering, full of questions and interruptions. He saw them as 'complete in Him.' He saw, not just the rough stone, but the cut and shining diamond. He saw these men as we too shall see them in a coming day when at last, they, and we, shall be like Him, 'for we shall see Him as He is.'"[1] In verse 11, Christ turns His thoughts from how the disciples have glorified Him to His return to the Father.

> "Now I am no longer in the world, but these are in the world, and I come to You. Holy Father, keep through Your name those whom You have given Me, that they may be one as We are." (John 17:11)

Jesus says He is *no longer in the world*, and yet, at this moment, He was still bodily present on the earth. So, what is He saying? Jesus' departure from the world was so near, so imminent, that He uses the present tense to describe it. He was finished with the world, as far as His physical presence was concerned. By three o'clock the coming afternoon, the world would be finished with Him. He is leaving this world, but His disciples are not. His thoughts go back to the eleven disciples with these words: *but these are in the world*. They are still among the wicked and the rebellious. And then His thoughts go to Heaven, to home, to His Father. He says *and I come to You*. His coming to the Father is so near that He, again, uses the present tense to describe it. What joy this must have been for Christ! I think of many of my friends who have died of cancer, and each of them could not wait to see the Lord. "I am coming Lord, I am coming!" Can you imagine what this must have meant to the Lord? I am coming to My rest, My home, to My Father's right hand, where there are pleasures forevermore. I am coming! I think of some of my grandchildren who, when they see me, will run to me with outstretched arms, "Grandma, I'm coming! I'm coming!" It floods my heart with joy! And yet, this human joy doesn't even compare to the spiritual joy of coming home to Heaven.

At this point, Christ begins His petitions to the Father for the ones He is soon to leave behind. But, first, He calls God *Holy Father*. This is the

---

[1] John Phillips, *Exploring the Gospel of John*, 323.

only time this word is used to describe the Father in the Gospel accounts. Holy, or separate, Father. It signifies that God is far removed from evil. He is pure in Himself. He is holy, holy, holy, as Isaiah says in Isaiah 6:3. Jesus calls God Holy because it is the crown of all His attributes. He is pleading on the holiness of God because Jesus knows He is leaving these eleven disciples in an unholy world.

Christ goes on to offer His first petition for the Eleven, *His **first** selfless supplication: Keep them through Your name.* He says *keep through Your name those whom You have given Me.* The word *keep* means to preserve, to defend, to sustain them in trials, and to save them from apostasy. This is a much-needed request at this time, because soon all of them will forsake Him and flee. And so, He prays for the Father to protect them and keep them while He is away from them. He's pleading, "Help them not to apostatize!" The image is one of a divine watchman or protector. And how will God keep them? Through His name—His character, His power, His love, His wisdom, all that His name represents. They will be kept by the power of God!

Next, Christ prays the *His **second** selfless supplication: that they would be unified.* His words are *that they may be one as We are.* By being kept and preserved, the disciples would be united as one for the purpose of bringing glory to God. The oneness that Jesus is speaking of here is a oneness of will and spirit, not of one person or personality. The oneness that Christ asks for here is also a constant unity. Up to this point, the disciples lacked this oneness of spirit, as was evident that very evening. According to Luke 22:24, they had been arguing about who would be the greatest in the Kingdom of Heaven. Perhaps that is why Jesus prays for unity four times in this prayer, here in verse 11, and also in verses 21, 22 and 23. We will see that Christ desires this for you and me as well, when we consider verses 21-23. Notice that Jesus prays here that the disciples would be one as He and the Father are: *that they may be one as We are.* This does not refer to a union of nature, but a union of affection or spirit. The Father and the Son have unity of spirit, unity of purpose.

Now, before we go on to verse 12, it's important to clarify that this verse does not mean, as some have taken it to mean, that Christ is praying for some big ecumenical movement. We cannot sacrifice truth for oneness! In fact, there is no true oneness without the truth. This is evidenced by what the Lord prays in verse 12, as one of the twelve disciples did not possess this spirit of unity, this same heart and purpose, as the other eleven.

> "While I was with them in the world, I kept them in Your name. Those whom You gave Me I have kept; and none of them is lost except the son of perdition, that the Scripture might be fulfilled." (John 17:12)

Jesus says while *I was in the world, I kept*, or guarded and watched over, *them in Your name.* The ones *You,* God, *gave Me, I have kept.* While Christ was on the earth, He *kept* the disciples by the power, love, and wisdom of God, by His *name*. He guarded them like a shepherd guards a flock or a soldier guards a treasure, and He did it constantly. And He goes on to say, *and none of them is lost except the son of perdition, that the Scripture might be fulfilled.* The *son of perdition* means the son of a destroyer. The word comes from the Greek word for perish. The word literally refers to damnation. Now, the question might arise in your mind, "Did Jesus lose Judas?" No, because Judas was never given to Jesus by the Father in the sense of being chosen for salvation. Did Jesus fail in the case of Judas? Some say, yes, Jesus did fail in regard to Judas, and that this proves we can fall from grace. But that is totally contrary to the Word of God! John 6:39 (LSB) states, "Now this is the will of Him who sent Me, that of all that He has given Me I lose nothing, but raise it up on the last day." Jesus kept all who were given to Him, but the son of perdition was lost and was never given by the Father as a love gift to Jesus. Judas was lost, not because Christ didn't have the power to keep him, but *so that the Scripture might be fulfilled.* This happened in order that *the Scripture*, the prophecy concerning Judas, might be fulfilled. The Scripture that Jesus is referring to is Psalm 41:9 and Psalm 109:4-8. We won't take the time to consider these verses now because we looked at them extensively when we studied Judas in John 13:21-30.

Now, when Jesus says Judas is *lost*, He uses one of the strongest Greek words for stating final and hopeless destruction. Jesus says in Mark 14:21, "It would have been good for that man if he had never been born."

Peter says in Acts 1:25, "Judas by transgression fell, that he might go to his own place." Judas is a sober warning to all of us. Beware of attaching yourself to Jesus Christ for the purpose of learning and curiosity, but not for the purpose of following His Lordship. If you do, yours, too, will be a hopeless destruction! Christ then shifts back to the fact of His coming home to the Father and says,

> "But now I come to You, and these things I speak in the world, that they may have My joy fulfilled in themselves." (John 17:13)

Again, we see that Jesus does not mention the soon-coming cross, but only the glory and the rest beyond it. He simply says *now I come to You*. But then He says *and these things I speak in the world*. *These things* I say aloud. This means that Jesus was deliberately praying out loud instead of praying silently, so that the disciples might hear His intercession for them. Why does Christ pray this prayer out loud? So that *they may have My joy fulfilled in themselves. This is His **third** selfless supplication: that their joy would be fulfilled.* Christ prays all these things out loud for their benefit, for their joy. Amazing! This is a request for their joy. How their hearts must have leaped with joy as Christ said this. He is praying this for me? For my joy? What love! He said something very similar in John 15:11, when He said to the disciples, "These things I have spoken to you, that My joy may remain in you, and that your joy may be full." Christ wanted His disciples to be filled with joy. Sometimes people will tell you they will pray for you or that they have been praying for you, and that is an encouragement, indeed, but to actually hear someone audibly pray for you in your presence is totally different, is it not? It is a joyful experience.

At this point in His prayer, Christ shifts from the joy that comes from Him to the hate that comes from the world, in verse 14.

> "I have given them Your word; and the world has hated them because they are not of the world, just as I am not of the world." (John 17:14)

Christ says *I have given them Your word* and the result was that *the world hated them*. The world *hates* or detests anyone who lives out the Word. If you don't think this is true, just start talking about the Word to unbelievers and notice how uncomfortable they get. They hate it! In fact, I have noticed over the years, as I have attended numerous funerals, that people are usually quiet and pensive when the eulogy is read, the songs are song, and the videos are played. But when the preacher gets up to preach the sermon or read Scripture, all of a sudden the audience gets fidgety. Why? Because so many are not of the Word but of the world, which is what Jesus emphasizes next when He says *because they are not of the world, just as I am not of the world*. This was something Jesus had already warned His disciples of. He already mentioned in chapters 15 and 16 that the world would hate them, persecute them, cast them out of the synagogue, and even kill them—all *because they are not of the world*, in the same way that Jesus is *not of the world*! I imagine, as Christ sees forward to the hatred and even martyrdom that the disciples will encounter, it grieves Him because of His love for them. And yet, they must stay in the world to complete the mission they were sent to do. And so, He continues on with His fourth petition for them in verse 15.

> "I do not pray that You should take them out of the world, but that You should keep them from the evil one." (John 17:15)

*Christ's **fourth** selfless supplication is this: Don't take them out of the world.* Jesus is asking the Father here to not take them out of the world: *I do not pray that You should take them out of the world*. To *take them out* means to lift them up and out. Jesus does not want His disciples to be taken out of the world; otherwise they would not be able to fulfill their mission. Remember, in John 15:27, He said to them, "And you also will bear witness, because you have been with Me from the beginning." What if Christ had prayed, "Father, you know how much I love these men, and I really don't think they can handle life without me. And God, I really don't want them to have to go through all that suffering, so, why don't we just bring them home with me right now?" That would have been a disaster! What would the rest of the New Testament look like? Where would you and I be? How thankful I am that Christ prayed for the Eleven! I know many times we feel like we would like to be taken out of the world and get on with glory. But there may be jobs left for us to do. We would do well to trust God with our lives and with our deaths and occupy till He comes, redeeming the time because we know the days are evil. Would that we all had Paul's attitude in Philippians 1:21-24 (LSB), where he says, "For to me, to live is Christ and to die is gain. But if I am to live on in the flesh, this will mean fruitful labor for me; and I do not know what I will choose. But I am hard-pressed between the two, having the desire to depart and be with Christ, for that is very much better, yet to remain on in the flesh is more necessary for your sake."

Instead of Christ praying to take the disciples out of the world, He prays, in contrast, *but that You should keep them from the evil one. This is His **fifth** selfless supplication: Keep them from the evil one.* Because they will be left in the world, Father, *keep them from the evil one*. Now, the Greek word *evil* can refer to either evil that exists in the world, in a moral or spiritual sense, or it can also refer to the evil one, meaning Satan or evil man. Jesus is praying that the Father will keep them from the author of evil and from evil itself. We should be praying this for ourselves as well as for our families. It is ever so important because Satan is always seeking whom He may devour. Next, Christ repeats in verse 16 what He had already prayed in verse 14.

> "They are not of the world, just as I am not of the world." (John 17:16)

Why does Jesus say this again? Usually, when something is repeated in Scripture, it is done for emphasis and means that whatever has been repeated is important for us to remember. Perhaps the disciples needed to be reminded that they are not of the world, just as, perhaps, many of us need the same reminder. Because we are not of this world, we should not love the world, as John tells us in 1 John 2:15-17; if we do love the world or the things in the world, John tells us that the love of the Father is not in us. Next, we come to Christ's sixth selfless supplication in verse 17.

> "Sanctify them by Your truth. Your word is truth." (John 17:17)

*Christ's **sixth** selfless supplication: sanctify them through your truth.* The word *sanctify* means to consecrate or set apart a person or thing to God. It comes from the Greek word *hagiazo*, which has two meanings. The first meaning has to do with someone or something being set apart for a special task. As God said to Jeremiah, "Before I formed you in the innermost parts I knew you, and before you came out from the womb *I set you apart*; I have given you as a prophet to the nations" (Jeremiah 1:5 LSB, emphasis mine). Before Jeremiah's mother even conceived him, God had ordained that Jeremiah should be a prophet. God had set apart, or sanctified, Jeremiah for that special task. Likewise, the disciples were set apart for a special service. The second meaning of this word has to do with equipping a man with the qualities of mind and heart and character that are necessary for that task. So, inherent in the idea of being sanctified is not only this being setting apart for a special service but God also equipping us with what we need to carry out that service. It is God who equips us. I guess this is an area that has grieved me so much over the years of my Christian life—so many professing Christians who are not set apart for service to their Lord. They have set themselves apart for so many other things—like sports, entertainment, exercise, endless diets, hobbies, and countless other things that will never satisfy, but they are not set apart to God for His service and glory. This does not mean that you have to be in full time, vocational ministry! You can be set apart for God as a homemaker, a mother, a grandmother, but we all, as Christians, should be set apart for service to God.

Now, how is it that God is going to *sanctify* the disciples? Jesus says *by Your truth*. And then He says *Your word is truth*. What does He mean here? The term *word* is *logos* in the Greek, which is the utterance of God's thought. It is all that is contained in the Bible. The Word of God must govern the disciple's service for God. Our equipping for service must be all governed by the Word of God. We should not be influenced by man's ideas and philosophies and the world's system of doing things. The Word of God should be the final authority by which we do everything. It is the Word that changes lives (see Hebrews 4:12-13 and John 15:3). It is the Word by which we are cleansed and made into the image of Christ. It should be the plumb line by which we serve God. This idea of the disciples being set apart for service goes right along with what Christ prays next in verse 18.

> "As You sent Me into the world, I also have sent them into the world." (John 17:18)

Christ was sent on a mission that culminated in His death for the lost. And just as God sent Jesus Christ *into the world* on a mission, Jesus says here that *I also have sent* the disciples *into the world* for a mission, a purpose. The disciples were his *sent* ones; the Greek word is *apostello*, from which we get our English word apostle. One of the last things Jesus said to His disciples before He ascended into Heaven was, "Peace be with you; as the Father has sent Me, I also send you." (John 20:21b LSB). We can read the book of Acts and see how their mission was fulfilled. And you know you and I have a mission as well! Christ didn't save us to have us sit around. We have been chosen so that we would go and bring forth fruit, as we have already seen from John 15. What is your mission? Do you know what your purpose is for which God has chosen you? We should know what our spiritual gifts are, and we should be using them for the glory of God. Christ ends this portion of His prayer for the eleven disciples with an incredible statement that is, again, just for their benefit.

> "And for their sakes I sanctify Myself, that they also may be sanctified by the truth." (John 17:19)

How does Christ *sanctify* Himself? When Christ says *I sanctify Myself*, it does not mean that He made Himself more righteous. Rather, it goes right along with the definition of sanctification we just considered: to be set apart for service. The word also carries the idea of consecration or dedication. Jesus set Himself apart for a special task, the work which God gave Him to do, the special task of providing salvation for mankind. Hebrews 10:14 gives a glimpse of this: "For by one offering He has perfected for all time those who are being sanctified" (LSB).

Christ goes on to say that the reason He sanctifies Himself is *that they also may be sanctified by the truth*. Once again, the writer to the Hebrews helps us here, in Hebrews 2:11: "For both He who sanctifies and those who are being sanctified are all of One; for which reason He is not ashamed to call them brothers" (LSB). The death of Christ sets us apart from the world and sets us apart to God. As Christ was set apart for a special service and as our supreme example, so the disciples and you and I have been set apart for a special work too. That work, primarily, is for carrying the gospel to all men everywhere and expanding the Kingdom of God. As Titus 2:14 says, Jesus is the one "who gave Himself for us that He might redeem us from all lawlessness, and purify for Himself a people for His own possession, zealous for good works" (LSB).

Summary

Jesus has approached His final hour, and He prays for His eleven disciples. He prays for His own. In that prayer, He makes six summary statements about His disciples:

1. Jesus manifested God's name to the disciples.

2. The disciples kept God's Word.

3. The disciples understood that Jesus is God.

4. Jesus gave the disciples God's Words.

5. The disciples received God's Words.

6. The disciples believed that God sent Jesus.

Jesus also prayed six selfless supplications for His disciples:

1. Keep them through Your name.

2. Cause them to be unified.

3. Fulfill their joy.

4. Don't take them out of the world.

5. Keep them from the evil one.

6. Sanctify them through Your truth.

Jesus doesn't ask for selfish requests for Himself. Instead, His requests are for the good of His disciples, for those whom He loved to the end.

If you and I were facing our final hours, would we be able to pray for others, and, if we did, would we pray such selfless prayers? Most of us are not right now in our final hours, or at least not that we're aware of. What do our prayers for others consist of at this time in our lives? We would all do well to ponder deeply the prayers of Christ for the disciples in John 17. Doing so will keep us from praying selfishly and keep us praying in the name of Jesus and for His glory.

QUESTIONS TO CONSIDER

1. Read John 17 out loud. (a) What elements of Jesus' prayer are missing from your own prayer life? (b) What are the words and phrases that are repeated in John 17, and what is the significance of each of these?

2. Memorize John 17:15.

3. Christ says, in John 17:9, "I do not pray for the world." (a) For whom are the following prayers given? Matthew 5:44; Luke 23:34; John 17:20; 1 Timothy 2:1-4. (b) How do these verses reconcile with what Jesus says in John 17:9?

4. In John 17:10, Christ mentions that the disciples glorified Him. In what ways did the disciples bring glory to the Lord during His earthly ministry? Share your thoughts and back them up with Scripture.

5. (a) What do the following verses say about the importance of unity among the brethren? Psalm 133; Romans 15:5-6; 1 Corinthians 1:10; 1 Corinthians 12:12-27; Philippians 2:1-4. (b) How do these verses help you to understand Christ's request for the Eleven in John 17:11? (c) In what practical ways can we strive to protect the unity in the body of Christ? (d) Do others characterize you as a woman who gets along with others in the body of Christ? Are you causing divisions, stirring up strife, or criticizing others, including those in leadership? (These are serious sins that the Lord does not look upon lightly!)

6. Jesus does not desire that the disciples be taken out of the world (see John 17:15). (a) Read the following passages and note who prayed to be taken out of the world and why. Numbers 11:10-15; 1 Kings 19:1-8; Jonah 4. (b) What do these verses teach you about the desire to be taken out of the world? (c) Why does Christ desire for us to be left in the world? See Ephesians 2:10 and Titus 2:14.

7. What do you think Christ meant in John 17:19 when He said, "I sanctify Myself"?

8. The disciples were sent out into the world for a purpose, a mission (see John 17:18). (a) Do you know what your purpose or mission is in the world? (b) Write it down in 20 words or less to share.

9. Write out a prayer that includes petitions for someone else. Concentrate on asking God for their spiritual welfare and try to avoid asking for physical needs. Be prepared to read them (or pray them) in class. These do not necessarily need to be lengthy. (Remember, the High Priestly Prayer is only about 3 minutes long.)

The High Priestly Prayer, Part 3: Christ Prays for Future Believers
John 17:20-26

RECENTLY, at my church in Tulsa, Oklahoma, we have had the joy of having several of the ladies in our church give birth to new babies. It is always fun to witness their joy at their baby shower, to go visit them in the hospital and see their new little one, and to witness the parents' joy in their new little bundle! (Of course, it is a personal joy for me to get to hold the new little one!) As most of us know, there is a great deal of preparation that goes in to getting ready for these new little ones. Though I am older now, I remember the things I had to do to prepare for the birth of each of my children. The room had to be readied, the crib had to be set up, clothes needed to be purchased, and, of course, we needed diapers, diapers, and more diapers! Then there was the scheduling of someone to come and help when we arrived home with that little one. On and on the list went!

As we consider all the physical preparations necessary for a precious new one's arrival, do we also stop and consider one of the most important preparations, that of praying for this little one who is about to come into the world? How much time do we spend on our knees praying for this little one's birth in comparison to the time we dedicate to all the necessary physical preparations? You might be thinking to yourself, "Praying for one who isn't even born yet? Isn't that rather silly?" Not really. Jesus prayed for us before we were ever born in the physical sense and before we were born again in the spiritual sense. If the incarnate Christ sensed a need to pray for those yet unborn, both spiritually and physically, how much more should we?

We have come to the last portion of the High Priestly Prayer, the portion where Christ prays for us, for future believers. We have already seen Christ praying for Himself, in verses 1-5. And in our last chapter, we saw Christ praying for the eleven disciples, in verses 6-19. In that chapter, we considered six summary statements Christ makes regarding the eleven disciples, in verses 6-8 as well as six selfless supplications Christ makes regarding the eleven disciples, in verses 9-19. In this chapter, Christ shifts from praying for the eleven disciples to praying for future believers, in verses 20-26. He says:

> "I do not pray for these alone, but also for those who will believe in Me through their word; that they all may be one, as You, Father, are in Me, and I in You; that they also may be one in Us, that the world may believe that You sent Me. And the glory which You gave Me I have given them, that they may be one just as We are one: I in them, and You in Me; that they may be made perfect in one, and that the world may know that You have sent Me, and have loved them as You have loved Me.
>
> "Father, I desire that they also whom You gave Me may be with Me where I am, that they may behold My glory which You have given Me; for You loved Me before the foundation of the world. O righteous Father! The world has not known You, but I have known You; and these have known that You sent Me. And I have declared to them Your name, and will declare it, that the love with which You loved Me may be in them, and I in them."

As we close our study of the Upper Room Discourse by examining this final portion of the Lord's High Priestly Prayer, we will see four prayer requests that Jesus makes on our behalf. I have put them in the form of an acrostic that spells out the word **FOUR**. That should be easy for you to remember as you think about the Lord praying *four* requests for you! What are these requests? Well, let's discover what they are, beginning in verse 20:

> "I do not pray for these alone, but also for those who will believe in Me through their word;" (John 17:20)

Included in Jesus' High Priestly Prayer are not just prayers for Himself and for the eleven disciples, but also prayers for another group of people that is on His heart. That's why Jesus says *I do not pray for these alone, but for those who will believe in Me through their word.* The word for *pray* here means to make request. So, Jesus isn't only making request for the eleven disciples with Him at that moment, but for those, He says, *who will believe in Me through their word*, that is, future believers. Jesus indicated the reality of future believers in John 10:16 (LSB), when He said, "And I have other sheep, which are not from this fold; I must bring them also, and they will hear My voice; and they will become one flock with one shepherd." There would be future sheep brought into the fold, and this would include all future believers who have come to Christ because of the disciples' message, the proclamation of the gospel. Ladies, this includes you and me! Through the disciples' preaching of God's message of salvation, many will be brought to saving faith. In fact, not too long after Christ ascended into Heaven, Acts records for us that through the preaching of the disciples, 3,000 souls, and then later 5,000 more souls, came to faith in Christ. As we saw from Christ's prayer in our last chapter (in verse 18), He had sent the Eleven on a mission: to proclaim the gospel. We owe much thanks to them, and countless believers who followed after them, for their obedience to faithfully proclaim the gospel to the world. Without their obedience, you and I might not have heard the gospel.

As the disciples heard this prayer, I imagine that some of them must have been wondering, "How will all future believers believe on Jesus through my word?" It must have been a humbling thought. Ladies, we too must be obedient to proclaim the gospel message. Like the disciples, we do not know who will come to saving faith in Christ in the future because of our proclamation of the gospel. It just might be our own children and grandchildren.

Before we go on to the next verse, I want you to notice one more thing in this verse. Jesus says that it is *belief*, or faith in Christ, that brings us into His fold. This is the only way to salvation. Jesus has already made this clear in the upper room, in John 14:6: "Jesus said to him, 'I am the way, the truth, and the life. No one comes to the Father except through Me.'" Then, in John 17:3, He also says, "And this is eternal life, that they may know You, the only true God, and Jesus Christ whom You have sent." In verse 21, Christ begins with His first petition for future believers. And it is one He repeats several times in the next few verses. *His prayer is for* **Unity: this will be the U on your acrostic.**

> "that they all may be one, as You, Father, are in Me, and I in You; that they also may be one in Us, that the world may believe that You sent Me." (John 17:21)

Petition number one that Christ makes for future believers is for unity. The Greek is more literally rendered as: "That they all may constantly be one." This is something Christ also prays for in verses 22 and 23 of this same prayer. The repetition of this request tells us that it must be of vital importance. We know that Christ also prayed this for the eleven disciples, back in verse 11. When we examined that verse, we learned that unity means oneness of spirit and purpose, not a oneness in nature. This same concept of oneness is communicated in a number of other New Testament Scriptures: the one heart and one soul, mentioned in Acts 4:32; the same mind and judgment, mentioned in 1 Corinthians 1:10; the unity of the Spirit in the bond of peace spoken of in Ephesians 4:3; the unity of the faith and of the knowledge of the Son of God, seen in Ephesians 4:13; and the being knit together in love, mentioned in Colossians 2:2. Unity is vital in the body of Jesus Christ. But what kind of unity does Christ ask the Father for here? *As You, Father, are in Me, and I in You; that they also may be one in Us.* Christ's clarification here helps us understand that He is referring to a union among all Christians that is founded on and resulting from a union of the Father and the Son. God the Father and Jesus Christ His Son are *one* in matters pertaining to salvation, grace, and glorifying God. Christ was praying for a unity among future believers of spirit and purpose, a unity of obedience to God and to His Word. You might be wondering, "Does this mean I have to be just like you and you have to be just like me?" No. Jesus and God are one, the Son and the Father are one, yet they are two distinct Persons. One, yet different. You and I are different, and we have different roles in life, different spiritual gifts, and different functions within the body of Christ, but we must be of one mind and strive for one purpose. We should work together as a body using our gifts and promoting unity. And again, as we brought out before, in verse 11, Jesus is not praying for some ecumenical church where heresy would be tolerated; oneness necessarily includes a unity of obedience to God and to His word. Jesus and the Father are one, this is true. But they are united when it comes to truth. They never tolerate heresy or error.

Since we are on this important topic of unity, I want to remind you of the biblically prescribed way of handling offenses. These things should be handled in a private matter, if possible according to Matthew 18:15-17, and with a spirit of meekness, according to Galatians 6:1. We should not be women who are accused of spreading gossip and slander and causing dissension within the church. Proverbs 6:16-19 is clear: "These six things the LORD hates, yes, seven are an abomination to Him: A proud look, a lying tongue, hands that shed innocent blood, a heart that devises wicked plans, feet that are swift in running to evil, a false witness who speaks lies, and one who sows discord among brethren." We must strive hard to preserve unity in the church.

Christ now gives a reason for why He petitions the Father for our unity. What is the reason? Jesus says *that the world may believe that You sent Me.* The unity of Christians will impress upon on the world the truth that Jesus Christ was indeed sent by the Father to die for the sins of the world. They will see Jesus lived out in us. As the songwriter once wrote, "You may be the only Jesus some will ever see." Have you ever asked yourself, "What kind of Jesus does the world see in me?" The church of Jesus Christ can do much damage to an unbelieving world by their strife and division. Such disunity hinders the unbelieving world and gives them excuses for not embracing Christ and Christianity; too often, the world rightly claims that there are too many hypocrites in the church. Our unity is one of the greatest evangelism tools we have as a church. We should guard it jealously and pray that nothing will divide us. Jesus again prays for our unity, in verse 22, but before that repeated request, He speaks of His glory.

> "And the glory which You gave Me I have given them, that they may be one just as We are one:" (John 17:22)

What does Jesus mean by this statement? Jesus is basically stating that God the Father was manifested, or glorified, in the person of His Son Jesus Christ, and now that glory has been manifested in the lives of all believers. The word *glory* means to recognize a person for what they are; to render what is due. Paul speaks of this in 2 Corinthians 3:18 (LSB), when he says, "But we all, with unveiled face, beholding as in a mirror the glory of the Lord, are being transformed into the same image from glory to glory, just as from the Lord, the Spirit." It is also what Jesus spoke of verse 10 of John 17, regarding the fact that He was glorified in the disciples. Have you ever known people who radiate the glory of Christ? Over the many years of our ministry, my husband and I have seen the glory of Christ in countless believers, and it produces in me a desire to be with them and learn from them and to become more like Christ! They manifest the glory of God by their lives! You might object, "Susan, I think you are taking this a bit too far. Christ's glory in us?!" Sure! Paul tells us in Colossians 1:27, "To them God willed to make known what are the riches of the glory of this mystery among the Gentiles: which is Christ in you, the hope of glory." Peter says something similar in 2 Peter 1:4 (LSB), "For by these He has granted to us His precious and magnificent promises, so that by them you may become partakers of the divine nature, having escaped the corruption that is in the world by lust."

You might be thinking, "Well, if this is true, then how do I practically glorify God?" I would like to share four ways we can practically glorify Him, and by no means is this list exhaustive:

1. *By being willing to suffer as He did.* And as we suffer, we should do so with a proper attitude of rejoicing and being willing to see all that God has for us through the suffering. That brings glory to Him. Paul states in Romans 8:18 (LSB), "For I consider that the sufferings of this present time are not worthy to be compared with the glory that is to be revealed to us." The glory which is revealed in us in Heaven will be even greater than any we experience here!

2. *By being obedient to Him.* The writer to the Hebrews says in Hebrews 5:8, speaking of Christ, "Although He was a Son, He learned obedience from the things which He suffered" (LSB). Jesus was obedient to the Father in everything, even in death, and, ladies, that brought glory to God! The more you and I are yielded to His will, the more His glory will be seen in us. There is something concerning about a believer who does not glorify God, and there is something beautiful about a believer who does glorify God!

3. *By declaring who God is through the person of His Son Jesus Christ.* Christ declared or manifested God while on the earth, thus bringing glory to Him. You and I can also declare who God is by declaring Him through the person of His Son, Jesus Christ. We glorify God by sharing the gospel.

4. *By our Unity.* It glorifies our Lord when we are one. In fact, Jesus ends this verse with that very request: *that they may be one just as We are one.* The unity of the body is one of the biggest ways we give God glory. We must always fight to protect it. Christ further describes this unity, this oneness, in verse 23.

> "I in them, and You in Me; that they may be made perfect in one, and that the world may know that You have sent Me, and have loved them as You have loved Me." (John 17:23)

This beginning statement, *I in them*, is similar to what Paul says in Galatians 2:20 (LSB), "I have been crucified with Christ, and it is no longer I who live, but Christ lives in me. And the life which I now live in the flesh I live by faith in the Son of God, who loved me and gave Himself up for me." Now, Christ says something a little different here in this request for unity than in His previous requests. The difference is that this is the first time He uses the word *perfect* to describe our unity. To *be made perfect* means to be made complete or finished. Lenski says of this oneness among believers, "All are to be completely brought to oneness."[1] Christ is asking that our union might be complete. And His reason for this request is twofold. The first reason is so *that the world may know that You have sent Me*. Christ wants the world to know or to realize and to keep on knowing that God sent Him. The second reason Christ prays for our unity is that the world might know that God has *loved them as You have loved Me*. Both words for *love* here are the Greek word *agapao*, which indicates a direction of the will and finding one's joy in something. This is a wonderful statement that Jesus makes here—that God loves you and me in the same way that He loves Jesus! Amazing! As Jeremiah 31:3 tells us, He has loved us with an everlasting love. By our unity, we

---

[1] R. C. H. Lenski, *The Interpretation of St. John's Gospel,* 1162.

prove to the world that indeed God sent Jesus Christ into the world, and we also prove that God is love. Would others look at your walk and say, "There goes a woman who proves by her life and her unity with the body that indeed Jesus really came and that God is love"? They should be able to! In verse 24, we have two more petitions Christ prays for us.

> "Father, I desire that they also whom You gave Me may be with Me where I am, that they may behold My glory which You have given Me; for You loved Me before the foundation of the world." (John 17:24)

*Christ's second petition is the **F** on your acrostic: that we would be **F**orever with Him.* Jesus prays that we will be with Him! The word *desire* is a Greek word which is used to express a strong and earnest desire, but also it suggests delight. You might be thinking, "Well, Jesus uses the past tense here, as evidenced by the words *whom you gave Me*, and yet you are telling me these are future believers He's speaking of?" The Greek tense here indicates a past act with a continuous present effect. All believers—past, present, and future—were given to Jesus, and they are His, even those who are still unborn. Jesus' desire is that all His children be *with* Him, which means to be constantly with Him. He wants to be constantly with us, but do you and I want to be constantly with Him? Hopefully we can answer that question with a definite "Yes!" He wants us to be with Him. And just where will that be? He says *with Me where I am*, which means "in My company." This same idea is communicated in John 14:1-3; Romans 8:17; Colossians 3:4; 2 Timothy 2:11-12; and Revelation 21:3.

Ladies, have you let this sink into your heart and mind?! Jesus Christ wants to spend eternity with you and me! Amazing! You can have a lovely home, but without people being present in it, it is just a home. It is incomplete. Likewise, Heaven is just a place without the family present. It is incomplete without us. Jesus wants us with Him there. Charles Spurgeon says, "Every time a believer mounts from this earth to paradise, it is an answer to Christ's prayer."[2] As the Psalmist says in Psalm 116:15, "Precious in the sight of the LORD is the death of His saints."

---

2 Charles H. Spurgeon, "Evening by Evening-March 22," *The Spurgeon Center*, https://www.spurgeon.org/resource-library/books/evening-by-evening-march/#flipbook/. Accessed 10/5/2023.

Now, you might be wondering, "Why does Christ want us with Him?" He answers that by saying *that they may behold My glory which You have given Me*. This is the third petition Christ prays for us and the **O** on your acrostic: *that we may **O**bserve His glory*. The word *behold* means to gaze, to look with interest and for a purpose, usually indicating the careful observation of details; it is to gaze upon something as a spectator, and it is used of objects that are extraordinary. 1 John 3:2 pictures this well: "Beloved, now we are children of God; and it has not yet been revealed what we shall be, but we know that when He is revealed, we shall be like Him, for we shall see Him as He is." Suppose at this moment that God were to answer this request of His Son and take us to where Christ is that we should behold His glory. Would we be content to gaze upon His glory forever, to be in His presence serving Him forever? I think we must ask ourselves honestly these questions. My friend, if you are not satisfied in Him alone now, you would not be satisfied with Him alone in eternity.

Why did God give Jesus Christ this glory? Jesus says *for You loved Me before the foundation of the world*. The word *foundation* means to throw down, a casting or laying down—in this case, before time began. The Father's love to the Son is dated in timeless eternity past. This means that in all eternity past the Father loved His Son. And because of the Father's love, He gave the Son glory. We saw in verse 5 that Jesus asked the Father to restore the glory that the Son had with the Father before the world was, and that request was answered. Christ now returns to thoughts of the world He is soon to leave, in verse 25.

> "O righteous Father! The world has not known You, but I have known You; and these have known that You sent Me." (John 17:25)

Jesus calls God "Holy Father" in verse 11, and now He calls Him *righteous Father*. *Righteous* means that which is straight. Everything God does is right and just. He acts conformably to justice and righteousness, without any deficiency or failure. Everything that the Father does is right! But why does Jesus call God righteous here? Perhaps Jesus uses this word as a contrast to the unrighteous world, as He immediately says *the world has not known You*. This is a sad lament, a final grievous thought before He goes to the cross: "The world I am getting ready to be crucified for does not know You." *But* [in contrast to the world] *I have known You.* Jesus said something similar to the Jews, in John 8:54-55 (LSB), "Jesus answered, 'If I glorify Myself, My glory is nothing; it is My Father who glorifies Me, of whom you say, "He is our God"; and you have not known Him, but I know Him; and if I say that I do not know Him, I will be a liar like you, but I do know Him and keep His word.'"

Jesus then says *and these have known that You sent Me*. Jesus is referring to the eleven disciples when He says *these*, but what He says applies to all true believers. All true disciples know that God sent Jesus Christ into the world. Then in the final verse, the final portion of this prayer, the Lord sums up briefly what He has done for the disciples and what He will still do, and He offers a final petition for future believers.

> "And I have declared to them Your name, and will declare it, that the love with which You loved Me may be in them, and I in them." (John 17:26)

Jesus closes His prayer by communicating that He had *declared* God's *name* to them in the past and that He *will declare it* in the future. We saw in verse 6 how Christ had declared God's name. But now He says He *will declare it*, which refers to a declaration in the future. What is He referring to? When we read Luke 24:44-45 and Acts 1:3, we see that Jesus declared God after His death and after His resurrection and before He ascended to Heaven. It's also possible that Jesus may be referring to the fact that the Holy Spirit would be their teacher and would be manifesting God to them.

Why did Jesus declare God's name and why will He declare it again? Jesus says *that the love with which You loved Me may be in them, and I in them. This is the fourth petition and the **R** on your acrostic: that the **R**emarkable Love of the Father and the Son would be in us.* Jesus' final request is that the love of God would be in our hearts. It is interesting that Christ closes this magnificent prayer with a petition that Christians would love one another. Christ's love for His people and their love for one another is predominant on our Lord's mind throughout this entire Upper Room Discourse. We began our first chapter with what verse?

John 13:1, "Having loved His own who were in the world, He loved them to the end." We began our study with Christ's act of love of washing the disciples' feet. The entire Upper Room Discourse has been filled with admonition and encouragement motivated by the love of Jesus and the Father and a desire that the disciples—and you and I—would continue on with that same love in us. What does Paul say in 1 Corinthians 13:13 (LSB), "But now abide faith, hope, love—these three; but the greatest of these is love." It is a shame, as one man says, that "instead of seeing how these Christians love one another, the world has too much reason to say 'see how they carp at one another, see how they judge one another, and see how they malign one another.'"[3]

Summary

In the final portion of His High Priestly Prayer, Christ prays for us, and as He does, He prays **FOUR** wonderful requests:

1. That we would be **F**orever with Him.
2. That we would **O**bserve His glory.
3. That we would be marked by **U**nity.
4. That we would have the **R**emarkable love of the Father and the Son in us.

Let's consider each of these as we close out this chapter.

1. That we would be marked by **U**nity (vv 21-23): Are you an answer to the Savior's request for unity? Are you striving to maintain unity in the body of Christ? Is there anyone with whom you need to reconcile?

2. That we would be **F**orever with Him (v 24): Are you an answer to the Savior's request in your desire to be with Him? Do you look forward to future glory when you will be in His presence forever? What about now? Do you enjoy His presence now? Do you make time to spend with Him?

3. That we would **O**bserve His glory (v 24): Are you an answer to the Savior's request to behold His glory? Will you be among those on that day

---
3 Marcus Rainsford, *Our Lord Prays for His Own* (Chicago: Moody Press, 1950), 404.

who will behold His glory? Are you content in this life with worshiping the Savior and giving Him glory?

4. That we would have the **R**emarkable love of the Father and the Son in us (v 26): Are you an answer to the Savior's request that Christians would love one another? Are you known as a woman who loves the brethren? Is there anyone you are finding difficult to love? What are you doing about it? Does the world see God's love in you?

What powerful prayers for you and me! And to think that Jesus hasn't stopped praying for us! He is ever interceding for us! When you think about the fact that your heavenly Father prayed for you and is still praying for you, does it not motivate you to pray for those who have yet to believe—your children and grandchildren? Even those who are not yet born? If it does not motivate you in that way, why doesn't it? Praying for them is one of the most profound ways we can show love to our children and grandchildren. As E. M. Bounds says,

> Woe to the generation of sons who find their censers empty of the rich incense of prayer; whose fathers have been too busy or too unbelieving to pray. Perils inexpressible and consequences untold are their unhappy heritage. Fortunate are they whose fathers and mothers have left them a wealthy patrimony of prayer.[4]

I personally am thankful for a heavenly Father and an earthly Father who have prayed for me. Where would I be without their prayers? And, I would add, where would we be without the prayers of our precious Lord? The High Priestly Prayer is now over, and the Passion is now upon our Lord.

---

[4] E. M. Bounds, "Purpose in Prayer," *Christian Classics Ethereal Library,* 2, https://www.ccel.org/ccel/b/bounds/purpose/cache/purpose.pdf. Accessed 9/29/2023.

QUESTIONS TO CONSIDER

1. Read John 13-17 reflectively. (a) Write down any new truths you have learned as a result of this study. (b) What changes have you made as a result of this study?

2. Memorize John 17:24.

3. The following question came from chapter one of this study: *What do you hope to gain from our study, "With the Master In the Upper Room"? (Hold on to your answer until the end of the book!)* Looking back on your answer from that very first chapter and considering all you have learned as you've studied John 13-17, can you say that you gained what you hoped to gain from this study?

4. (a) What do the following verses say about the righteousness of God? Psalm 36:6; Psalm 45:6-7; Psalm 50:6; Psalm 71:19; Romans 1:16-17; Romans 3:5-6; Romans 3:21-26; James 1:20; 2 Peter 1:1; 1 John 3:7. (b) How do these verses help you to understand why Jesus calls God "righteous Father" in John 17:25?

5. Jesus says, in John 17:24, that the Father loved Him before the foundation of the world. (a) According to the following verses, what else happened before the foundation of the world? Matthew 25:34; Luke 11:49-51; Ephesians 1:4; Hebrews 4:3; 1 Peter 1:18-20; Revelation 13:8; Revelation 17:8. (b) What does this teach you about eternity past?

6. (a) Read 1 Corinthians 3:1-9, noting how Paul addressed the issue of disunity in the church. What do you glean from Paul's words about what our attitudes should be? (b) How *should* the body be functioning? See 1 Corinthians 12. (c) How do these verses relate to Christ's prayers for us in John 17:20-26?

7. (a) Do you pray for your children and/or grandchildren who are not yet born, and for the future spouses of your children and/or grandchildren? (b) What types of prayers have you prayed for them? I encourage you to start including them in your prayers. (Jesus prayed for us before we were even born!)

8. What challenge have you come away with regarding your own prayer life after studying John 17? Please write it down in the form of a prayer request.

God's Plan of Salvation

Everyone is destined to die, but life does not end with death. The Bible says that after death there will be a judgment where each person will give an account of his life to God (Hebrews 4:13; 9:27). When God created Adam and Eve in His own image in the garden of Eden, He gave them an abundant life, and the freedom to choose between good and evil (Genesis 2:9). They chose to disobey God and go their own way. As a consequence, death was introduced into the human race; not only physical death, but also spiritual death (Romans 5:12). For this reason, all human beings are separated from God.

Unfortunately, man's sinful nature and his ongoing choices to sin result in men living in continual disobedience to God: *for all have sinned and fall short of the glory of God* (Romans 3:23). This is humanity's problem: because of sin, everyone is separated from God (Isaiah 59:2).

People have tried to overcome this separation in many ways: by doing good, by practicing religion, by creating their own ideas of salvation, or by attempting to live a good moral life. However, none of these things is enough to cross the barrier of separation between God and humanity, because God is holy and human beings are sinful (Isaiah 64:6; Philippians 3:7). Regardless of how good you think you are, every human has lied, stolen, hated, or otherwise disobeyed God's perfect will.

This spiritual separation has become the condition of mankind, and because of this all humanity is condemned: *He who believes in Him is not judged; he who does not believe has been judged already, because he has not believed in the name of the only begotten Son of God* (John 3:18).

God's Love and Plan

Jesus Christ said:

>*For God so loved the world, that He gave His only begotten Son, that whoever believes in Him shall not perish, but have eternal life* (John 3:16).
>*...I came that they may have life, and have it abundantly* (John 10:10).
>*He who believes in the Son has eternal life; but he who does not obey the Son will not see life, but the wrath of God abides on him* (John 3:36).
>*...I am the way, and the truth, and the life; no one comes to the Father but through Me* (John 14:6).

God's holiness makes it impossible for Him to have a loving relationship with sinful people (Habakkuk 1:13). His justice demands that every sinner be judged and condemned to an eternal separation from God. Because of this, all people have become enemies of God. Although God has every right to condemn every person, because of His love He provided a solution through His Son, Jesus Christ. God sent Jesus, who is truly God and truly man, to bear the sins of the whole world on the cross (1 John 2:2). Jesus' death was the only acceptable sacrifice for sin: *And there is salvation in no one else; for there is no other name under heaven that has been given among men by which we must be saved* (Acts 4:12).

Through Jesus' death for us on the cross, He establishes a loving relationship that unites us with the Father. Because of this sacrifice, every person who is born again can have true fellowship with God both now and forever.

Jesus Christ Is Alive Today

After Jesus Christ died on the cross at Calvary, where He received the punishment that we deserved, the Bible says that He was buried in a tomb. But He did not remain there: Christ rose from the dead! For all those who believe in Jesus Christ, His resurrection is a guarantee that they will also be resurrected to eternal life in the presence of God forever. This is very good news! *Christ died for our sins...was buried, and...He was raised on the third day according to the Scriptures* (1 Corinthians 15:3-4).

How to Receive God's Love and Plan

In His mercy, God has determined that salvation is free. To receive it, agree with and believe these four things:
1. Acknowledge the problem: separation from God because of sin (Romans 3:10-12).
2. Admit to being a sinner, and that you need salvation (Ephesians 2:3).
3. Repent by turning from your sins, and put your faith in Christ, who paid the penalty for the forgiveness of your sins (Acts 2:38).
4. Commit yourself to Jesus Christ as your Savior and Lord (2 Peter 3:18).

The Bible says:

> *that if you confess with your mouth Jesus as Lord, and believe in your heart that God raised Him from the dead, you will be saved* (Romans 10:9).
> *for "Whoever will call on the name of the Lord will be saved"* (Romans 10:13).

A Prayer for Salvation

Lord Jesus, I know that I have sinned against You and that I do not live according to Your plan; therefore, I plead with You to forgive me of my sins. I believe that You love me and died for me, and in doing so, You paid the debt for my sins. I repent of my sin and want to live every day with You and for You. Please come into my life and be my Savior. Help me to follow You and to obey You as Lord. I love you, thank you for loving me and redeeming me.

Living As a New Creation in Christ

When Jesus makes you born again, several things take place: your sins are forgiven (Colossians 2:13), you become a child of God (John 1:12), and you receive eternal life (John 3:16).

You may feel strong emotions, but don't put your confidence in the way you felt when you prayed to Christ because feelings can change day to day. Daily put your complete confidence for salvation in what Jesus did for us on the cross (1 John 4:10).

You are not saved by a one-time confession, but a lifetime of devotion to Christ as your Lord and Savior (1 Corinthians 15:2). It is important to have daily fellowship with God through prayer and reading the Bible. Also, have fellowship with other Christians, especially the local church, so that you can receive support and Biblical wisdom (Hebrews 10:25).

This presentation is courtesy of Three Sixteen Publishing

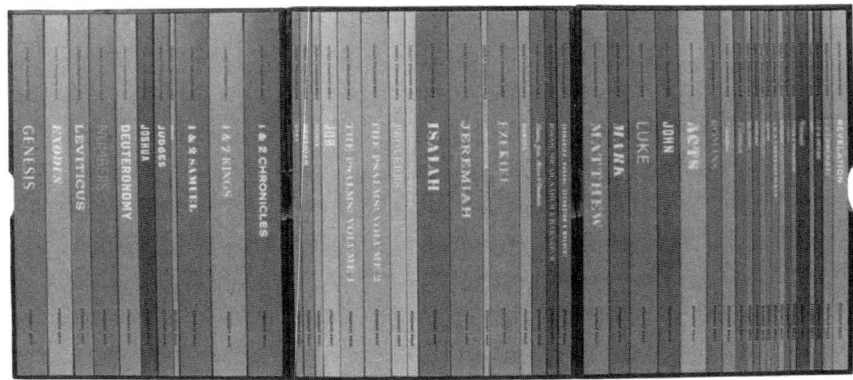

LSB Scripture Study Notebooks
For the Entire Old and New Testaments!

The LSB Scripture Study Notebooks are perfect for sermon notes, lesson preparation, and personal reflection. Available individually or as a set. Features include:

- 1.25-inch side margins
- Easy-to-read 10-point font
- Single-column, verse-by-verse format
- Space to write above and below each verse
- Lined page opposite each Scripture page
- Extra lined pages in the front & back
- Thick, opaque paper
- Each notebook is 6.5 x 9.5 inches

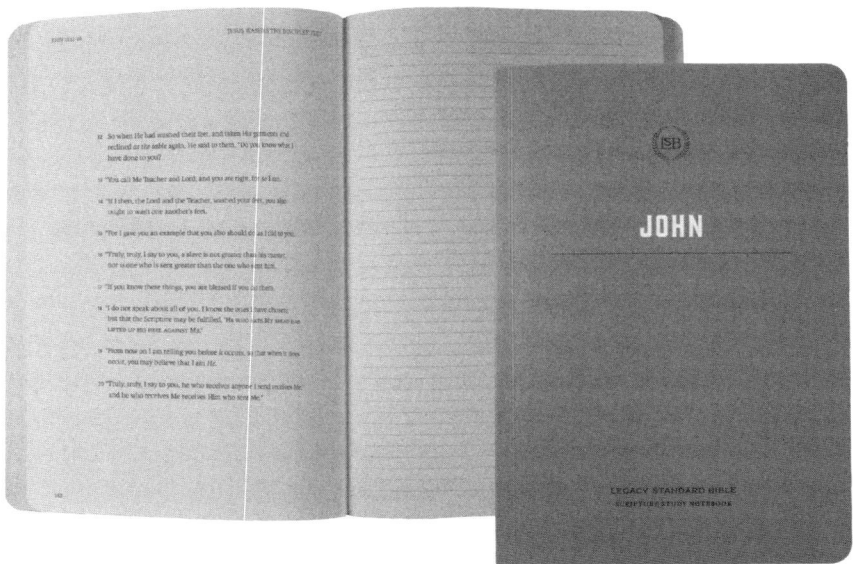

Visit the Free Resources tab at 316Publishing.com to download a free sample layout!